Transforming Cities with Transit

Transforming Cities with Transit

Transit and Land-Use Integration for Sustainable Urban Development

Hiroaki Suzuki
Robert Cervero
Kanako Iuchi

THE WORLD BANK
Washington, DC

© 2013 International Bank for Reconstruction and Development / The World Bank
1818 H Street NW, Washington DC 20433
Telephone: 202-473-1000; Internet: www.worldbank.org

Some rights reserved
1 2 3 4   15 14 13 12

This work is a product of the staff of The World Bank with external contributions. Note that The World Bank does not necessarily own each component of the content included in the work. The World Bank therefore does not warrant that the use of the content contained in the work will not infringe on the rights of third parties. The risk of claims resulting from such infringement rests solely with you.

The findings, interpretations, and conclusions expressed in this work do not necessarily reflect the views of The World Bank, its Board of Executive Directors, or the governments they represent. The World Bank does not guarantee the accuracy of the data included in this work. The boundaries, colors, denominations, and other information shown on any map in this work do not imply any judgment on the part of The World Bank concerning the legal status of any territory or the endorsement or acceptance of such boundaries.

Nothing herein shall constitute or be considered to be a limitation upon or waiver of the privileges and immunities of The World Bank, all of which are specifically reserved.

Rights and Permissions

This work is available under the Creative Commons Attribution 3.0 Unported license (CC BY 3.0) http://creativecommons.org/licenses/by/3.0. Under the Creative Commons Attribution license, you are free to copy, distribute, transmit, and adapt this work, including for commercial purposes, under the following conditions:

Attribution—Please cite the work as follows: Suzuki, Hiroaki, Robert Cervero, and Kanako Iuchi. 2013. *Transforming Cities with Transit: Transit and Land-Use Integration for Sustainable Urban Development.* Washington, DC: World Bank. DOI: 10.1596/978-0-8213-9745-9 License: Creative Commons Attribution CC BY 3.0.

Translations—If you create a translation of this work, please add the following disclaimer along with the attribution: *This translation was not created by The World Bank and should not be considered an official World Bank translation. The World Bank shall not be liable for any content or error in this translation.*

All queries on rights and licenses should be addressed to the Office of the Publisher, The World Bank, 1818 H Street NW, Washington, DC 20433, USA; fax: 202-522-2625; e-mail: pubrights@worldbank.org.

ISBN (paper): 978-0-8213-9745-9
ISBN (electronic): 978-0-8213-9750-3
DOI: 10.1596/978-0-8213-9745-9

Cover photo: Bogota, Colombia; photo taken by Karl Fjellstrom, ITDP (www.transportphoto.net)

Cover design: Debra Naylor

Library of Congress Cataloging-in-Publication Data

Suzuki, Hiroaki, 1951–
  Transforming cities with transit : transit and land-use integration for sustainable urban development / Hiroaki Suzuki, Robert Cervero, and Kanako Iuchi.
       p. cm. — (Urban development series)
  Includes bibliographical references and index.
  ISBN 978-0-8213-9745-9 (alk. paper) — ISBN 978-0-8213-9750-3 (electronic : alk. paper)
  1. City planning. 2. Sustainable urban development. 3. Urban transportation. 4. Land use. I. Title.
  HT166.S96 2013
  307.1'216—dc23

2012045174

Contents

Acknowledgments xi

About the Authors xv

Abbreviations xvii

Glossary xix

Message to City Leaders in Developing Countries xxii

Overview 1
    Transit and Land-Use Integration 3
    Global Best Cases of Transit and Land-Use Integration 3
    Lessons from Case Studies in Developing Countries 7
    Toward Transit and Land-Use Integration 14
    Core Lessons on Transit Investments and Urban Growth 20
    Roles of Development Financial Institutions 21
    Conclusion 21
    References 23

1. Introduction: Critical Challenges Facing Cities and Urban Transport 25
    Expanding Cities, Shrinking Green Space 26
    Cities for Cars, Not for People 29
    Integrating Transit and Land Use toward Sustainable Urban Development 33
    Study Objectives, Framework, and Methodology 42
    Structure of This Book 45
    Notes 45
    References 46

2. Lessons from Sustainable Transit-Oriented Cities   49
Transit and Land-Use Integration in Adaptive Cities   52
Integrating Transit and Land-Use Planning through Adaptive Transit and Bus Rapid Transit   82
Conclusion   89
Note   91
References   91

3. Integrating Transit and Urban Development in Cities in the Developing World   95
Ahmedabad: A City at a Critical Juncture   96
Bogota: Beyond TransMilenio   109
Guangzhou: Adaptive Bus Rapid Transit   129
Ho Chi Minh City: Building a Green Transit Corridor   138
Notes   142
References   145

4. Toward Sustainable Urban Futures   147
Barriers to Integrating Transit and Urban Development   147
The Challenge of Inclusive Transit-Oriented Development   165
Toward Successful Integration: Recommendations   167
Conclusion   189
Notes   191
References   192

Index   195

Boxes
O.1	Transforming a vision into a conceptual image of the future metropolis	4
O.2	Articulated versus average density	11
1.1	What is bus rapid transit?	26
1.2	Urban growth in Tehran	27
1.3	Urban expansion in the Jakarta metropolitan area	28
1.4	A tale of two cities: Atlanta and Barcelona	34
1.5	What is transit-oriented development?	37
1.6	Economic cities as ecological cities: The World Bank's Eco^2 initiative	40
3.1	Ahmedabad's Sabarmati Riverfront Development Project	101
3.2	Ahmedabad's Town Planning Scheme	105
3.3	Ahmedabad and its bus rapid transit system at a glance	110
3.4	How has Bogota's TransMilenio affected the built environment?	114
3.5	Bogota and its bus rapid transit system at a glance	130
4.1	Articulated versus average density	155
4.2	How land speculation contributes to sprawl	163

4.3	Reducing housing costs and improving livability in Vancouver	166
4.4	Integrating land-use and transit policy planning in India	170

Figures

BO.1.1	Copenhagen's "Finger Plan" for urban development	4
BO.1.2	Singapore's "Constellation Plan" for urban development	5
O.1	The Maritime Square residential-retail project developed by the Mass Transit Railway of Hong Kong SAR, China	7
BO.2.1	Importance of articulated density for mass transit	11
BO.2.2	Transit-oriented spatial development in Curitiba and Bogota	11
O.2	A healthy conversation between transit and land-use planning officials	16
O.3	Preconditions for successful integration of transit and land use	18
B1.1.1	Bus rapid transit in Curitiba, Brazil	26
B1.2.1	Aerial views of metropolitan Tehran, 1986 and 2009	27
B1.3.1	Aerial views of metropolitan Jakarta, 1976–2004	28
B1.3.2	Density of metropolitan Jakarta, 1988 and 2011	28
1.1	Actual and projected number of motorized vehicles in the world, 1975–2050	30
1.2	Urban density and transport-related energy consumption in selected cities	31
1.3	Actual and projected global CO_2 emissions from the transport sector, 1980–2030	32
B1.4.1	Built-up area of Atlanta and Barcelona, 1990	34
1.4	Urban space taken up by cars, motorbikes, and buses	35
B1.5.1	Key features of the eco-block concept	37
B1.5.2	Transit-oriented development in metropolitan Washington, DC	38
B1.6.1	The Eco^2 integrated approach to development	40
1.5	Urban form of Curitiba and São Paulo, Brazil	42
1.6	Study framework	43
2.1	Transit ridership and vehicle kilometers traveled per capita in selected global cities	51
2.2	Population density and transit ridership in selected global cities	51
2.3	Evolution of Copenhagen's "transit first" plan	53
2.4	Copenhagen's "finger plan" for urban development	56
2.5	The Maritime Square residential-retail project developed by the Mass Transit Railway of Hong Kong SAR, China	63
2.6	Transformation of Seoul's Cheong Gye Cheon from an elevated freeway to an urban greenway	66
2.7	Bus rapid transit corridors in central Seoul	67
2.8	Residential property values before and after transformation of Seoul's Cheong Gye Cheon freeway into an urban greenway	70
2.9	Singapore's Constellation Plan	71
2.10	Rates of return of private railway corporations in metropolitan Tokyo, 1980–96	75
2.11	Street life near Shinjuku metrorail station, Tokyo	76

2.12	Tokyo Station City	77
2.13	Average commercial land values within five kilometers of Shinkansen line stations in Tokyo, 2000 and 2010	78
2.14	"Bull's eye" concept of rail development in Arlington County, Virginia	80
2.15	Curitiba's trinary road system	83
2.16	Transitway development in Ottawa, Canada	85
2.17	Passengers per guideway mile in selected North American busway and light rail systems	87
2.18	Ottawa's Transitway network, including O-Train light rail line linked to busway	88
3.1	Phases I, II, and III of Ahmedabad's Janmarg bus rapid transit system	98
3.2	Before and after Janmarg at the Anjal station area	99
B3.1.1	International kite festival at the riverfront, 2006	101
3.3	Closed textile mill sites and development progress in Ahmedabad	102
B3.2.1	Land adjustment in Ahmedabad	105
B3.3.1	Map of Ahmedabad, India	110
B3.3.2	Janmarg bus	110
3.4	Phases I, II, and III of Bogota's TransMilenio bus rapid transit system	112
B3.4.1	Changes in building density in areas of Bogota affected by the TransMilenio	114
3.5	Development at end station of Bogota's TransMilenio, 1998 and 2011	115
3.6	Distribution of building volume in Bogota by floor area ratio, 2010	117
3.7	Floor area ratio in areas of Bogota affected by the TransMilenio, 2004 and 2010	118
3.8	Joggers along Bogota's Ciclovia	118
3.9	Bike parking spaces at Portal de Suba, Bogota	119
3.10	Location of Metrovivienda development sites in Bogota	121
3.11	City offices in Bogota responsible for transportation and urban development	123
3.12	Bogota's regional territorial occupation model	125
3.13	Unattractive, disconnected space in the TransMilenio corridors	127
3.14	Proposed metro network in Bogota	128
B3.5.1	Map of Bogota, Colombia	130
B3.5.2	TransMilenio bus in Bogota, Colombia	130
3.15	Aerial view of Guangzhou's bus rapid transit system	132
3.16	Area around the Gangding station in Guangzhou before and after construction of the bus rapid transit system	133
3.17	Green connectors in Guangzhou's bus rapid transit system	134
3.18	Bike-sharing station in Guangzhou	135
3.19	Restoration of the Donghaochong Canal in Guangzhou	135

3.20	Enhanced mixed land use of existing multistory apartment in Liuyun Xiaoqu community of Guangzhou	137
3.21	Proposed bus rapid transit system in Ho Chi Minh City	139
3.22	Current state of green transit corridor in Ho Chi Minh City	140
3.23	Typical working sessions held to plan the Ho Chi Minh City bus rapid transit system	140
3.24	Preliminary sketches of the "island-valley" concept adopted for the Ho Chi Minh City bus rapid transit system	141
3.25	Sketches of the concept designs for iconic bus rapid transit station areas in Ho Chi Minh City	142
4.1	Average population densities in built-up areas in 60 global metropolitan areas	153
B4.1.1	Importance of articulated density for mass transit	155
B4.1.2	Densities along the bus rapid transit corridors in Curitiba and Bogota	155
4.2	Fragmented land use in Chengdu, China	157
4.3	Street without footpath in Ahmedabad, India	160
4.4	Flyover in Bogota's TransMilenio bus rapid transit system	161
4.5	Integrated solutions proposed for greenway corridor in Ho Chi Minh City	161
4.6	Automobile-dependent urban development in Kuala Lumpur, Malaysia	164
B4.3.1	Laneway housing	166
4.7	A healthy conversation between transit and land-use planning officials	172
4.8	Relationship between urban form and cost-effective public transit	174
4.9	Preconditions for successful integration of transit and land use	177
4.10	Likely land-use outcomes when urban rail investments are proactively leveraged	187

Tables

1.1	Constraints on coordinating transit and land-use planning	41
2.1	Transit ridership, vehicle kilometers traveled, and GDP in selected cities	52
2.2	Green transit-oriented development attributes of Hammarby Sjöstad, Sweden	59
2.3	Mode splits for journeys in various parts of Stockholm County	60
2.4	Operating speeds of cars and buses in Seoul before and after opening of exclusive median-lane bus lanes	69
2A.1	Modes of transportation in selected cities	90
B3.3.1	Population statistics for Ahmedabad, India	110
B3.3.2	Capacity and infrastructure of the Janmarg bus rapid transit system	110
B3.5.1	Population statistics for Bogota, Colombia	130
B3.5.2	Capacity and infrastructure of the TransMilenio bus rapid transit (BRT) system	130

Acknowledgments

This book was written by Hiroaki Suzuki and Kanako Iuchi of the World Bank and Robert Cervero of the University of California at Berkeley. It draws on in-depth case studies of Ahmedabad, India, and Bogota, Colombia, and two shorter case studies on Guangzhou, China and Ho Chi Minh City, Vietnam.

A team from the Centre of Excellence (CoE) in Urban Transport, Centre for Environmental Planning and Technology (CEPT) University, Ahmedabad, led by Professor H. M. Shivand Swamy, which included Shalini Shinha (Associate Professor), Nitika Bhakuni (Associate Professor), and Sungdi Imchen (Researcher), prepared the in-depth case study on Ahmedabad and assisted the World Bank team's field research. The Bank team and the CoE CEPT team obtained strong support and collaboration from the state government of Gujarat; including from I. P. Guatam (IAS), Principal Secretary of the Urban Development and Housing Department; Guruprasad Mohapatra (IAS), Municipal Commissioner of the Ahmedabad Municipal Corporation; Mamta Verma (IAS), Chief Executive of the Ahmedabad Urban Development Authority; and Neela Munshi, Senior Town Planner of the Ahmedabad Urban Development Authority. Executive Director U. C. Padia and Mr. Harshadray J. Solanki of the Ahmedabad Janmarg, Limited also provided support.

A team from Geografía Urbana, led by Alejandro Rodriguez, which included Hernando Arenas, Jill Fortune, Daniel Garavito, and Luis Hernan Saenz, prepared the in-depth case study on Bogota and assisted the Bank team's field research. Other agencies and supporters of the Bogota case study included Cristina Arango, Head of Secretary of Planning of Bogota; William Camargo, Director of Transportation and Secretary of Planning of Bogota; Claudia Hoshino, Coordinator for the United Nations Centre for Regional Development (UNCRD), Latin America Office; Gustavo

Marulanda, Director de la Unidad Administrativa de Catastro Distrital; Felipe Targa Rodriguez, Vice Minister of Transportation, Government of Colombia; and Mario Valbuena, Director of Operations of TransMilenio.

The Guangzhou case study was developed with substantial support from the Institute for Transportation and Development (ITDP); the case study was based on ITDP's report "Guangzhou, China Bus Rapid Transit: Emission Impact Analysis," by Colin Hughes, Global Policy Analyst, and Xianyuan Zhu, ITDP China. The authors also conducted interviews and held discussions with ITDP staff in Washington, DC and Guangzhou. Karl Fjellstrom, ITDP China Director; Xianyuan Zhu; and Xiaomei Duan have also contributed substantially to the editing of this case study. The Ho Chi Minh City case study was prepared with substantial input by Andre A. Bald, Senior Urban Specialist, World Bank.

This book greatly benefited from peer reviews by World Bank staff: Om Prakash Agarwal, Andreas Dietrich Kopp, Zhi Liu, Augustin Pierre Maria, Shomik Raj Mehndiratta, Taimur Samad, Harris Selod, and Victor M. Vergara. Important comments and suggestions were also received from Mauricio Cuellar, Ke Fang, Artulo Ardila Gomez, Roger Gorham, Nancy Lozano Gracia, Stephane Hallegatte, Austin Kilroy, Somik V. Lall, Marcus John Jin Sarn Lee, Pedro Ortiz, Paul Procee, Robin Rajack, Camila Rodriguez, Shigeyuki Sakaki, Andrew Salzberg, Daniel Sellen, Maria Catalina Ochoa Sepulveda, Christopher Willoughby (former OED Director), and Kwai Peng Belinda Yuen.

Valuable insights and support were provided by Clever Almeida, President, Institute for Research and Urban Planning of Curitiba; Luciano Ducci, Mayor of Curitiba; Shreya Gadepalli, Senior Program Director for India, ITDP; Ralph Gakenheimer, Professor Emeritus, MIT; Darío Hidalgo, Director for Research and Practice, EMBARQ (World Resources Institute); Walter Hook, Executive Director, ITDP; Henry Edward Jewell (former World Bank staff); Kiyonobu Kaidou, Professor, Meijo University; Tadashi Matsumoto, Senior Policy Analyst, Organisation for Economic Co-operation and Development (OECD); Slobodan Mitric (former World Bank staff); and Yasushi Yoshida, Head of the Regional Policies for Sustainable Development Division, OECD.

Beth Tamayose assisted with research and the editing of the first version of the manuscript. Special thanks go to Fernando Armendaris, Adelaide Barra, Vivian R. Cherian, Laura Lewis De Brular, Xiaofeng Li, Hafida Sahraoui, Berenice Sanchez Suarez, and Juliet Teodosio, who provided logistical and administrative assistance.

The Sustainable Development Network of the World Bank sponsored this report. The Royal Norwegian Ministry of Foreign Affairs, through the Multi-Donor Trust Fund for Sustainable Urban Development, and the Cities Alliance, through a noncore contribution of the Japanese Government, also provided financial support.

The report was produced under the supervision of Abha Joshi Ghani, Sector Manager for the Urban Development and Local Government Unit, and with the overall direction of Zoubida Allaoua, Director of the Finance, Economics and Urban Department.

The publication of *Transforming Cities with Transit* was managed by the World Bank's Office of the Publisher, under the supervision of Susan Graham and Patricia Katayama and with help from Andres Meneses and Dan Nikolitis. The book was edited by Barbara Karni.

About the Authors

Hiroaki Suzuki is the Lead Urban Specialist of the Urban and Resilience Management Unit of the Urban and Disaster Risk Management Department at the World Bank. He has more than 20 years of operational experience within the infrastructure and public sectors at the World Bank, and in 2009 he joined the Bank's corporate urban sector unit. Suzuki is the main author of *Eco^2 Cities: Ecological Cities as Economic Cities* and its implementation guide, *Eco^2 Cities Guide*, and he is the Task Team Leader of the Integrated Spatial Development study *Transforming Cities with Transit: Transit and Land-Use Integration for Sustainable Urban Development*. Before joining the Bank, he assumed the management responsibilities in the Overseas Economic Cooperation Fund, (currently JICA) and a management consulting firm in Japan. He graduated from Yokohama City University and the MIT Sloan School of Management and obtained a Diploma in French from the University of Caen in France.

Robert Cervero is the Carmel P. Friesen Distinguished Chair of Urban Studies and Professor of City and Regional Planning at the University of California, Berkeley, where he also directs two research institutes. His research focuses on the nexus between transportation and urban development. Cervero currently chairs the International Association of Urban Environments and the National Advisory Committee of the Robert Wood Johnson Foundation's Active Living Research Program. He also serves on the Advisory Committee on Urban Development of the World Economic Forum and the International Panel on Climate Change, contributing to the chapter on human settlements and infrastructure in the IPCC's Fifth Assessment Report. He holds a BA from the University of North Carolina, Chapel Hill; MS and MCP degrees from Georgia Tech; and a PhD from UCLA.

Kanako Iuchi has been an Urban Specialist in the Urban and Resilience Management Unit of the Urban and Disaster Risk Management Department of the World Bank since 2010. Her areas of expertise include urban and regional planning, disaster management planning, and community development, and she has co-led this Integrated Spatial Development study. Prior to joining the Bank, she worked as an international development planner and researcher with bi- and multi-lateral organizations; national, regional, and local governments; and communities in more than ten countries across East and South Asia, South America, and Eastern Europe. She holds a BS from Tsukuba University, an MRP from Cornell University, and a PhD from University of Illinois, Urbana-Champaign, in urban and regional planning.

Abbreviations

AJL	Ahmedabad Janmarg Ltd
AMC	Ahmedabad Municipal Corporation
AMTS	Ahmedabad Municipal Transport Services
AUDA	Ahmedabad Urban Development Authority
BRT	Bus rapid transit
CBD	Central business district
CEPT	Centre for Environmental Planning and Technology
CGC	Cheong Gye Cheon
CO$_2$	Carbon dioxide
COE	Centre of Excellence
DANE	National Department of Statistics (Departamento Administrativo Nacional de Estadistica)
Eco^2	Ecological Cities as Economic Cities
EIU	Economic Intelligence Unit
ERP	Electronic road pricing
ERU	Urban Renovation Company (Empresa de Renovación Urbana)
FAR	Floor area ratio
FSI	Floor space index
FSR	Floor space ratio
GDP	Gross domestic product
HOV	High occupancy vehicle
IDU	Urban Development Institute (Instituto de Desarrollo Urbano)

IPPUC	Institute for Research and Urban Planning of Curitiba (Instituto de Pesquisa e Planejamento Urbano de Curitiba)
ITDP	Institute for Transportation and Development Policy
JnNURM	Jawaharlal Nehru Urban Renewal Mission
LOOT	Territorial Ordinance Organic Law (Ley Organica do Ordemamiento Territorial)
LPG	Liquefied petroleum gas
MTR	Mass Transit Railway
MTRC	Mass Transit Railway Corporation
NGO	Nongovernmental organization
NMT	Nonmotorized transport
NO_2	Nitrogen dioxide
OC-Transpo	Ottawa-Carleton Regional Transit Commission
OECD	Organisation for Economic Co-operation and Development
PM_{10}	Fine-grained particulate matter
POT	Territorial Ordinance Plan (Plan de Ordenamiento Territorial)
PPP	Public-private partnership
PZ	Zonal plans (Planeamiento zonal)
R+P	Rail+Property
REIT	Real Estate Investment Trust
RMB	Renminbi
ROB	Rail over bridge
SAR	Special administrative region
SITP	Public transportation integrated system
TDM	Transportation demand management
TIF	Tax increment financing
TOD	Transit-oriented development
TPS	Town planning scheme
UITP	International Association of Public Transport
ULCA	Urban Land Ceiling Act
UNCRD	United Nations Centre for Regional Development
UPZ	Zonal planning units (Unidades de planeamiento zonal)
UTF	Urban Transport Fund
UTTIPEC	Unified Traffic and Transportation (Planning and Engineering) Centre
VKT	Vehicle kilometers traveled
WMATA	Washington Metropolitan Transit Authority

Glossary

Brownfield development. Development on sites once used mainly for industrial purposes, which are often polluted as a result. Many require site remediation to treat and remove soil toxins, water contaminants, and other hazards. Brownfield sites are often found in premier locations of a city and are typically underutilized. Redevelopment increases the value of the land.

Bus rapid transit (BRT). High-quality bus-based services that mimic many of the features of high-capacity metrorail systems but at a fraction of the cost. Buses most closely resemble metrorail services when they operate on specially designated lanes or have physically separated lanes for their exclusive use. Grade separation of busways at critical intersections and junctures also expedite flows. BRT systems often include bus stations instead of stops to provide weather protection and allow passengers to pay before boarding.

Central business district (CBD). An area where cities' major businesses (financial institutions, stores, major convention and sport facilities, and hotels) are concentrated. CBDs produce agglomeration economies.

Charrette. A collaborative design and planning workshop that occurs over four to seven consecutive days, is held on site, and involves stakeholders at critical decision-making points. During a *charrette*, workshop participants identify key concepts, discuss design considerations and options, and come up with plans and policies. A main feature is the use of designs and drawings to visualize various concepts and options.

Eco^2 (Ecological Cities as Economic Cities). A sustainable urban development initiative intended to help developing countries achieve greater ecological and economic sustainability by drawing on the synergy between the two processes. Launched by the World Bank as an integral part of its urban and local government strategy, this city-based approach enables local governments to lead a development process that takes into account their specific circumstances, including their ecology, and to realize the benefits of integration by planning, designing, and managing the whole urban system.

Floor area ratio (FAR). The ratio of a building's total floor area to the size of the land on which it is built. The higher the FAR, the higher the density. Also referred to as floor space ratio (FSR) and floor space index (FSI).

Greenfield development. New development that takes place on lands that were not previously developed as urban land, including agricultural, rural, and unused land.

Land consolidation and readjustment scheme. A land development process that groups individual, irregular-shaped land parcels and returns smaller but rectilinear-shaped and better-serviced parcels to landholders. The sale of extra land or remnant parcels to private interests generates revenues that go to providing public infrastructure, including roads, public parks, water lines, and a sewerage system. The scheme can benefit landowners if land value in the neighborhood increases as a result. Also referred to as Town Planning Scheme (TPS) in places such as Ahmedabad, India.

Mixed use. A pattern of development characterized by a mixture of diversified land uses, typically including housing, retail activities, and private businesses, either within the same building space (for example, vertical mixing) or in close proximity (for example, horizontal mixing).

Nonmotorized transport. Any type of transport mode that is not motorized, such as walking and bicycling. Nonmotorized transport, or NMT, has gained popularity as not only a clean, carbon-free form of mobility with a very small footprint but also as a means to improve public health through increased physical activity.

Pedestrian-friendly design. Design intended to enhance the pedestrian experience, typically through improved amenities (for example, attractive landscaping, lighting, and seating areas) and by improving the efficiency of walking (for example, small city blocks, grid street patterns, and high road connectivity that provide direct, less circuitous pathways).

Public-private partnership (PPP). A formal partnership between a public sector entity and a private corporation, often used to construct and operate infrastructure facilities or develop certain urban areas.

Sprawl. A pattern of development characterized by uniform low density, lack of a distinctive core, poor accessibility, dependence on automobiles, and uncontrolled and noncontiguous land expansion.

Tax increment financing (TIF). A financing method that mobilizes funds for redevelopment by issuing bonds against future incremental tax revenue generated from improvement in a targeted area. Property tax revenue gains also get rechanneled to the redevelopment zone to help retire bonds and finance future infrastructure and neighborhood enhancements.

Transit-oriented development (TOD). Compact, mixed-use, pedestrian-friendly development organized around a transit station. TOD embraces the idea that locating amenities, employment, retail shops, and housing around transit hubs promotes transit usage and nonmotorized travel.

Transportation demand management (TDM). Policy and incentive measures to reduce demand for travel, particularly by automobile, and induce use of nonmotorized transport or public transit. Typical measures include removal or reduction of fuel subsidies, congestion pricing, parking regulations and fee increases, higher car registration costs and associated taxes, and introduction of car-free zones or days. TDM reduces or redistributes travel demand by time, mode, or corridor.

Value capture. An opportunity to generate revenues by capitalizing on the value created by infrastructure investments (often transit and other government-backed projects) by developing or selling property or collecting fees or taxes. Value capture can be facilitated through direct measures, such as the sale of properties or the granting of a development franchise, or through indirect methods, such as extracting surplus from other property owners (through a betterment tax, for example) or reaping higher proceeds from regular property taxes.

Message to City Leaders in Developing Countries

Transport differs from other problems developing societies face, because it gets worse rather than better with economic development. While sanitation, education, and other challenges improve with economic growth, transport gets worse.

—Enrique Peñalosa, president of the Institute for Transportation and Development and former mayor of Bogota, 2005

Sustainable cities will never appear if the transport system is not sustainable. Increasing energy consumption, extensive travel and poor natural resource management must be redirected. Urban sprawl and the need to commute great distances for work and shopping must be curbed.

—Natalija Kazlauskiene, director, Directorate General for Regional Policy, European Commission, 2009

The integration of transit and land use is one of the most important strategic initiatives for developing more sustainable urban futures. Achieving effective integration requires a cogent, forward-looking strategic vision of the future city; an enabling institutional framework; and sustainable financial models.

Cities need to envisage their long-term futures, crafting visions that are eventually articulated into spatial plans and specific land-use initiatives. A spatial framework should guide transit and other infrastructure investments. The channeling of higher urban densities along high-capacity transit corridors is of particular importance.

Also critical is a robust institutional framework and regulatory and planning tools that facilitate regional collaboration and cross-sector cooperation. An inclusive planning framework is also important to give voice to all segments of society, especially disadvantaged and marginalized populations.

Sustainable financial models are vital to attaining hoped-for long-term visions of the city. At the macro level, cities that are compact and have a rich mix of land use—as a result of transit-oriented development (TOD)—are highly livable. They can increase their global competitiveness by attracting firms, especially knowledge-based industries and outside investments, which are drawn to such environments. At the micro level, financial sustainability can take the form of "value capture" as a tool for generating revenue from TOD to recoup the costs of investment and finance additional improvements of TOD precincts.

Unprecedented opportunities exist in much of the developing world for successfully integrating transit and land development. For bus rapid transit and railway investments to trigger meaningful land-use changes in economically and financially viable ways, cities need rapid growth, rising real incomes, and increased motorization and congestion levels—conditions that already exist in many cities in the developing world.

This report builds on the World Bank's Eco^2 (Ecological Cities as Economic Cities; www.worldbank.org/eco2) concept, which promotes sustainable urban development through cross-sector integration by focusing on the careful coordination of transit and land development. This strategy holds enormous promise for advancing environmental sustainability, economic development, and socially inclusive development in rapidly growing cities. Done well, integrated spatial development—particularly the physical linkage of transit investments and urban development—can create Eco^2 outcomes that enhance cities' competitiveness and livability and help address the number one challenge facing cities in the developing world: reducing poverty and the hardships of extreme deprivation. Improving the economic well-being of urban residents of all backgrounds opens the way to a future of social justice and prosperity.

Transforming Cities with Transit

- Global, transit-oriented cities
- Case study cities of the developing world

Overview

This study explores the complex process of transit and land-use integration in rapidly growing cities in developing countries. It first identifies barriers to and opportunities for effective coordination of transit infrastructure and urban development. It then recommends a set of policies and implementation measures for overcoming these barriers and exploiting these opportunities.

Well-integrated transit and land development create urban forms and spaces that reduce the need for travel by private motorized vehicles. Areas with good access to public transit and well-designed urban spaces that are walkable and bikeable become highly attractive places for people to live, work, learn, play, and interact. Such environments enhance a city's economic competitiveness, reduce local pollution and global greenhouse gas emissions, and promote inclusive development. These goals are at the heart of transit-oriented development (TOD), an urban form that is increasingly important to sustainable urban futures.

This book uses a case study approach. It draws lessons from global best-case examples of transit-oriented metropolises that have direct relevance to cities in developing countries and elsewhere that are currently investing in bus rapid transit (BRT) and other high-capacity transit systems. It also reports the results of two original in-depth case studies of rapidly growing and motorizing cities that introduced extended BRT systems: Ahmedabad, India and Bogota, Colombia. Two shorter case studies—of Guangzhou, China and Ho Chi Minh City, Vietnam—enrich the understanding of factors that are critical to "transforming cities with transit."

The mechanisms for successfully integrating transit and urban development are complex. The multitude of factors involved includes inherent characteristics of a city (for example, natural and historical conditions); governance structures; institutional settings; public sector initiatives and actions (for example, transit investments, planning regulations, tax policies, and financial incentives); financing instruments; and market responses.

Transit shapes urban development by enhancing accessibility; attributes of land, such as residential and job densities and the degree of land-use mixing, affect travel demand. The case studies presented in this book focus mainly on the impact of transit investment on land use and urban form rather than on the impact of land use on transit demand, as it takes many years for shifts in land use and their eventual impacts on transit demand to unfold and reveal themselves.

Analysis of the interaction between public sector initiatives and market response is especially challenging, because the mechanisms of these interactions are not fully understood. The study probes market response, which reflects consumer and market preferences indirectly, by studying, for example, the influences of BRT improvements on residential land prices and private real estate investment decisions. Cases show that the private market does not always respond to transit investments as would be expected, opting instead to build new housing enclaves away from BRT corridors. Case studies hint at factors that would explain such responses, but much more research is needed on this topic. Accordingly, this study focuses on public sector initiatives and actions (for example, public policy interventions such as zoning reforms and improved feeder bus connections to BRT stations) that work with, react to, and shape the marketplace.

The case analyses reveal key institutional, regulatory, and financial constraints that hamper successful transit and land-use integration. They also highlight opportunities for charting sustainable pathways. The last chapter of the book offers policy recommendations and suggests steps needed to implement them. The recommendations are drawn from best-practice experiences worldwide as well as insights gained in studying the unique challenges faced by Ahmedabad and Bogota as they strive to become more sustainable.

Most of the cases reviewed are from developed countries. Their experiences cannot be directly applied and transplanted without some adaptation and adjustments to local realities. The aim is less to identify specific practices and more to impart key principles and core lessons that can guide the planning and practice of cities currently planning or investing in large-scale transit systems. Recommendations for creating more sustainable cities of the future range from macro-level strategies that influence land development and governance at the metropolitan scale to micro-level initiatives, such as TOD, which can radically transform development patterns at the neighborhood level.

The book will be of interest to a wide and diverse audience, including mayors, city council members, national and local policy makers, urban and transport planners, transit agency officials, developers, staffs of development financial institutions, and others involved with TOD projects in rapidly growing and motorizing cities in the developing world.

Transit and Land-Use Integration

Cities in developing countries are growing at an unprecedented rate. Their population is projected to increase from 2.0 billion in 2000 to 5.5 billion by 2050, accounting for 95 percent of the increase in the world's urban population. With rising incomes, urban residents will expand outward, following the trajectory of automobile-dependent sprawl evident in developed countries.

This trend must be reversed if significant headway is to be made in increasing cities' economic competitiveness through energy- and time-efficiency improvements. Negative externalities such as air pollution and greenhouse gas emissions cannot be reduced and social equity cannot be promoted without action to prevent urban populations in developing countries from following this path of automobile-dependent sprawl.

Transit and land-use integration is one of the most promising means of reversing the trend of automobile-dependent sprawl and placing cities in developing countries on a sustainable pathway. BRT systems deserve special attention, as the majority of future urban growth is expected to take place in medium-size cities (cities with no more than 500,000 people) (UN Habitat 2011) with limited fiscal capacities. BRT systems, which are less costly than other forms of mass transit, such as metros, can meet these cities' traffic demand. With more than 130 BRT systems having commenced operation in the past decade, promoting TOD will be particularly important.

Global Best Cases of Transit and Land-Use Integration

All global best-case examples of transit and land-use integration had a cogent land-use vision—a vision that shaped regional transit investments more than vice versa. Transit was one of several important tools, along with supportive zoning and creative financing, used to make urban visions a reality. Transportation demand management (TDM) measures, including congestion charges and streetscape enhancements that promote nonmotorized transport modes, have also been important. Cities like Hong Kong SAR, China and Tokyo reveal that successful transit and land-use integration can generate revenue and capture value through the development of property and air rights.

Cities like Copenhagen and Singapore have benefited from cogent regional visions that ensure that high-capacity transit investments produce desired urban-form outcomes (box O.1). Experiences from these and other cities suggest that station area planning needs to be carried out selectively and judiciously. In many instances, planning efforts should be devoted to developing or redeveloping no more than a handful of rail and BRT stations, in order to allow resources to be concentrated effectively. Doing so increases the odds of a "win-win" arrangement in which both public and private interests can co-participate in the benefits new transit investments

> **Box O.1 Transforming a vision into a conceptual image of the future metropolis**
>
> The first steps in moving transit and land-use integration from theory to reality are formulating a vision and transforming it into a conceptual image of the future metropolis. Prime examples of such a process include Copenhagen's "Finger Plan" and Singapore's "Constellation Plan."
>
> Copenhagen's Finger Plan is a textbook example of a long-range planning vision shaping rail investments, which in turn shaped urban growth (figure BO.1.1). Local planners identified corridors to channel overspill growth from urban centers early in the planning process. Rail infrastructure was built, often in advance of demand, to steer growth along desired growth axes.
>
> **Figure BO.1.1 Copenhagen's "Finger Plan" for urban development**
>
> *Source:* Cervero 1998; reproduced with permission from Island Press, Washington, DC.

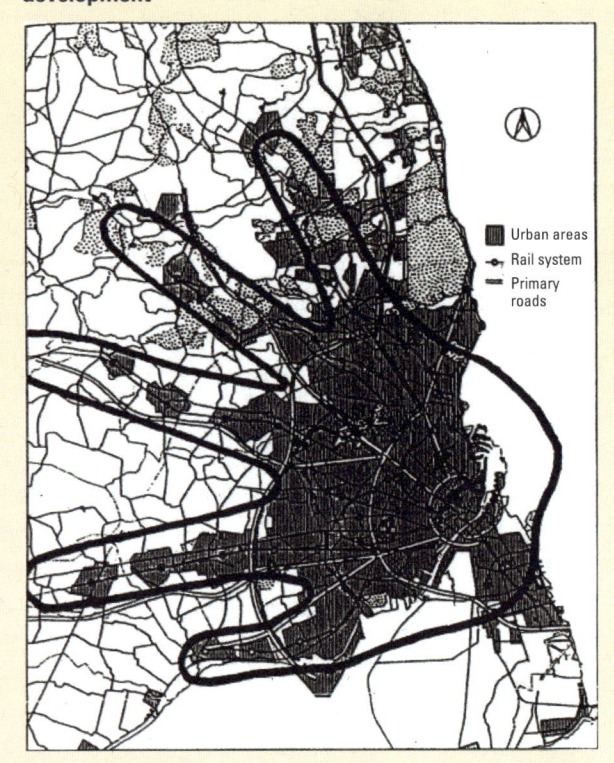

yield. Demonstrating that positive land-use changes are possible in conjunction with transit investment is important for producing models that the larger development community can emulate as well as for convincing lenders that investing in station area projects can be financially remunerative.

Planning visions of transit and land-use integration are important, but adequate funding is needed for successful execution. An important lesson from international experience is that transit and land-use integration can yield the income needed to expedite and support the process. Experiences in cities like Hong Kong SAR, China and Tokyo show that "value capture"— an infrastructure financing concept that seeks to capture land value created

Box O.1 Transforming a vision into a conceptual image of the future metropolis (continued)

Figure BO.1.2 Singapore's "Constellation Plan" for urban development

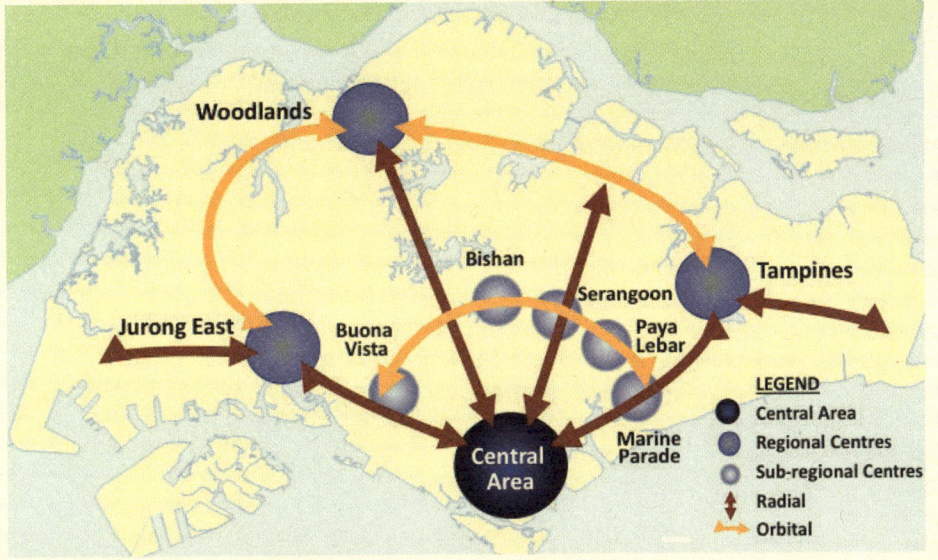

Source: Singapore Land Transport Authority 2008; reproduced with permission.

Singapore has embraced Scandinavian planning principles that call for radial corridors that interconnect the central core with master-planned new towns (figure BO.1.2). Its spatial plan has the appearance of a constellation of satellite "planets" (new towns), which surround the central core, interspersed by protective greenbelts and interlaced by high-capacity, high-performance rail transit.

Source: Authors.

by new infrastructure, particularly transit—is effective not only for sustainable finance but also for sustainable urbanism. Value capture is particularly well suited for financing transit infrastructure in dense, congested settings, where a high premium is placed on accessibility and the institutional capacity exists to administer the program. Accessibility benefits, which get capitalized into land values, present enormous opportunities for recapturing some of the value created by transit investment, at least as a supplement to fare-box income and other traditional revenue sources.

Even in ultra-dense, transit-friendly Hong Kong SAR, China, rail investments are not financially viable on their own: the Hong Kong Mass Transit Railway (MTR) meets investors' demands for return on equity only as a result of its property development. Value capture and joint development not only generate income to help retire rail-capital investment bonds and finance operations, they also create market demand that ensures high-ridership services. Hong Kong SAR, China's version of a public-private partnership is not about off-loading the cost of building railways to the private sector. Rather, it is about "co-development"—development in which each sector brings its natural advantage to the table (for example, land acquisition powers in the case of the public sector, access to equity capital in the case of the private sector). The resulting "win-win" situation leads to financially viable investments and forges a close connection between rail systems and nearby real estate development that attracts tenants, investors, and transit riders.

Greater Tokyo's private railways have historically practiced transit value capture on an even grander scale, building massive new towns along rail-served corridors and cashing in on the construction, retail, and household service opportunities created by these investments. In both Hong Kong SAR, China and Tokyo, rail and property development has created a virtuous cycle of viable railway operations and a highly transit-oriented built form.

Important to capturing transit value in both cities has been institutional adaptation and change. In Hong Kong SAR, China, MTR executives gained an appreciation over time of the importance of urban design, pedestrian circulation, and public amenities, all of which are particularly important in dense, crowded cities. They also created financially successful Rail + Property (R+P) projects (figure O.1). The emergence of the city as an international gateway, combined with its economic transformation from traditional manufacturing to a service-based economy, opened up new possibilities for R+P in both shaping growth and serving new market demands. To its credit, MTR made a conscious decision to build high-quality, mixed-use R+P projects on greenfields en route to the new international airport as well as on brownfields served by central-city railway extensions. These projects have proven to be wise investments: recent-generation R+P projects that functionally and architecturally blend with surrounding communities have outperformed earlier projects in terms of ridership gains and real estate market returns.

Experiences in Tokyo, and to a lesser degree Seoul and Stockholm, also underscore the importance of market adaptation. In Tokyo, the downturn in the real estate market, slower economic growth, and a changing demographic structure prompted private railway companies—both new and old—to seek new market opportunities, most notably infill housing and mixed-use developments around major central-city railway terminals. Such redevelopment complements the earlier towns built by private companies. To appeal to professionals and a more youthful labor force, planners are placing greater emphasis on creating high-quality urban spaces in and around joint development projects. Resiliency in the design and planning of "new-towns/in-towns" has also been a hallmark of recent urban regeneration successes in Seoul and Stockholm.

Successful value capture schemes depend to a significant degree on a supportive institutional environment. In Washington, DC, a single

Figure O.1 The Maritime Square residential-retail project developed by the Mass Transit Railway of Hong Kong SAR, China

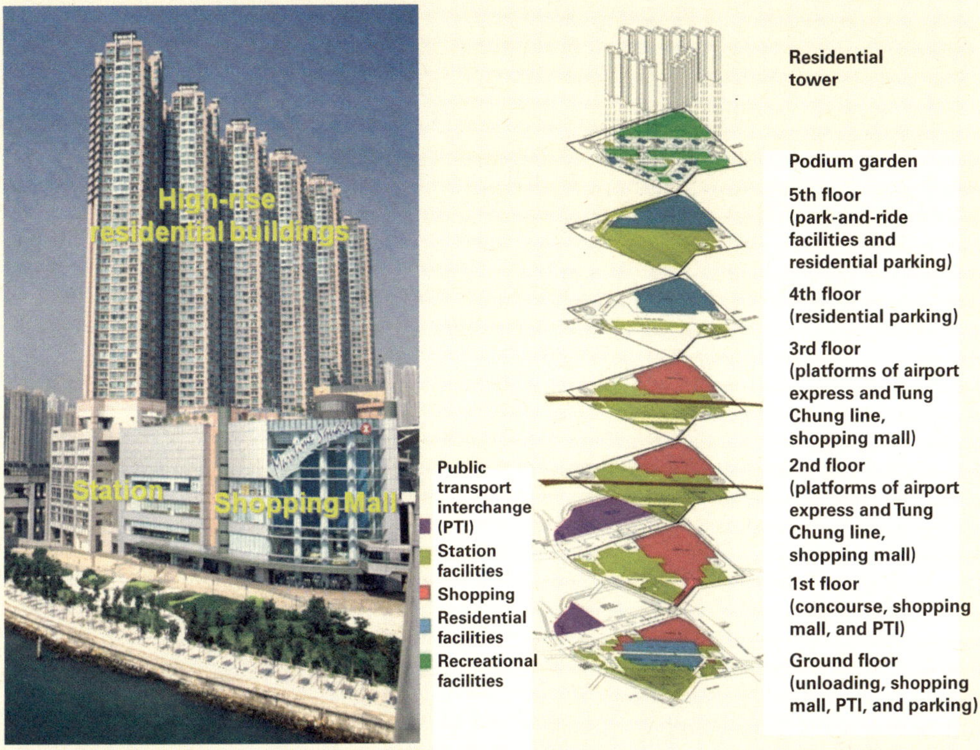

[Image labels: High-rise residential buildings; Station; Shopping Mall]

Legend:
- Public transport interchange (PTI)
- Station facilities
- Shopping
- Residential facilities
- Recreational facilities

Residential tower

Podium garden

5th floor (park-and-ride facilities and residential parking)

4th floor (residential parking)

3rd floor (platforms of airport express and Tung Chung line, shopping mall)

2nd floor (platforms of airport express and Tung Chung line, shopping mall)

1st floor (concourse, shopping mall, and PTI)

Ground floor (unloading, shopping mall, PTI, and parking)

Source: Courtesy of MTR Corporation Ltd.
Note: Situated above the Tsing Yi Station between the center of the city and the new international airport, Maritime Square features a hierarchy of integrated uses: a shopping mall extends from the ground floor to the third level; the station concourse sits on the first floor, with rail lines and platforms above and ancillary/logistical functions (such as public transit/bus interchange and parking) at or below; above the fourth and fifth floor residential parking lies a podium garden, and above that are luxury residential towers.

transit authority—the Washington Metropolitan Area Transit Authority (WMATA)—was formed and given the resources needed to leverage TOD. Particularly important was the formation of a proactive real estate development department within the organization, staffed by individuals with private sector experience to create a more entrepreneurial approach to land development. Creating a town planning and urban design department to ensure that joint development projects are of high quality and architecturally integrated is another key institutional reform, as demonstrated by the case of Hong Kong SAR, China.

Lessons from Case Studies in Developing Countries

Faced with ever-worsening traffic congestion and deteriorating environmental conditions, many cities in developing countries have turned to public transit systems in an effort to reverse course. Transit investments, proponents hope, will also help reverse automobile-dependent patterns of urban growth.

Case studies reveal that transit in developing countries has been guided primarily by the almost singular objective of enhancing mobility (that is, the ease and speed of moving about cities). Motivated by the need to see results while current city leaders are still in office, city administrations and transit agencies often adopt a short-term, narrow focus—for example, on rapidly relieving congestion. In this process, the long-term visions of promoting sustainable patterns of urban growth are often lost. This mindset is reflected in the absence of strategies and regulations to create higher densities along transit corridors and high-quality urban spaces. Both can be vital to increasing transit and nonmotorized transit use, thus reducing private automobile travel.

Two cities—Ahmedabad, India and Bogota, Colombia—serve as case studies for probing the opportunities and challenges posed by integrated transit and urban development. Careful analysis of their BRT projects and urban development trends identified eight major barriers to transit and land-use integration:

- lack of regional coordination at the metropolitan level
- sector silo behavior and practices at the city level
- inadequate policies and regulations for strategically creating "articulated densities" (densities that are strategically distributed across parts of a metropolitan area)
- restrictive national regulations and administrative constraints
- inconsistencies in the planning instruments and deficiencies in their implementation
- inadequate policies, regulations, and supporting mechanisms for redeveloping built-up areas, particularly brownfields or distressed and blighted districts
- neglected urban design at the neighborhood and street level
- financial constraints.

Although their BRT systems have improved overall mobility, these two cities have yet to fully explore the potential benefits of transit and land-use integration. Quantifiable evidence on land-use impacts is limited in both cases, as the initial phases of the BRT systems were constructed primarily to meet existing traffic demand in built-up areas. Since then, market responses to new development opportunities have emerged, particularly along corridors close to economically strategic locations, such as large-scale riverfront development sites or areas closest to international airports.

Lack of regional coordination at the metropolitan level

At the metropolitan scale, governments need to closely coordinate land-use plans, infrastructure investments, and urban services. The management of a metropolitan region is an exceedingly complex task, because it involves diversified governmental entities at multiple governing levels. Through decentralization, the national government devolves some of its decision-making powers and fiscal functions to lower-level governments. However, devolution can sometimes isolate municipalities, making regional collaboration more difficult unless proper regulatory and institutional coordination mechanisms are incorporated.

Political and economic competition among municipalities often impedes the coordination of planning, investment, and service provision across administrative boundaries, a challenge Bogota and its neighboring municipalities currently face. For example, the city's BRT (the TransMilenio) and other regional bus services are not well connected, making commuting for many low-income people who work in Bogota but live in neighboring municipalities difficult. This deficiency arises from the fact that TransMilenio's service jurisdiction does not align with the regional context under which Bogota-Cundinamarca (Bogota's regional department) planning and policy making occurs. Recognizing these institutional shortcomings, in 2011, the national government enacted the Territorial Ordinance Organic Law (Ley Organica do Ordemamiento Territorial [LOOT]) to promote regional coordination. It is too early to gauge its effectiveness.

Sector silo behavior and practices at the city level

At the city level, departments and agencies have varying missions, objectives, budgets, management styles, governance structures, and staff profiles. These differences often hinder the types of cross-sector and interagency coordination needed for transit and land-use integration.

Transportation department staffs often have little knowledge of urban planning and design, and urban planners have little knowledge of transportation, making seamless integration and implementation of the two difficult. Transportation department staffs have limited capacity to take proactive measures toward integrating transit and land use (and often limited interest as well). Staff members from the two departments work under different management and budgetary constraints, and they have little incentive for uncertain cross-sector coordination.

The mobility secretariat and TransMilenio S.A. developed TransMilenio with little coordination with the city's other relevant secretariats, particularly the urban planning secretariat. New urban development near the BRT stations or corridors is limited, for example, except in the airport corridor and some commercial complex developments close to BRT terminal stations. The paucity of development near many TransMilenio stops may be related to the fact that the floor area ratios (FAR) of these areas (which had been kept low, at less than 2.0, except in the central business district and a few other areas) have not been adjusted, even though land values near the BRT stations and corridors have increased. In addition, the BRT station designs are not well integrated with the urban fabric of nearby neighborhoods and streets.

Inadequate policies and regulations for strategically creating articulated densities

Most large cities in Asia and in most developing countries have higher average population densities than land-rich Australia, Canada, and the United States. Ahmedabad (with 18,430 people per square kilometer, according to the 2001 census) and Bogota (with 21,276 people per square kilometer in 2010, according to the Secretary of Planning for the City of Bogota) are among the densest cities in the world. For various reasons, politicians, planners, and residents of most high-density cities in developing countries have a desire to "de-concentrate" and spread development to new areas rather than increase density in existing built-up areas.

It is widely believed that cities in developing countries cannot accommodate additional growth or densification in built-up areas. Indeed, city authorities tend to consider population growth and the limited "carrying capacity" of the city as prime causes of chronic gaps between the demand for and supply of urban services or their low quality. They tend to prefer development of peripheral greenfields rather than urban redevelopment in the city core, because greenfield development is faster and costs less up front (Burchell and others 2002).

Although expansion of the urban area of rapidly growing cities in developing countries is unavoidable to some extent, these arguments suggest that the only way to accommodate urban growth is to expand outward. This belief ignores the high life-cycle costs related to expanding the infrastructure network (for example, water pipelines and sewerage networks); operating and maintaining that network; and forgoing the high opportunity costs of expanded urban land use.

Although it logically follows that higher densities require an increased level of infrastructure investments, the perception that density leads to the deterioration of urban service provision is not necessarily true. Seoul (with 16,589 people per square kilometer in 2009, according to the UN Department of Economic and Social Affairs [UNDESA]) and Singapore (with 7,025 people per square kilometer [according to UNDESA]), for example, provide efficient and high-quality urban services while maintaining good environmental conditions.

Because of the prevalence of this negative perception of high average urban population density, policy makers and city planners in developing countries are often reluctant to ramp up urban density by allowing a higher FAR (box O.2). They also tend to apply either a uniform or too narrow a band of ratios across all city areas, without capitalizing on location premiums, such as proximity to transit stations or corridors. Controlling density without considering the land's economic value prevents cities from effectively managing their land use. In Ahmedabad, for example, the FAR of urban areas is kept low (1.80–2.25) for the entire urban area. In Bogota, except for the central business district and several peripheral areas, where

Box O.2 Articulated versus average density

What matters most for transit and land-use integration is not average population densities but "articulated densities"—densities that are strategically distributed across parts of a metropolitan area. The layout depicted in panel c of figure BO.2.1 is better suited for mass transit than the one in panel a, even though the two forms have the same average population density.

Figure BO.2.1 Importance of articulated density for mass transit

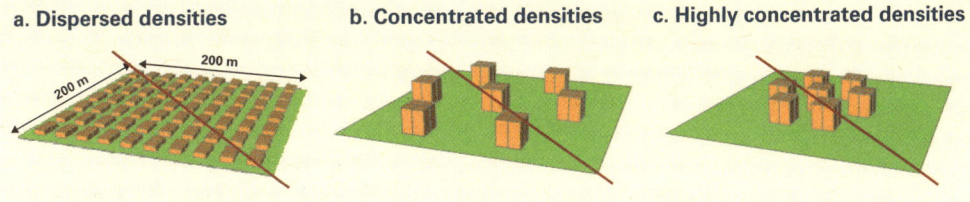

a. Dispersed densities   b. Concentrated densities   c. Highly concentrated densities

Source: Adapted from OECD 2012.
Note: Red line represents a mass transit line.

Curitiba, Brazil has created articulated densities along its BRT corridors (figure BO.2.2a). Bogota, Colombia has not done so along its TransMilenio corridors (figure BO.2.2b). It maintains a low FAR (0–2), except within the central business district and a few other selected spots.

Figure BO.2.2 Transit-oriented spatial development in Curitiba and Bogota

a. Curitiba, Brazil

Source: IPPUC 2009.
Note: Buildings in Curitiba, represented in bright yellow and orange, are strategically built along the BRT corridors with good urban planning. The current urban form was developed under a long-term vision; a TOD concept was first outlined in its 1965 Master Plan. Today, the city has lower greenhouse gas emission levels, less traffic congestion, and more livable urban spaces compared with other similar Brazilian cities. The red, green, and orange lines indicate the city boundaries.

b. Bogota, Colombia

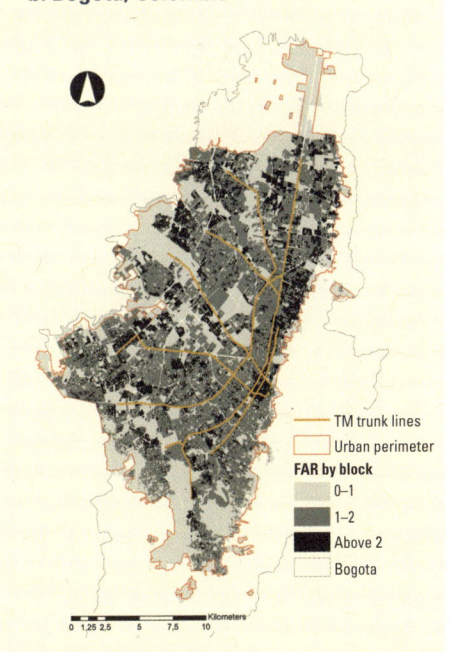

TM trunk lines
Urban perimeter
FAR by block
0–1
1–2
Above 2
Bogota

Source: World Bank.

no FAR restriction exists, the FAR is either 0–1.0 or 1.1–2.0, including near BRT stations and corridors.

The transit-oriented cities analyzed in chapter 2 of the book adopt much wider variations. Within the central business district area alone, these ratios range from 12 to 25 in Singapore, 8 to 10 in Seoul, 1 to 20 in Tokyo, and 1 to 12 in Hong Kong SAR, China. Each of these cities has developed different density ranges in different areas, taking social and economic features into consideration. In general, all allow for high-density construction around transit lines and stations.

Restrictive national regulations and administrative constraints

In addition to the FAR, certain national and local government regulations and administrative deficiencies adversely affect the smooth functioning of land markets. The result is the under- or oversupply of land, noncontiguous spatial development, and changes in land-use patterns that respond slowly to the values created by transit infrastructure. These regulations are major barriers to transit-oriented spatial development.

In India, many national regulations restricting the market's rational response significantly limit the ability of city planning instruments to redirect real estate development in a way that is consistent with a long-term spatial vision. For example, the Urban Land Ceiling Act (ULCA) of 1976 prevented developers or individuals from owning large parcels, thus hindering the redevelopment of vacant land of the closed textile mills until the law's abolishment in 1999. A high stamp duty on land sales, control over minimum plot sizes, and rent control are other examples of regulations that impede market-based property transactions and development.

Colombia has fewer national or local restrictive regulations hindering the smooth functioning of the real estate market. Problems there relate to the deficiency of the planning process and its implementation rather than regulatory constraints. In Bogota, because of the inconsistency between the Territorial Ordinance Plan (POT) and development plans, it usually takes four to five years to obtain a construction permit or approval to consolidate land (Samad, Lozano-Gracia, and Panman 2012). This problem is one reason why it is difficult for developers to undertake urban redevelopment projects, particularly large-scale, mixed-land, urban regeneration projects that require the consolidation of several pieces of land. These deficiencies in planning and administrative process make it difficult for the private sector to respond to the new development opportunities provided by the increase in the economic value of land near BRT stations and its corridors.

Inadequate policies, regulations, and supporting mechanisms for redeveloping built-up areas

Most transit investments in cities in developing countries take place first in already urbanized areas (as shown in the four case cities in developing countries), because the priority is to address existing unmet traffic demand and reduce congestion. Retrofitting these areas in response to new development opportunities created by transit is more complex and difficult than implementing TOD in greenfield development.

Retrofitting built-up areas is difficult for two reasons. First, private businesses or households own the majority of TOD precinct property; the government has little control over this land. In contrast, the government can control the construction of transit systems, once it secures the right of way and the funds for construction. Second, as its name indicates, the redevelopment of "built-up" areas—whether they be publicly owned or private property—requires the demolition of physical assets, such as infrastructure and housing stock, and their reconstruction. Such requirements have both economic and social implications, as redevelopment requires substantial costs and resettlement arrangements.

Neglected urban design at the neighborhood and street level

Transit shapes urban development, and land-use patterns influence travel demand. Land-use variables reflect not only trip interchange attributes (for example, travel time and the cost of travel from origin to destination) but also the attributes of the origins and destinations themselves (for example, density and degree of land-use mixture).

Density is not the only important element of land use and built environments. Other elements—including carefully articulated land-use mixtures; safe and smooth accessibility to transit stations (enabled by foot paths, cycle paths, and street lights, for example); and amenities such as benches, parks, landscaping, and libraries—contribute to the development of a good built environment. Some BRT stations in Bogota are located in the medians of six- to eight-lane highways, requiring passengers to walk across long steel access flyovers. The city has not been able to improve the quality of public places along BRT corridors, because the neighborhood redevelopment plan has not yet been implemented. A long line of unadorned walls occupies the space between the BRT corridors. The lack of urban design elements creates a disconnect between the transit system and the surrounding neighborhoods. This lack of integration does not promote the reconfiguration of the city layout along the BRT lines in a way that fosters vibrant urban life and economic activities.

Financial constraints

The huge upfront capital investment required to develop a transit system is one of the greatest obstacles to integrating transit and land use. This obstacle is particularly difficult to surmount because unprecedented urban growth has put severe pressure on the ability of local governments to finance infrastructure investments and urban services.

At the operation stage, cities sometimes need to provide subsidies, either to make up operational deficits or to provide vouchers for low-income riders. Scarce financial resources also sometimes oblige transit companies to choose routes based on the cost of right-of-way acquisition rather than on the long-term development potential of the areas to be served. In such cases, system design is driven primarily by the desire to minimize construction costs—by, for example, siting stations in the median of thoroughfares, reducing costly land takings and disruptions. Opportunities to maximize development are forgone.

Both Ahmedabad and Bogota recognize the benefits of integrating BRT or planned metros and urban development. Building on their experiences, both cities have huge potential to generate sizable revenues through value capture. Both cities recognize that improving the quality of pedestrian access and providing high-quality urban spaces next to transit stations will be pivotal in promoting TOD in future phases. True to the World Bank's Ecological Cities as Economic Cities (Eco^2) concept promoting sustainable urban development through cross-sector integration, this planning approach toward integrated urban space will facilitate the creation of cities that are not only cleaner, more livable, and more inclusive but cities that are more prosperous and economically competitive as well.

Toward Transit and Land-Use Integration

Case studies of cities that have aggressively invested in mass transit systems highlight the unique contexts and challenges of integration. Collectively, the insights gleaned from these case experiences point to policy recommendations and implementation measures that deserve careful consideration at different levels of strategic decisions and planning exercises.

Strategic vision and enabling institutional and regulatory framework

1. Develop strategic plans. A strategic vision is indispensable for successfully integrating transit and urban development. Transit is a means to help create desirable patterns of urban growth, not the other way around. It is, literally and figuratively, a vehicle for connecting people to places, thus contributing to creating the kinds of cities and neighborhoods in which people want to live, work, play, learn, and interact. Cities need to translate their visions of the future into the land-use and infrastructure elements of a statutory master plan, which must be market sensitive, socially inclusive, and rooted in fiscal realities.

2. Create a supportive institutional and government environment. Effective integration requires a robust regional governance structure that gives rise to intermunicipal cooperation; fosters accountability, in order to reduce negative spillovers across jurisdictions; and provides a territorial context for coordinating growth within a region's commuter and labor sheds. Regional institutions need to be endowed with the power of regulatory oversight and the funding capacities to finance investments required for integration. At the city level, the administration must have the capacity and political backing to overcome the inertia formed by parochial, unisectoral entities that view the world in silo terms. Creation of a super-organization that absorbs various agencies to redress this problem is rarely effective. Instead, the administration should focus on establishing consensus on critical, urgent issues that require institutional coordination and involve key stakeholders in the process. The administration also needs to align budgetary and human resource policies with the objectives of cross-sector cooperation. Walker (2012) states:

> The land planners do a long-range sketch of urban structure and this goes up on the wall in the transit planner's office, so that it guides daily thinking as well as long-range planning. The transit planner does a similar sketch of a long-range transit network, and this goes up on the wall in the land-use planner's office. That way, when developments are being approved, the short-term land-use planner can check whether the location is a good or bad one for transit and can judge developments accordingly. Meanwhile, as the long-term land-use planners stare at the transit map, they have new ideas for how to build communities around the proposed line and stations (figure O.2).

3. **Remove restrictive regulations and set appropriate prices on land.** Some national and local government regulations adversely affect the smooth functioning of land markets by distorting prices. The result is an under- or oversupply of land and noncontiguous spatial development. Regulations such as India's ULCA also inhibit the ability of transit infrastructure to change land-use patterns. These regulatory barriers to transit and land integration need to be removed in order to ensure the rational functioning of the land market. It is also important that the national government help manage the balance between private automobile and public transit use by removing various incentives for car use, such as subsidized fuel prices, low parking prices, and low toll charges.

4. **Aim for short-term mobility objectives and long-term sustainable urban-form goals, in parallel.** Cities are encouraged to try to realize both short-term mobility enhancement objectives and long-term sustainable development. Global best practices indicate that investing in more roads and transportation infrastructure in order to improve mobility in the short term eventually leads to more and longer-distance trips—what is called "induced traffic." By itself, supply-side expansion often provides only ephemeral congestion relief. Successful integrated spatial development can provide both near-term congestion relief and longer-term urban-form benefits. Effective integration is not automatic, however; it requires strong leadership and institutional efforts and support.

City-level planning approach

5. **Create articulated densities.** Simply stated, mass transit needs mass. Cities need to promote higher densities along transit-served corridors to ensure a critical mass of trip origins and destinations that will drive up ridership and thus increase cost effectiveness. How densities are organized in relationship to high-capacity transit services, not average densities, matters.

Figure O.2 A healthy conversation between transit and land-use planning officials

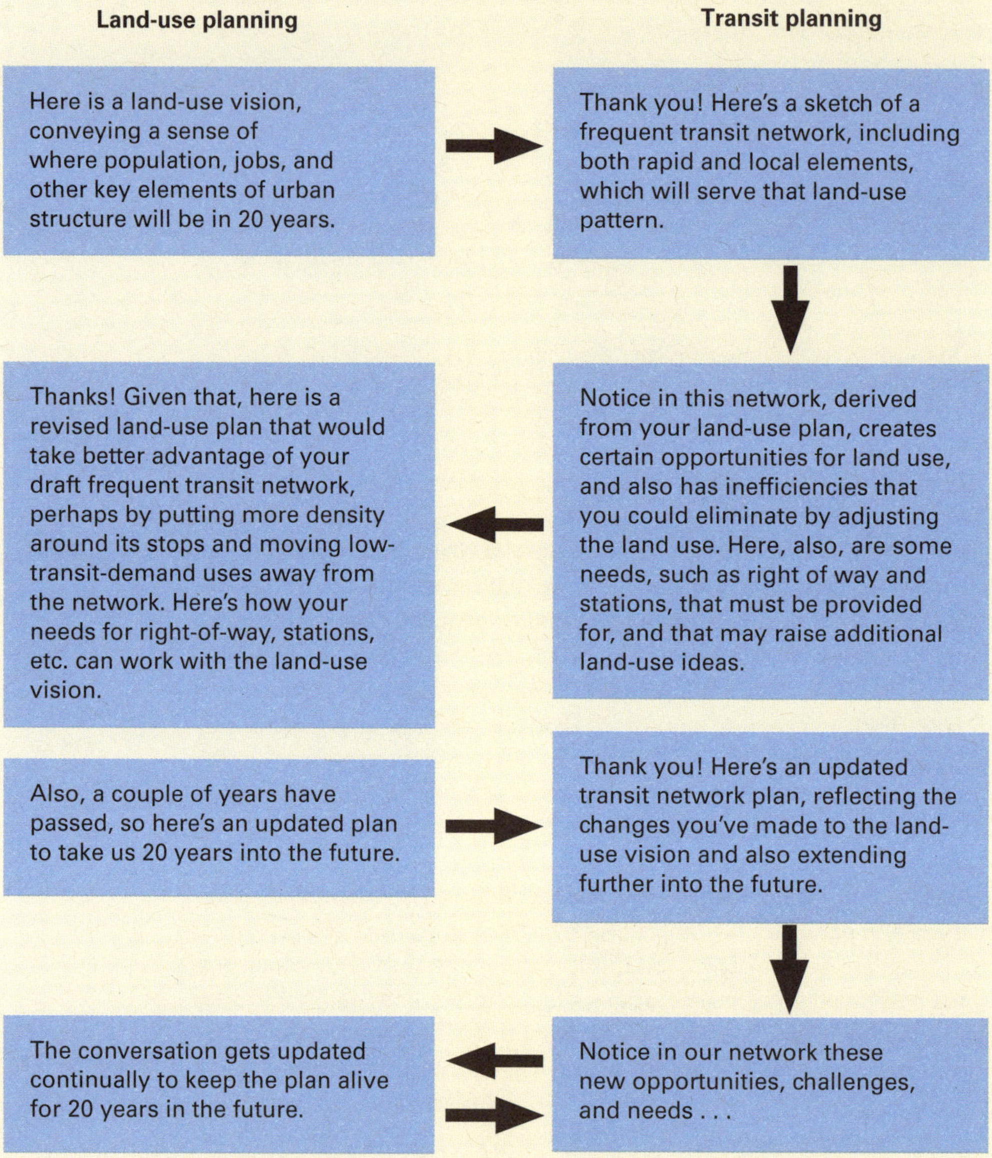

Land-use planning

- Here is a land-use vision, conveying a sense of where population, jobs, and other key elements of urban structure will be in 20 years.

- Thanks! Given that, here is a revised land-use plan that would take better advantage of your draft frequent transit network, perhaps by putting more density around its stops and moving low-transit-demand uses away from the network. Here's how your needs for right-of-way, stations, etc. can work with the land-use vision.

- Also, a couple of years have passed, so here's an updated plan to take us 20 years into the future.

- The conversation gets updated continually to keep the plan alive for 20 years in the future.

Transit planning

- Thank you! Here's a sketch of a frequent transit network, including both rapid and local elements, which will serve that land-use pattern.

- Notice in this network, derived from your land-use plan, creates certain opportunities for land use, and also has inefficiencies that you could eliminate by adjusting the land use. Here, also, are some needs, such as right of way and stations, that must be provided for, and that may raise additional land-use ideas.

- Thank you! Here's an updated transit network plan, reflecting the changes you've made to the land-use vision and also extending further into the future.

- Notice in our network these new opportunities, challenges, and needs . . .

Source: Walker 2012; adapted with permission from Island Press, Washington, DC.
Note: Similar conversations happen between land use and road planning, or between transit and road planning, etc., for other infrastructure or government objectives.

6. **Combine higher densities with diverse land uses and pedestrian-friendly design.** By themselves, higher densities are insufficient for promoting sustainable urban development. Experience shows that to promote sustainable travel and city form, higher densities must be complemented

by diverse land uses, high-quality public places, and pedestrian-friendly street designs. Such physical interventions can shorten trips, encourage nonmotorized travel, keep many trips within the TOD neighborhood, and increase transit use.

7. **Create a supportive environment to leverage TOD.** Enhancing accessibility through urban transit investments is rarely sufficient to trigger significant land-use changes. A number of factors must be in place if significant land-use shifts are to occur as a result of newly opened transit stations (figure O.3):

- the presence of other new nearby land developments, spurred perhaps by public sector urban renewal projects or private developers reacting to market opportunities
- the availability of developable land
- the existence of strong regional demand for new growth
- supportive government policies and measures, including tax incentives, infrastructure investments, and community involvement through participatory planning.

8. **Exploit implementation tools.** A host of regulatory and incentive-based tools for promoting transit and land-use integration is available, including the following:

- establishment of a redevelopment authority to convert brownfields and distressed urban districts, with the power to underwrite the cost of land development through such mechanisms as tax-increment financing and assistance with land assemblage/acquisition through eminent domain powers
- land consolidation and readjustment schemes to assemble land and finance local infrastructure improvements around major transit stations
- process-related tools, such as streamlining development reviews and fast-tracking the permitting of projects
- TOD and site and street guidelines that illustrate how TODs can contribute to an efficient arrangement of land uses and increase ridership.

Such implementation tools often require the passage of enabling legislation by higher levels of government before introduction by local authorities.

9. **Rationalize mainline transit investments and feeder systems.** High-quality transit services must be provided if TOD is to yield significant accessibility benefits. Such services are not only time competitive with private automobiles, they are also free of extreme overcrowding, they are reasonably on time, and they provide exceptionally high-quality feeder access. Global

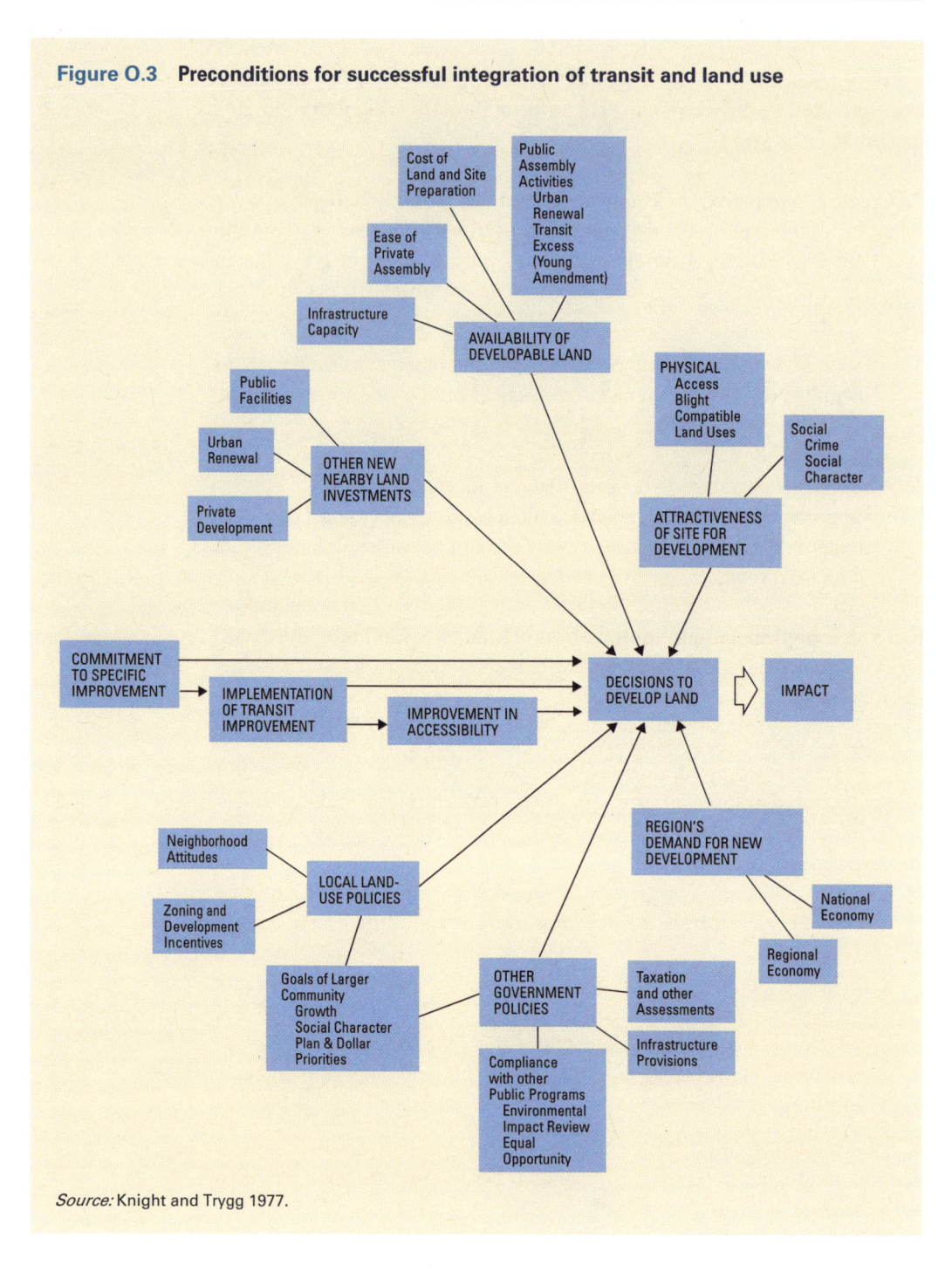

Figure O.3 Preconditions for successful integration of transit and land use

Source: Knight and Trygg 1977.

experiences point to the importance of providing well-integrated, seamless pedestrian connections between surrounding neighborhoods and transit stops. Particularly important are "green connectors," which provide perpendicular bikeway and pedway linkages to transit stations and surrounding areas.

Promoting and implementing transit-oriented development

10. Create TOD typologies. Cities in developing countries need to build a typology of transit station environments and TODs, backed by realistic market assessments and illustrative design templates. A diverse portfolio of plans and layouts is more likely to reflect market realities and regulatory factors—such as responding to emerging consumer preferences and ensuring the availability of usable land—than a standardized, one-size-fits-all approach.

11. Create TOD prototypes. For cities with little history of TOD, or even transit and land-use integration, it is important that prototypes be introduced as a way to test the waters in both market and political terms. Each city presents a unique context for creating such prototypes.

12. Combine TOD with transportation demand management (TDM). TOD hardware—the physical design that promotes transit ridership and nonmotorized access—needs supportive software. When introduced with TOD, TDM measures such as congestion pricing and parking controls can yield synergies, such as increases in transit ridership from combining incentives for using public transit with disincentives for using automobiles.

13. Mainstream social development in TOD (make cities inclusive). TOD should not be just about creating economically efficient and environmentally friendly urban spaces. It should also help address the most serious problem facing many cities in developing countries: crippling urban poverty and deprivation. Land markets typically respond by increasing land prices in and around transit stations, which often displaces low-income households. Where possible, city authorities should aggressively pursue affordable housing policies and developer incentives to ensure that affordable housing is built close to transit stops.

Financing scheme

14. Pursue sustainable finance through value capture. Vertical growth, rather than horizontal expansion, is vital to accommodating urbanization pressures and combating the negative impacts of automobile-dependent sprawl. Strategically targeted densities suitable for transit use can create a more compact city. However, higher densities require expanded or upgraded urban infrastructure, including transit services. Ahmedabad plans to construct a new metro connecting its downtown and the state capital, Gandhinagar. Bogota plans to construct a new metro system to increase passenger capacity in the extended central business district. As rail is more expensive than BRT, the biggest challenge for cities planning major transit upgrades is to secure adequate financial resources in light of limited budgets.

Value capture is the most promising fiscal tool available for generating new revenue. It can directly occur through land ownership or joint development, as the cases of Hong Kong SAR, China and Tokyo reveal. It can also occur indirectly, by extracting surplus from other property owners through the imposition of betterment taxes, the creation of benefit assessment districts, and the reaping of higher regular property tax proceeds, for example.

Successful value capture schemes depend, to a significant degree, on a supportive institutional environment. Particularly important is the formation of a proactive real estate development department within a transit agency, staffed by seasoned professionals with private sector experience who bring an entrepreneurial approach to land development. Transit company management should foster an organizational culture that embraces property development as a legitimate mission of the organization, as successful transit operations are not just about running trains and buses on time but also about shaping markets and ensuring high levels of future ridership through carefully placed development. Equally important to increasing urban densities and creating needed institutional capacity is ensuring a supportive legislative environment that empowers transit authorities to pursue joint development projects.

The most challenging issue in applying value capture in developing countries is the lack of transparency in property rights registration systems and the complex procedures associated with land acquisition and transaction. Without straightforward, transparent, and efficient regulations and procedures for land registration and transactions, the successful application of value capture financing schemes is difficult, if not impossible.

Core Lessons on Transit Investments and Urban Growth

Seven lessons about using transit investments to reshape urban forms can be drawn from global experiences:

1. *The impacts of transit-related land use are greatest before an upswing in regional growth.* Investment timing strongly influences whether significant land-use shifts will occur. For many rapidly developing cities, investing in transit during growth spurts can translate into appreciable land-use impacts, assuming the institutional capacity and wherewithal to leverage land development opportunities are present.
2. *Transit systems generally reinforce and often accelerate decentralization.* By improving accessibility to different parts of a region, extensive railway and BRT networks, like their highway counterparts, generally encourage suburbanization to some degree. However, transit-oriented growth can follow a much more sustainable pattern than the one fostered by highways.
3. *Proactive planning is necessary if decentralized growth is to take the form of subcenters.* An aggressive effort to leverage the benefits of mass transit services can lead to more concentrated forms of decentralized growth.

4. *Radial high-capacity transit systems such as BRT and metros help keep downtowns economically viable.* These systems lead to increased employment growth in urban centers, because such centers receive the largest incremental gains in regional accessibility. However, the regional shares of jobs and retailing that are downtown often still fall in the wake of new transit investments, because of the decentralization trends mentioned above. They would have fallen even more, however, were it not for central business district–focused railway services.
5. *Under the right conditions, railways and high-capacity busways can spur central city redevelopment.* When government agencies are willing to absorb some of the risks inherent in redeveloping depressed and economically stagnant neighborhoods, railways and high-capacity busways can help attract private capital and breathe new life into struggling areas. However, an unwavering public commitment is necessary to underwrite redevelopment costs and provide needed financial investments.
6. *Other pro-development measures must accompany railway and high-capacity busway investments.* In addition to financial incentives, software policies are needed to make transit hardware attractive to land developers. These policies include various financial and tax incentives and process basis tools.
7. *Network effects matter.* For fixed-guideway railway and high-capacity busway systems to induce large-scale land-use changes, they must provide the geographic coverage and regional accessibility of their chief competitors, limited-access freeways and highways. The addition of exclusive-guideway services can create spillovers and synergies, benefiting not only the newly served corridors but existing ones as well.

Roles of Development Financial Institutions

Given that a denser, transit-oriented, built form results in more cost-effective transit investments, a sensible policy position would tie outside financial assistance to bona fide local efforts to improve coordination and integration. In addition to providing financial assistance for physical investments, financial institutions must help national governments address regulatory constraints and help cities develop their institutional capacities to design and implement prototype TODs and value capture schemes. This approach requires a hybrid lending instrument that combines policy and regulatory reforms, capacity development, and physical investment components.

Conclusion

This report seeks to build on the Eco^2 concept (which promotes sustainable urban development through cross-sector integration) by focusing on integrated transit and land-use development as a promising strategy for advancing environmental sustainability, economic development, and inclusive development. If done well, integrated spatial development—particularly the physical linkage of transit investments and urban development—can create positive and meaningful Eco^2 outcomes. Achieving such effective integration requires a cogent, forward-looking strategic vision; an enabling institutional framework; and sustainable financial models.

A point emphasized throughout this report is the importance of developing visions of urban futures. Experiences from Scandinavian cities like Copenhagen and Stockholm reveal that a clear and compelling regional vision is critical if high-capacity transit investments are to produce desired urban-form outcomes.

It is also imperative that there be a financial model to sustain TODs. Such a model can occur at two levels and in two directions. The macro, top-down perspective of sustainable financing is critical for cities competing regionally or globally. Pursuing a strategy of compact, mixed-use, high-quality development—whether TOD or smart growth in general—at the citywide or even metropolitan level can become an effective regional economic development tool, making city regions more economically competitive in the global marketplace. A high-quality, functional regional transit system that links high-quality urban centers creates the kind of built environment that is of increasing importance to amenity-conscious firms, employers, and employees. Blending good urban design with compact, mixed-use TOD becomes an effective tool for attracting outside investments, knowledge-based companies, and businesses, which increasingly place a premium on livability and quality of place. Cities that manage to create great environments around transit stations can enjoy a competitive edge in recruiting and retaining highly sought firms, which are instrumental in fostering regional economies. Experiences with orienting growth in transit-served corridors matched by high-quality urban design—in cities such as Hong Kong SAR, China; Seoul; Singapore; and Stockholm—reveal that good urbanism is wholly compatible with economic prosperity and competitiveness. Given that cities globally contribute 75 percent of gross domestic product (GDP), this macro perspective should also be of prime interest to national governments.

At the micro, bottom-up level, financial sustainability can take the form of value capture as a tool for generating revenue—funds that go to pay for not only the stations, tracks, and vehicles but also for all the upgrades and enhancements that are needed within a half-kilometer, five-minute walkshed of the station to create a high-quality environment for living, working, playing, learning, and interacting. The revenue could also finance social housing and associated facilities for low-income people. As experiences in Hong Kong SAR, China and Tokyo reveal, using some of the profit from selling land or development rights to the private sector to embellish public spaces and pedestrian environments around stations can lead to better projects that generate higher profits as well as higher property tax revenues. The resulting TOD is not only environmentally but also financially sustainable.

A virtuous cycle is set in motion in which denser, high-quality TODs generate higher profits and fiscal revenue, some of which can go into creating additional high-quality TODs.

As new urban growth shifts to cities in the developing world, unprecedented opportunities will arise for linking land development and transit infrastructure. While motorization rates are subsiding in the developed world, they are growing exponentially elsewhere. The potential for payoffs from successful integration of transit and land use in the Nairobis, Jakartas, and Mexico Cities of the world is therefore enormous.

Given that the vast majority of future urban growth that is projected for cities will occur in cities with fewer than half a million people (UN Habitat 2011), a bus-based form of smaller-scale TOD interlaced with high-quality infrastructure for pedestrians and cyclists may be appropriate in many settings. Many cities in the developing world have the kinds of conditions needed if railway and BRT investments are to trigger meaningful land-use changes, including rapid growth, rising real incomes, and increased motorization and congestion levels.

Effective BRT requires supportive planning policies and zoning regulations, public sector leveraging and risk-sharing opportunities, and the capacity to manage the land-use shifts that are put in motion by transit infrastructure investments. Cities in developing countries are well positioned to learn from international experiences with transit-induced changes in land use. Few, however, have adopted the practices of cities like Hong Kong SAR, China; Tokyo; and Washington, DC in engaging private investors to co-finance capital investments through ancillary land development. Such value capture initiatives could go a long way toward putting cities in developing countries on more sustainable pathways—in terms of both facility financing and future patterns of urban development. Among all the tools available, TOD combined with value capture offers the most promise for putting the Eco^2 concept of sustainable growth and economic prosperity into practice.

References

Burchell, R. W., G. Lowenstein, W. Dolphin, and C. Galley. 2000. "Costs of Sprawl 2000." Report 74, Transportation Research Board, National Research Council, Washington, DC.

Cervero, R. 1998. *The Transit Metropolis: A Global Inquiry*. Washington, DC: Island Press.

IPPUC (Instituto de Pesquisa e Planejamento Urbano de Curitiba). 2009. Slide from presentation made on April 2, IPPUC, Curitiba, Brazil.

Knight, R. and L. Trygg. 1977. *Land Use Impacts of Rapid Transit: Implications of Recent Experience*. Washington, DC: Office of the Secretary of Transportation.

OECD (Organisation for Economic Co-operation and Development). 2012. *Compact City Policies: A Comparative Assessment.* OECD Green Growth Studies. Paris: OECD.

Samad, T., N. Lozano-Gracia, and A. Panman, eds. 2012. *Colombia Urbanization Review: Amplifying the Gains from the Urban Transition.* Directions in Development. Washington, DC: World Bank

Singapore Land Transport Authority (SLTA). 2008. *Long Term Master Plan: A People-Centered Land Transport System.* Singapore: SLTA.

UN Habitat (United Nations Human Settlements Programme). 2011. *Global Report on Human Settlements 2011: Cities and Climate Change.* Nairobi: UN Habitat.

Walker, J. 2012. *Human Transit: How Clearer Thinking about Public Transit Can Enrich Our Communities and Our Lives.* Washington, DC: Island Press.

CHAPTER 1

Introduction: Critical Challenges Facing Cities and Urban Transport

Worldwide, the urban transportation arena finds itself at a critical crossroads, as the growing presence of private automobiles influences not only the way people move about cities but the shape and form of cities themselves. This chapter examines the challenges posed by urban sprawl in the wake of rapidly increasing automobile ownership and usage as well as associated problems, such as the economic productivity losses from worsening traffic congestion, environmental deterioration, and social inequity. It highlights the need to integrate transit[1] and land use as a critical step toward achieving sustainable urban development, building on the World Bank's Ecological Cities as Economic Cities (Eco^2) model, which promotes sustainable urban development through cross-sector integration.

The role of transit in sustainable urban development is increasingly being recognized and promoted as a way to moderate climate change and increase the mobility of the poor. At the 2012 Rio+20 Conference, for example, international development banks, including the World Bank, announced a "game changer" commitment to sustainable transport and pledged substantial financial support over the next decade for this purpose (WRI 2012).[2]

This study explores the complex process of transit and land-use integration in rapidly growing cities in developing countries. It first identifies barriers to and opportunities for effective coordination of the transport infrastructure and urban development. It then recommends a set of policies and implementation measures for overcoming these barriers and exploiting these opportunities.

The study uses the comparative case study method to identify and learn from global best-case practices in promoting transit-oriented development (TOD)—compact, mixed-use, pedestrian-friendly development organized around a transit station—on a metropolitan scale. It analyzes the market-driven and policy-shaped interactions between bus rapid transit (BRT) systems (box 1.1) and urban development in four cities in developing countries.

Box 1.1 What is bus rapid transit?

Bus rapid transit (BRT) is the name given to sophisticated bus systems that have their own lanes on city streets. These systems use bus stations instead of bus stops, a design feature that allows passengers to pay before boarding the bus. Bus stations allow for faster, more orderly boarding similar to the procedures used on metro and light rail systems. Stations have elevated boarding platforms level with the bus floors, so that passengers do not need to climb steps to get on the bus. Electronic signage tells passengers when the next bus is arriving. BRT is faster, safer, more efficient, and more user-friendly than traditional bus systems.

Many cities are now choosing BRT, for two important reasons: cost and convenience. Building a heavy rail system can cost 10 times as much as building a BRT system. Light rail, which is common throughout Europe, is less expensive than heavy rail, but it can still cost more than four times as much as BRT. What's more, cities that opt for BRT can see results very quickly, as installing a system can take just two years. By contrast, building an underground metro can drag on for a decade.

Figure B1.1.1 Bus rapid transit in Curitiba, Brazil

Source: Photo of Curitiba, Brazil from EMBARQ website (http://www.embarq.org).

It pays particular attention to the impacts of public interventions—such as transit investments, planning regulations, tax policies, and financial incentives—on the ability to successfully integrate transit and urban development, all within the framework of the institutional and regulatory realities and constraints.

Expanding Cities, Shrinking Green Space

Cities in developing countries are growing at an unprecedented rate. Over the next several decades, most of the world's urban population growth

> **Box 1.2 Urban growth in Tehran**
>
> Tehran is one of the world's fastest-growing cities, with a population that increased from 6 million in 1985 to more than 10 million in 2009 (NASA Earth Observatory 2009). Color images of Tehran's expansion reveal that built-up areas have extended along roads along the city's outskirts (figure B1.2.1). To manage population growth and development, Tehran is currently upgrading and building new transport systems, including urban railways and BRT lines.
>
> **Figure B1.2.1 Aerial views of metropolitan Tehran, 1986 and 2009**
>
> a. 1986   b. 2009
>
> *Source:* NASA Earth Observatory 2009.

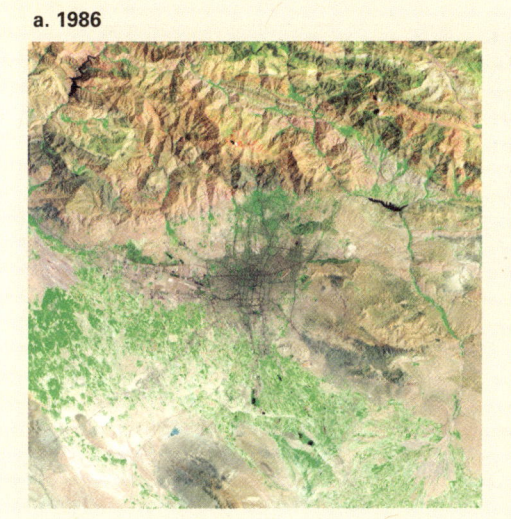

is projected to take place in developing countries, whose populations are expected to increase from 2.0 billion in 2000 to 5.5 billion by 2050. The number of urban inhabitants in developed countries, by contrast, is expected to stabilize at about 1 billion. Angel and others (2011) note that if developing countries continue to experience annual population growth rates of 2.5 percent and built-up densities continue to decline by 1.5 percent a year, their land coverage—often referred to as "sprawl"—will expand by 4.0 percent a year. At this rate, the world's cumulative area of built-up, impervious surfaces will double in 17 years and triple in 27 years. The long-term ecological consequences of converting land from natural habitats and open space to urban functions—diminished water supplies, the release of more pollutants into the air, heat-island effects, and lost agricultural land, for example—could be devastating.

Urban population growth and spatial expansion are expected to accelerate in the coming years, as migration from the countryside to cities continues (boxes 1.2 and 1.3). Cities have always attracted people from agrarian settings seeking better living, educational, and employment opportunities. At the same time, fast-growing cities create jobs that further accelerate their economic growth. Urbanization then further intensifies, as people and

Box 1.3 Urban expansion in the Jakarta metropolitan area

The population of Indonesia's capital city more than doubled in 30 years, rising from 6 million in the mid-1970s to 13 million in the early 2000s. In 1976, developed areas were mainly along Jakarta's northern coastal line (shown in light green in figure B1.3.1). By 1989, the city's urbanized area had expanded toward the eastern side of the metropolis. By 2004, Jakarta's land coverage extended southward, overtaking large amounts of land with vegetation and natural habitats (shown in red).

Figure B1.3.1 Aerial views of metropolitan Jakarta, 1976–2004

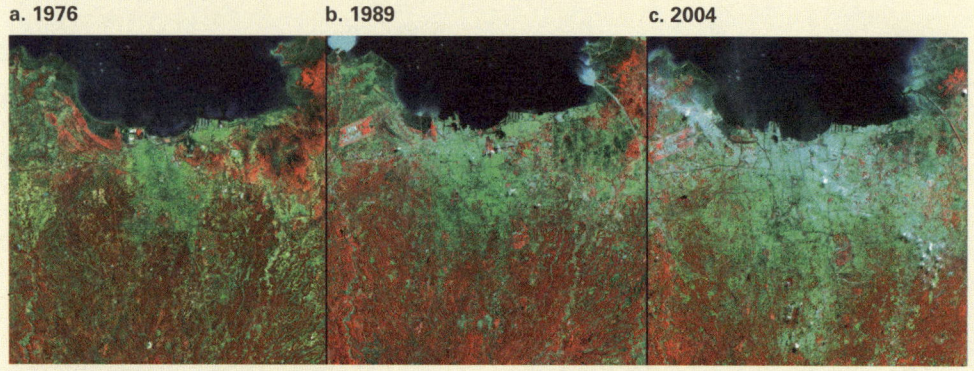

a. 1976   b. 1989   c. 2004

Source: NASA Earth Observatory 2005.

The images also reveal the transformation of Jakarta's built environment, marked not only by more land coverage but also by higher densities in general (figure B1.3.2). Many of the city's high-rise structures have been and continue to be built in an ad hoc, piecemeal manner, without a guiding long-range vision of physical form or institutional coordination.

Figure B1.3.2 Density of metropolitan Jakarta, 1988 and 2011

a. 1988   b. 2011

Photo by Sadao Orishimo.

growth spill out from city boundaries, sometimes in informal settlements that offer the only means of shelter to unskilled, poorly educated rural migrants.

The current speed of urbanization is extremely rapid. "Globally, towns and cities with populations equivalent to Malmö, Sweden—about 200,000 inhabitants—are built every day, 365 days a year" (Reutersward 2009).

Cities in the developing world are poised to play an increasingly central role in the global economy. They often provide relatively low-cost labor, less-stringent regulatory constraints, and a newly emerging consumer base. As they actively compete head-to-head regionally and globally, cities will continue to strive for agglomeration economies—that is, the economic benefits conferred by ease of access and face-to-face contact among specialized businesses and labor. Such market forces spawn economic clusters and concentrations within cities.

With rising incomes and population increases, cities will also expand spatially—more specifically, outward. The correlation between economic wealth and urban spatial coverage is strong and positive: big cities generally average higher gross domestic product (GDP) per capita than smaller ones.

Of concern is the fact that many rapidly growing cities around the world are poorly planned, managed, and governed. The absence of a long-term vision and spatial plans for where and how to develop, as well as a history of informal settlements or limited coordination among key institutions and stakeholders, undermine the ability to effectively and sustainably manage urban growth. When urban growth is poorly managed, cities and their inhabitants suffer the inescapable consequences: degraded urban environments, lost economic productivity, and widening income disparities and inequities.

To make matters worse, urbanization is outpacing the growth in municipal revenues, squeezing cities financially. As a consequence, cities in developing countries struggle to provide basic services like clean water, sanitation, and primary education, much less modern infrastructure like thoroughfares or high-capacity transit.

Cities for Cars, Not for People

One of the most critical challenges facing cities worldwide is automobile-dependent urban development.[3] With economic growth, many cities in developing countries have begun to follow the trajectory of motorization that developed countries once followed—but at a much faster rate. Worldwide, rising incomes are fueling automobile ownership, spurred by increasingly affordable vehicles. Many urban inhabitants—often the middle-income population—are shifting from public or nonmotorized transportation to private automobiles. In addition, higher incomes allow people to afford more spacious houses on large suburban lots, using their own cars to reach jobs and educational opportunities in the city. An automobile-oriented built form—marked by spread-out development, noncontiguous land uses, large city blocks that are unfriendly for pedestrians, and strip development—is an inevitable consequence of an automobile-dependent lifestyle.

Of particular concern is the fact that motorization rates are increasingly faster in the developing world. With rising incomes and modernization come more cars, trucks, and motorcycles. Motorcycles are viewed as stepping stones to full-blown car ownership; they also serve as an indicator of changes in income levels. The number of motorcycles in Bangkok increased

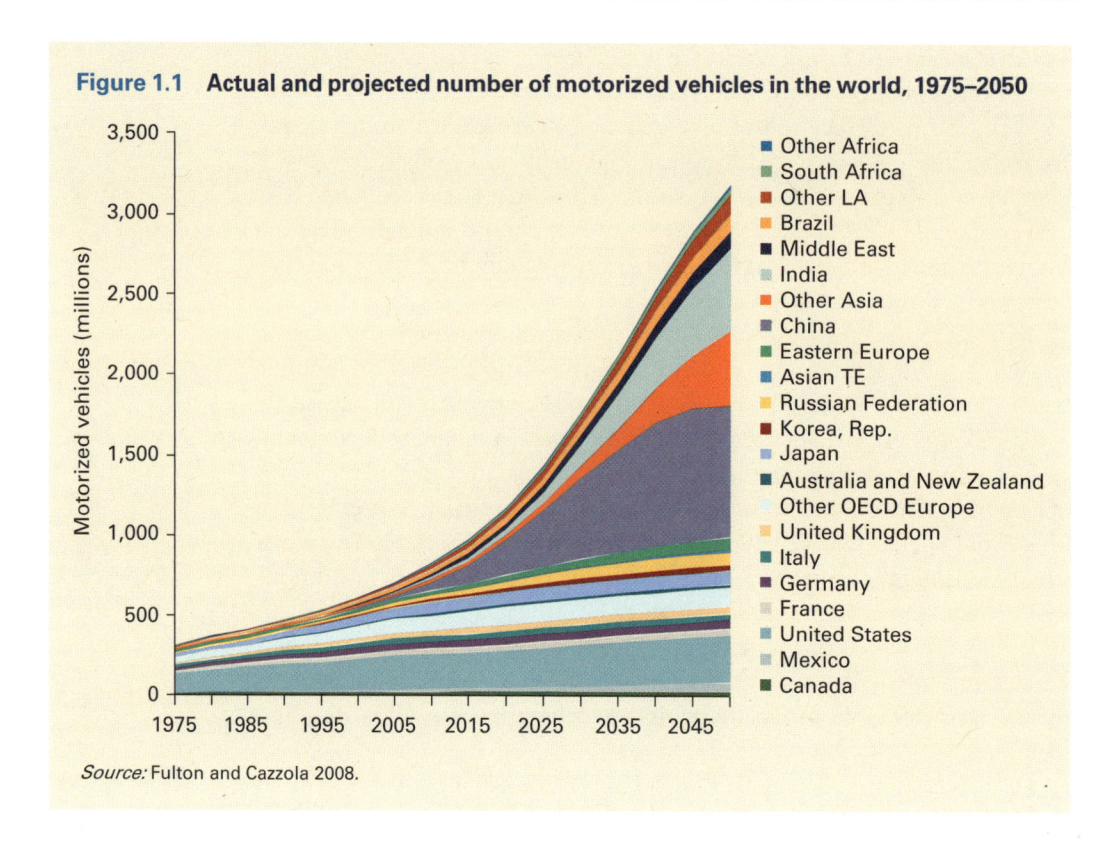

Figure 1.1 Actual and projected number of motorized vehicles in the world, 1975–2050

[Stacked area chart showing motorized vehicles (millions) from 1975 to 2045, ranging from 0 to 3,500 million. Categories from top to bottom in legend: Other Africa, South Africa, Other LA, Brazil, Middle East, India, Other Asia, China, Eastern Europe, Asian TE, Russian Federation, Korea, Rep., Japan, Australia and New Zealand, Other OECD Europe, United Kingdom, Italy, Germany, France, United States, Mexico, Canada.]

Source: Fulton and Cazzola 2008.

at an average annual rate of 34 percent in the 1990s (World Bank 1996). In many parts of China and India, motorization growth rates in cities today are believed to exceed 20 percent a year. These increases are, in part, supply driven. In China, for example, mainstreaming of the automotive industry and government investments in superhighways have contributed to the exponential increase in the numbers of motorized vehicles. By 2050, China is projected to have 900 million motor vehicles—more than the total number of cars, trucks, and motorcycles in the world today (figure 1.1). At the current rate of motorization, 2.3 billion automobiles will be added worldwide between 2005 and 2050, and more than 80 percent of them will end up on the roads and highways of developing countries (Chamon, Mauro, and Okawa 2008).

Rapid motorization has contributed to deteriorating traffic conditions worldwide, and congestion levels are worsening day by day. A 2010 study by IBM examined "global commuter pain" by polling 8,192 motorists in 20 global cities across 6 continents. According to the study, traffic congestion levels rose markedly between 2007 and 2010, despite the worldwide recession. With a 24 percent annual growth rate in registered vehicles, traffic conditions deteriorated the most in Beijing over this period.

In a follow-up survey in 2011, almost half of respondents reported that traffic had continued to worsen. Motorists in Moscow and Nairobi reported the worst commutes, with 45 percent of respondents in Moscow and 35 percent in Nairobi claiming they spent three or more hours a day stuck

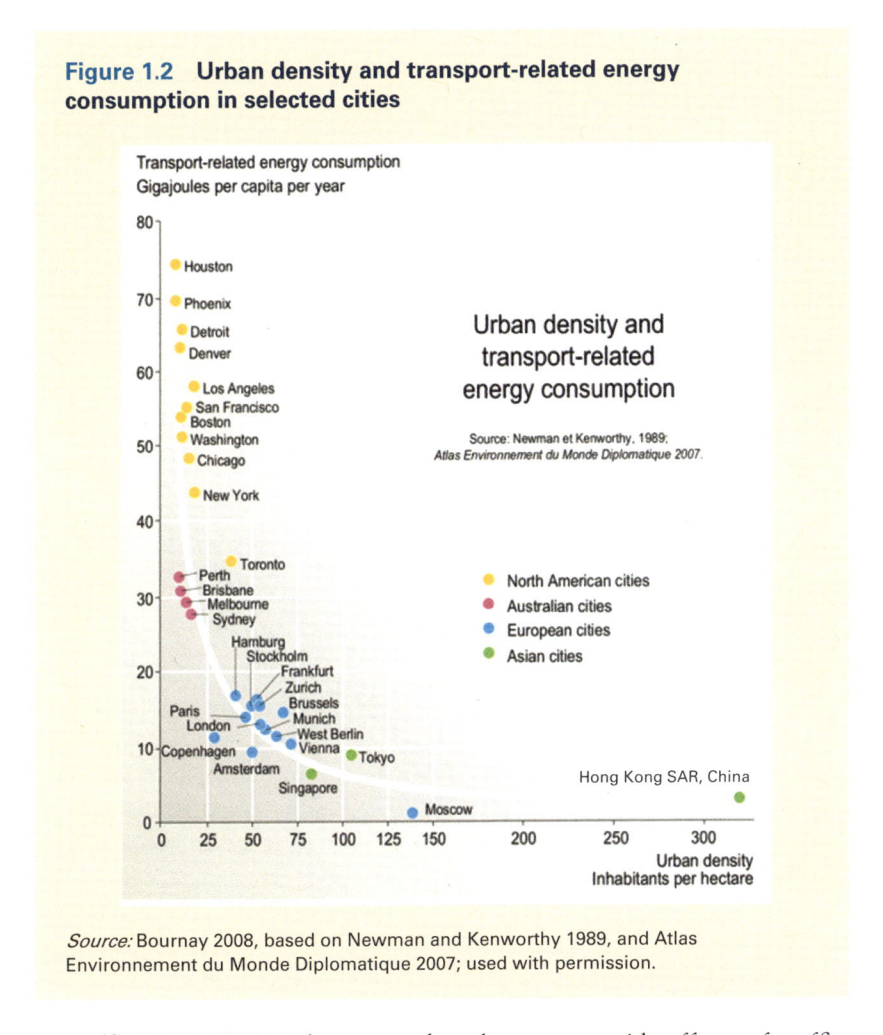

Figure 1.2 Urban density and transport-related energy consumption in selected cities

Urban density and transport-related energy consumption

Source: Newman et Kenworthy, 1989; Atlas Environnement du Monde Diplomatique 2007.

Source: Bournay 2008, based on Newman and Kenworthy 1989, and Atlas Environnement du Monde Diplomatique 2007; used with permission.

in traffic (IBM 2011). The survey found numerous side effects of traffic, including stress, road rage, respiratory ailments from dirty air, and bodily injuries and deaths from traffic accidents. Traffic congestion also has real and enduring economic consequences: over the course of a month, traffic caused about half of survey respondents to cancel a planned trip for work, shopping, recreation, entertainment, or dining out. Delays in the movement of people, goods, freight, and raw materials in and out of cities become a drag on economic productivity, reducing a city's competitiveness. One study estimates the economic loss from congestion-induced delays in Bangkok during the 1990s at more than $4 million a day (World Bank 1996).

Other negative consequences of automobile-dependent growth include excessive energy consumption and pollution. There is a strong association between urban density and energy consumption. One study finds that low-density cities made possible by high levels of car ownership average considerably higher energy consumption per capita than high-density cities (Newman and Kenworthy 1989) (figure 1.2). The difference partly reflects the fact that residents depend largely on private cars for travel in cities where fewer public transit services are available. In addition, air pollution worsens

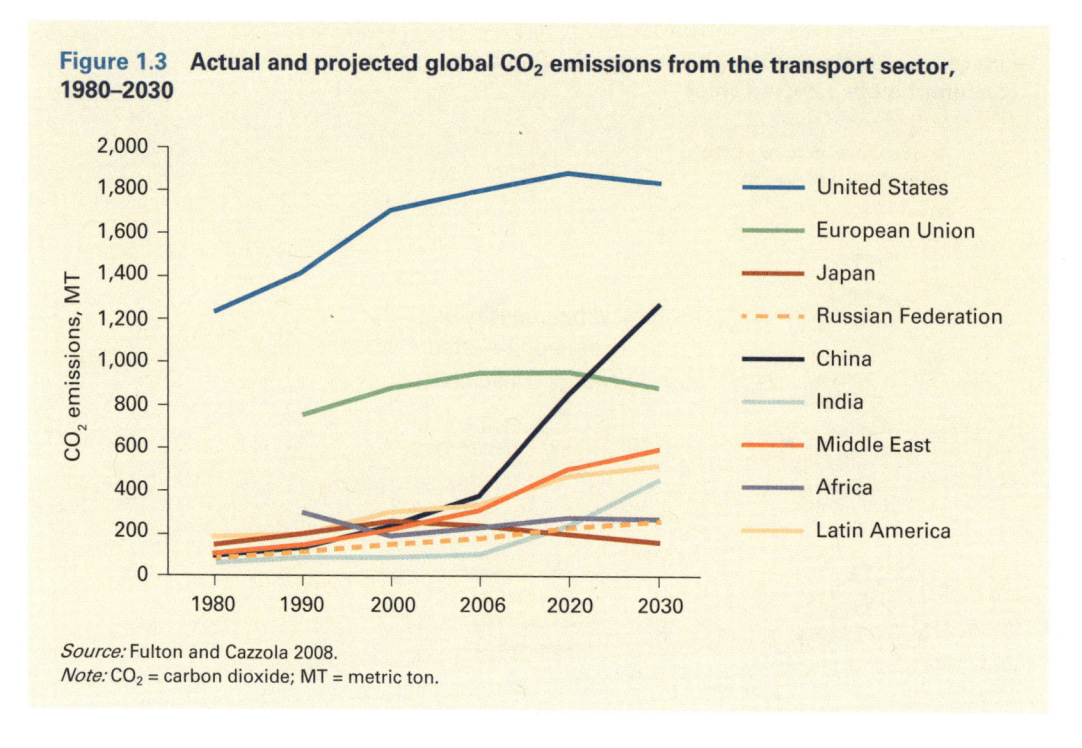

Figure 1.3 Actual and projected global CO_2 emissions from the transport sector, 1980–2030

[Line chart showing CO_2 emissions in MT from 1980 to 2030 for United States, European Union, Japan, Russian Federation, China, India, Middle East, Africa, and Latin America]

Source: Fulton and Cazzola 2008.
Note: CO_2 = carbon dioxide; MT = metric ton.

and the number of traffic accidents rises when car ownership rates increase. Pollutants emitted through the tailpipes of cars, trucks, and buses—including lead, ozone, and suspended particulates—can trigger debilitating upper-respiratory illnesses; over the long run, they can damage body organs from prolonged exposure. Carbon dioxide (CO_2) emissions from cars and trucks are increasingly worrisome, especially at the global scale, because their environmental effects threaten to destabilize climates, leading to rising sea levels, flooding, extreme heat waves, and droughts.

The transport sector is a major contributor to global climate change. It is a significant source of CO_2 emissions, generating about one-fourth of total emissions, with 18 percent coming from road transport (UNEP 2010). CO_2 emissions from the road sector continue to increase, with their share expected to reach one-third of the total by 2050. Over the next two decades, emissions from emerging markets, particularly China and India, are expected to grow the fastest (figure 1.3).

The frequency of traffic accidents, which has decreased in developed countries, has increased in developing countries: the number of road fatalities per 10,000 inhabitants is often four times higher in developing countries than in developed ones (World Bank 1996). In Africa, the number of road fatalities increased 26 percent between 1987 and 1995 (Jacobs, Aeron-Thomas, and Astrop 2000).

Social aspects are also important considerations. Low-income populations in cities are the most vulnerable in automobile-dominant cities, for several reasons. First, automobile-dependent urban forms provide limited choices on where to live, often forcing people who cannot afford a car to live in informal settlements on the urban fringe. As a consequence, they often have limited access to basic urban services, jobs, and educational opportunities.

Second, even where transit services are available, the cost is often substantial. One study found that poor families devote as much as 20 percent of total household income to transportation, compared with just 5 percent for wealthier households (Gomez-Ibanez and Meyer 1993). Money spent on transit is money that cannot go to meeting other pressing needs, such as food, shelter, health care, and education.

Third, in automobile-dependent cities, the majority of public investment goes to automobile-related facilities, such as roads and parking, taking money away from the upgrading of public transit or nonmotorized transport facilities, such as footpaths, bike lanes, and bike parking. Low-income residents benefit disproportionately from investments in public transit and bikeways, because they are much more reliant on these relatively low-cost modes than other income groups. Directing scarce national, regional, and municipal revenues to roads and highways does little to improve the livelihoods of people who do not own cars.

Fourth, "time pollution"—the amount of time wasted in trying to complete essential tasks, because of congestion or the need to travel long distances—often affects low-income people the most. Time spent traversing long distances in the city means less time available at the intended destination—working, studying, shopping, or socializing. Studies show that the poor spend much more time commuting than other income groups, often traveling from informal settlements on the urban periphery to city centers, where formal and informal employment opportunities exist. A study of Mexico City in the 1990s, for example, finds that 20 percent of the underprivileged respondents surveyed spent more than three hours a day commuting to work, and 10 percent spent more than five hours (Schwela and Zali 1999). When commuting long distances, they needed to make multiple transfers on privately operated transportation and other informal carriers (Cervero 2000).

Fifth, low-income residents are highly vulnerable to the health effects of airborne pollutants and traffic accidents. Walking, cycling, or using other micro paratransit vehicles to get around, they face exposure to polluted air and aggressive motor vehicles every day. In Bangladesh and India, more than three-quarters of deaths on roads are pedestrians and people transported by pedal power (World Bank 1996). In Manila, almost half of medication used by residents is for illnesses related to air pollution (Romualdez 2012).

Integrating Transit and Land Use toward Sustainable Urban Development

Reversing automobile dependency is not easy. Yet history shows that transit investments, if well integrated with urban development, promote

Box 1.4 A tale of two cities: Atlanta and Barcelona

Guiding development to reduce low-density expansion is a key feature of sustainable urbanization. Figure B1.4.1 reveals huge differences in the environmental footprints of two global cities, Atlanta and Barcelona. In 1990, the two cities had similar size populations of about 2.5 million people. Atlanta, however, had more than 26 times the built-up land area of Barcelona.

Figure B1.4.1 Built-up area of Atlanta and Barcelona, 1990

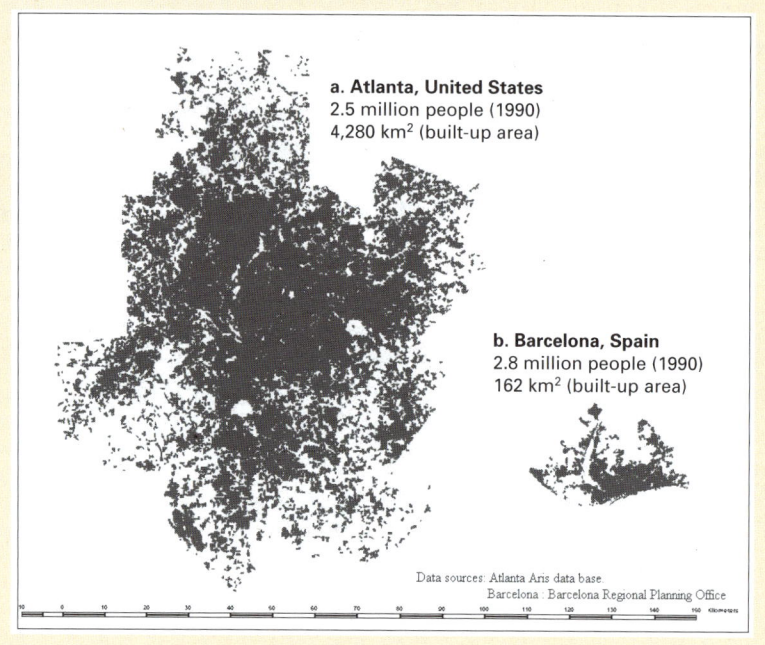

a. Atlanta, United States
2.5 million people (1990)
4,280 km² (built-up area)

b. Barcelona, Spain
2.8 million people (1990)
162 km² (built-up area)

Data sources: Atlanta Aris data base.
Barcelona : Barcelona Regional Planning Office

Source: Bertaud 2003.

Having less paved, built-up areas has allowed Barcelona to preserve green spaces. Less sprawling development reduces the cost of providing and extending urban infrastructure investments; it also makes transportation operation and maintenance, water and sanitation, and energy distribution systems less expensive.

Barcelona's energy use is considerably lower than Atlanta's. Because vehicle kilometers traveled per capita are much lower in Barcelona than Atlanta, far less fuel is consumed in the transport sector and CO_2 emissions are considerably lower. Additional benefits of compact urban form may include economic productivity gains from urban agglomeration and increased opportunities to instill a sense of community through increased social interactions.

---

sustainable urban forms with promising outcomes. Atlanta, a sprawled low-density city, and Barcelona, a compact high-density city, show dramatic differences in their private car use, energy consumption, and environmental footprints (box 1.4).

Reversing the Culture of Automobile-Oriented Development

Two key initiatives for reversing automobile dependency include (a) shifting travel from private motorized vehicles to nonmotorized and public transport, and (b) reducing sprawl by promoting TODs that are served by high-quality public transit services. Public transit is inherently the most resourceful form of mobility, measured in consumption of energy or land, as illustrated by figure 1.4, which compares the amount of road space required for about 80 travelers by different modes of transportation (GTZ 2004). Reducing the amount of impervious surfaces given over to roads and parking not only shortens trip distances, it also reduces heat-island effects and water pollution (from oil-stained run-off of rain into streams).

Cities designed to reduce travel distances encourage walking, cycling, and use of the public transit system. "Cities of short distances" are also cities with lower levels of air pollution, energy consumption, and CO_2 emissions. In the long term, efficient urban form makes cities more economically competitive and environmentally sustainable. It also helps build social capital by allowing people from all walks of life to come into regular, day-to-day contact with one another. Denser cities are also more socially just. By providing high levels of access to everyone, regardless of income, they enable the less-privileged segments of society to achieve upward mobility.

Figure 1.4 Urban space taken up by cars, motorbikes, and buses

Source: GTZ 2004.

One practical approach to reducing traffic congestion, greenhouse gas emissions, and other pressing environmental problems is to promote TOD (Calthorpe 1993; Cervero and others 2005; Curtis, Renne, and Bertolini 2009) (box 1.5). Experiences show that well-designed TOD not only increases ridership of public transit by drawing more travelers out of cars and into trains and buses, it can also serve as a hub for organizing community development and revitalizing long-distressed urban districts (Bernick and Cervero 1997; Cervero 1998).

Mixed land use is a particularly important element of TOD. Intermixing housing, offices, retail shops, and other urban amenities in close proximity to public transit stations integrates long-distance travel by transit and short-distance, within-neighborhood travel by foot.

TOD concepts should be carefully adapted to reflect the local urban context, social and cultural considerations, and market realities. A one-size-fits-all approach to TOD planning and design is not recommended, particularly for rapidly growing cities in developing countries. Instead, cities should develop typologies of transit station environments and TODs that correspond to local conditions.

When coupled with transportation demand management (TDM) measures, TOD can become even more effective. TDM aims to alter the demand for travel in order to reduce traffic congestion and improve environmental conditions. It includes measures that modify the physical designs of cities and streetscapes as well as various incentive mechanisms that change the cost of transportation to users. Physical design examples include pedestrian- and bicycle-friendly street designs, traffic calming, and intermixing of land uses to shorten trip distances. Examples of TDM include congestion pricing, parking controls, and car sharing. Experience shows that combining TOD and TDM measures can induce people to use public transit and nonmotorized transportation and to reduce levels of car ownership and usage (Guo and others 2011).

In general, cities take on a polycentric form as they grow. Connecting high-density centers—be they central business districts, residential areas, or mixed-use subcenters—by high-quality transit is critically important to sustainable urban development. Interlinking mixed-use urban centers with high-capacity transit can create two- or multiple-way travel flows, allowing travel demand to be more evenly spread out throughout the day.

Another way to materially enhance transit services is to design a superior system of feeder services that allows smooth and seamless transfers and connections among different transport modes. Trunk-line services, such as metros, provide economies of scale; smaller vehicle feeder services, such as minibuses, provide economies of scope. The two modes can be highly complementary. A well-integrated metropolitan-wide public transport system that links regional railways, metros, BRT systems, and local buses is essential if rising automobile usage and ownership is to be reversed. Physically linking nonmotorized transportation with public transit—through dedicated bike lanes that funnel into public transit stations, for example—is

Box 1.5 What is transit-oriented development?

Transit-oriented development (TOD) is characterized by two main features:

- proximity to and a functional relationship with transit stations and terminals and service provision by high-quality public transit (BRT systems, underground trains, and so forth)
- compact, mixed-use buildings and neighborhoods that, because of their design, encourage walking, cycling, and use of public transit by residents, employees, shoppers, and visitors.

The ingredients of successful TOD include strategic (macro) and design (micro) elements such as a strong development climate and master plans for multiuse, high-intensity developments supported by implementation plans. They also include investments that promote the following:

- easy and direct pedestrian, bicycle, and public transit access (figure B1.5.1)
- good signage and a pleasant environment to attract substantial pedestrian flows
- significant regional accessibility to major job and activity centers
- short, direct connections between transportation modes and transit facilities
- bicycle lanes and parking facilities that feed stations
- attractive facilities that are well integrated with the surroundings (public spaces, street furniture, and so forth)
- safe and secure designs, including adequate lighting
- effective parking management around stations
- environmentally friendly technology options, such as shared fleets of alternative (electric) vehicles located in neighborhoods.

Figure B1.5.1 Key features of the eco-block concept

Dedicated off-street paths

Primary sidewalks

Secondary sidewalks

BRT Station — 5-min. walk — 10-min. walk

High-level of pedestrian accessibility and connectivity

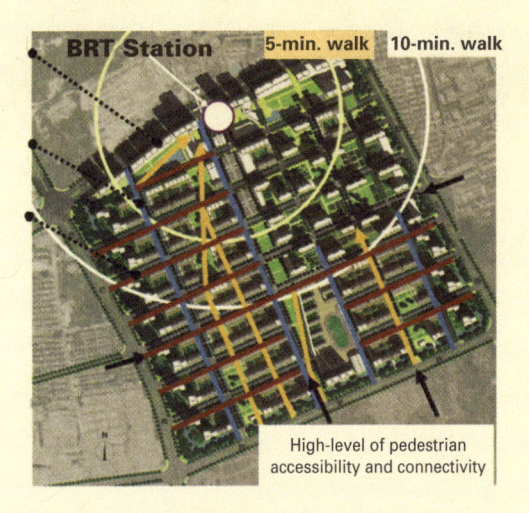

Source: Fraker 2009.
Note: The eco-block concept maximizes pedestrian access to transit stations. It is illustrated here using a location in China.

(Box continues on next page)

Box 1.5 What is transit-oriented development? *(continued)*

Research shows that the impacts of TOD are realized over the long term and depend on the quality of related microdesigns and the rate of an area's demographic and economic growth. Lund, Cervero, and Willson (2004) studied residential and commercial sites in major cities in California. They found that factors related to TOD, particularly proximity to urban and commuter rail stations, increased ridership on rail and buses by as much as a factor of three to four relative to control sites. The ridership benefits of TOD are also found in rapidly urbanizing settings. Cervero and Day (2008a, 2008b) surveyed households relocating to suburban TOD and non–TOD sites in Shanghai to assess the impacts on travel behavior. They found that TOD sites experienced increased public transit ridership, improved access to regional jobs (as measured by employment locations within a radius equivalent to one hour in travel time), and reduced commuter times per household worker.

Figure B1.5.2 Transit-oriented development in metropolitan Washington, DC

a. Connection between metrorail and feeder bus system

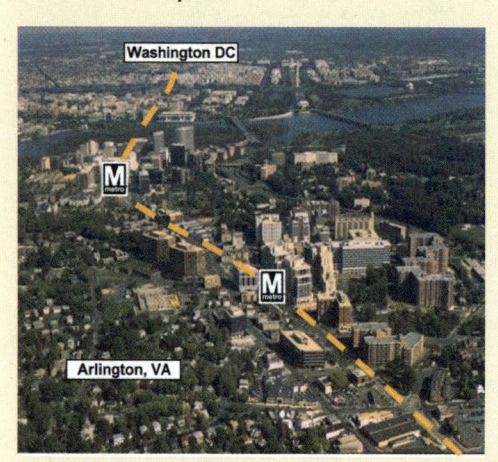

b. Road and metrorail connection at Clarendon, Virginia

Source: Zimmerman 2008.
Note: The photo in panel a shows a high-quality public transit corridor between Arlington, Virginia, and Washington, DC, with an underground metropolitan train and a feeder bus system. The corridor exhibits many elements of good macro-level planning and TOD, including higher densities around high-quality public transit (the metro) in an otherwise car-oriented environment. After 20 years of mixed-use development around stations (such as Clarendon, Virginia, pictured in panel b), the corridor has become transit supportive in its form and design.

another essential part of a highly interconnected and viable transportation network that offers mobility options to the private car.

Integration: Perceived Consensus and Neglected Reality

Interest in the role of transport investments and policies in fostering efficient urban growth has received considerable attention in recent years. In 2010, the World Bank launched an initiative called "Eco^2 Cities: Ecological Cities as Economic Cities" (Suzuki and others 2010). The initiative aims to help cities in developing countries achieve economic and environmental sustainability and enhance social equity. The "one-system approach," which promotes cross-sector integration in spatial development, is one of the four principles of Eco^2 (box 1.6). Integrating transit and land use is one of the most promising strategies for achieving urban sustainability.

City leaders and policy makers increasingly recognize that cities that enjoy high levels of mobility and accessibility are also economically more productive, vibrant places to live and attractive places to run a business. They also have a smaller environmental footprint and score high on the quality-of-life index. Thoughtful leaders realize that careful integration of transit with urban development is one of the best ways to place cities on a sustainable pathway.

History shows that transit investments powerfully shape the growth of cities by changing accessibility (the ease of traveling from one place to another) (Cervero and Seskin 1995; Giuliano 2004). In the absence of regulatory restrictions in a growing environment, investment in high-capacity, high-quality transit services unleashes land-use shifts and urban form adjustments by yielding accessibility benefits. Because there is a limited supply of highly accessible locations, enhanced accessibility prompts developers to acquire land, intensify development, and introduce land-use mixes to maximize profits. Land-use and location shifts in turn affect daily activity patterns and thus travel demand. Shifts in travel, as reflected by flows within the network, affect the performance of the transportation system.

Despite these benefits, urban development that integrates transit and land use rarely takes place—in developing countries or developed ones. Major reasons for this may lie in the distinctive nature of the planning and implementation of transportation and land use. Transportation planning often embraces a linear, technological perspective; land-use planning tends to be more flexible, ad hoc, and passive, thus making collaboration difficult (Gakenheimer 2011; table 1.1). Weak institutional and regulatory frameworks for regional and local planning, an orientation toward short-term project investments, and constrained technical and financial capacity also make urban development and management difficult. And a myriad of urban actors—including multiple layers of governments and their agencies, private developers, and informal sectors, including squatters—make coordination of transportation and urban growth exceedingly complex.

The difficulty of integrating transit and land development is evident in projects managed by the World Bank. "Cities on the Move" (2002), a strategy for urban transport developed by the Bank, underscored the need to link urban development and the transport sector in order to promote livable cities, economic competitiveness, financial sustainability, and good urban governance and management. But saying and doing are two different things. A review of the Bank's urban transport project portfolio from 1999 to 2009 indicates that only 2 of 55 projects addressed the linkage between transport and urban development (Mitric 2011). Over this period, uncoordinated growth continued in many cities in developing countries.

Coordinating transit and land use is not easy. As highlighted by the cases reviewed in this study, many barriers stand in the way, including deeply

Box 1.6 Economic cities as ecological cities: The World Bank's Eco² initiative

Eco² Cities is a World Bank initiative that helps cities in developing countries achieve greater ecological and economic sustainability, while increasing human and social well-being. It provides a framework to plan, manage, and invest in sustainable urban systems that are integrated and beneficial in the long term. Four principles underlie the Eco² framework:

- Principle 1, a city-based approach, focuses on the need to enable and strengthen the leadership, capacity, and decision-making abilities of cities and their regional planning institutions. It also emphasizes the need to enhance the unique historic, cultural, and ecological resources of each city.
- Principle 2, a platform for collaborative design and decision making, focuses on compounding the benefits of urbanization by leveraging and combining the unique capacities and resources of all stakeholders. It supports an inclusive and fair process of urban development and decision making that involves and empowers all stakeholders.
- Principle 3, a one-system approach, strives to create a "resource regenerative and multifunctional" city. Sectors, policies, and budgets—as well as natural and man-made systems—need to work together across spatial scales and administrative jurisdictions so that the city functions effectively as one system.
- Principle 4, an investment framework that values sustainability and resilience, focuses on broadening the scope and extending the timeframe within which policies, plans, and investment options are assessed for costs, benefits, and risks. It supports decision-making approaches that value natural, cultural, and social capital.

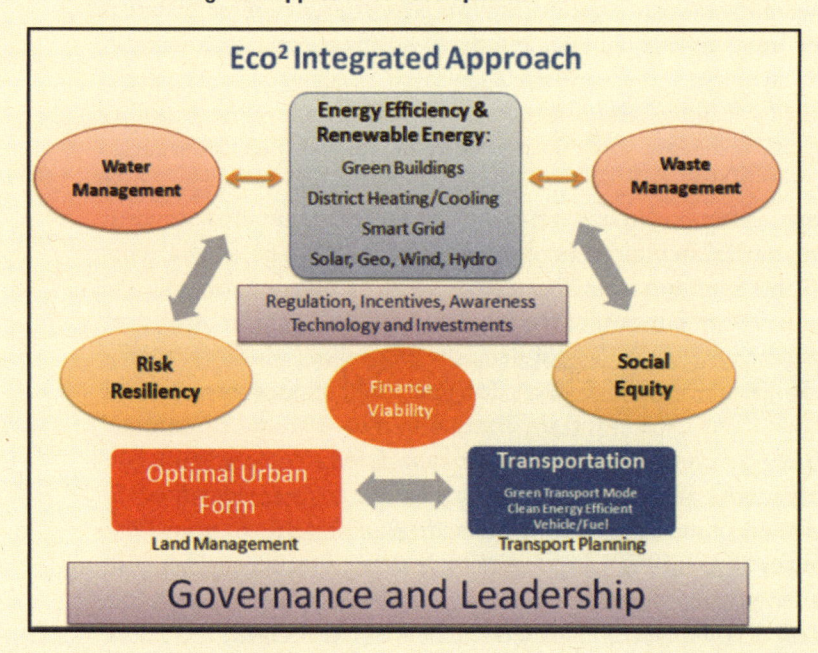

Figure B1.6.1 The Eco² integrated approach to development

Source: Suzuki and others 2010.
Note: Available online at www.worldbank.org/eco2.

Table 1.1 **Constraints on coordinating transit and land-use planning**

Feature	Transit planning	Land-use planning
Objectives	Objectives focus on economic and affordable accessibility.	Objectives are diverse, extending to housing, social equity, and economic development.
Planning approach	Planning involves analysis-based quantitative approach, focusing mainly on traffic demand.	Planning approaches are mixed, depending on area of focus.
Scale for planning and implementation	Planning focuses on metropolitan-wide integrated linear systems; infrastructure is indivisibly constructed.	Planning concerns are often locally focused on communities and districts; implementation is tied to parcels.
Implementation power	Governments have power to implement projects.	Individuals and private actors have more decision-making power than governments.
Scale of projects affecting administrative strength	Projects have large, publicly funded capital budgets, strengthening administrative power.	Projects involve smaller, publicly funded capital budgets, weakening the power of administration with respect to individuals and the private sector.
Length of planning vision	Sector requires long-term vision.	Ad hoc and shorter plans can exist in parallel with long-term visions.

Source: Authors, based on Gakenheimer 2011.

entrenched institutional and political ones. The articulation of a long-range vision and a spatial development strategy is critical to jump-starting the process. The political will and commitment to execute the vision is equally important.

Two cities in Brazil—Curitiba (population 3 million) and São Paolo (16 million)—have followed significantly different approaches to managing urban growth, with very different outcomes. Curitiba was planned as a city with well-defined linear densities along BRT–served corridors. In contrast, São Paulo has mostly unplanned densities, which are poorly linked to the city's transit system (Acioly 2000) (figure 1.5). Despite large differences in population sizes, the number of annual public transit trips per capita in 2000 was similar in the two cities (355 for Curitiba, 330 for São Paulo).

Curitiba's transit-oriented built form stems from good urban planning. Early in the planning process, Curitiba's leaders adopted a master plan that sought to channel growth along designated corridors, mix land uses, intensify land development at key BRT stations, and introduce high-quality urban designs that encouraged pedestrian access to the BRT corridor. In contrast, São Paulo's pattern of growth has been largely market driven, producing a more chaotic urban form that is difficult to serve by public transit and encourages people who can afford to travel by private car (Cervero 2000).

Figure 1.5 Urban form of Curitiba and São Paulo, Brazil

a. Linear densities in Curitiba

b. Unplanned densities in São Paulo

Photos by Robert Cervero.

Study Objectives, Framework, and Methodology

This study identifies ways to promote more sustainable forms of urban growth that result in increasingly sustainable travel behavior in rapidly developing cities of the world. It examines factors that encourage or hinder built forms that are conducive to the use of public transit; highlights lessons on the prerequisites to and policy outcomes of successful transit and land-use integration from around the world; and offers case-based insights on how cities can overcome barriers to sustainable urban growth and become more transit oriented when opportunities present themselves.

Figure 1.6 presents a normalized perspective on transit and urban-form relationships. It shows that transit investments can bring about urban form and land-use adjustments by enhancing accessibility, typically in the form of more compact TODs. Such shifts in the built environment can in turn influence the demand for public transit, as higher densities lead to higher ridership levels. Density, however, is but one dimension of the built environment that influences travel. Other variables that shape travel demand are diversity, design, destination accessibility, and distance to transit (the so-called "D" variables) (see Ewing and Cervero 2010 for detailed discussions). Transit and urban form are co-dependent; the need to carefully coordinate the two lies at the heart of promoting sustainable urban futures. The in-depth case studies presented in this book focus mainly on the right-hand side of figure 1.6: how public interventions—in particular, transit investments, planning strategies, regulation, tax policies, and incentives—influence urban form. Analysis of market responses to transit investments receives less attention, largely because data are constrained and the market response to public interventions requires further detailed analysis. Some insights are provided on the ridership-inducing effects of TOD, which are often a product of public interventions and private market forces. However, because it often takes time for these impacts to unfold and reveal themselves, this part of the relationship receives less empirical attention.

Figure 1.6 Study framework

Inherent Characteristics of a City
Natural and historical conditions
Urban development pattern
Governance and institutional setting

Macro forces: socioeconomic conditions

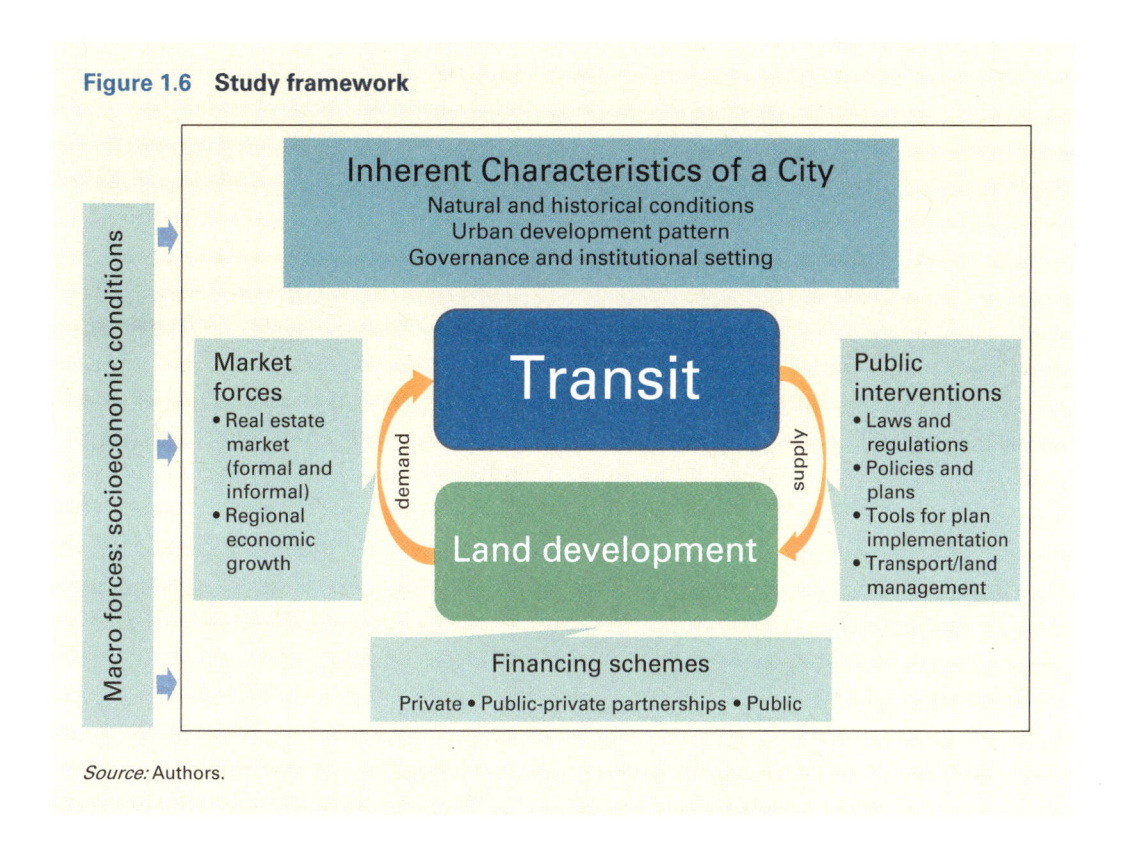

Market forces
- Real estate market (formal and informal)
- Regional economic growth

Transit ⇄ (demand/supplies) **Land development**

Public interventions
- Laws and regulations
- Policies and plans
- Tools for plan implementation
- Transport/land management

Financing schemes
Private • Public-private partnerships • Public

Source: Authors.

Figure 1.6 reveals other forces that shape the relationship between transit and urban form that are examined in this study. One is a set of macro forces that are outside the sphere of local policy influence, such as shifting socioeconomic trends and gasoline prices. Such forces can powerfully influence the relationship between transit and land use. Higher gasoline prices, for example, promote both mixed-use higher densities and transit ridership.

Also at play are market forces, which affect the choice of business and residential locations. For example, the shift toward knowledge-based industries in a city's economic base can encourage spatial clustering, prompting firms to seek denser, transit-served locations. Deliberate policy interventions, such as zoning regulations and parking codes, can influence private development around transit station areas and thus ridership. Financial instruments play a pivotal role in determining whether there is the fiscal capacity to create a transit-oriented built form.

This two-way dynamic between transit and land development, and the powerful array of forces that shape this relationship, occurs at multiple geographic scales: neighborhoods, corridors, districts, and regions. Correspondingly, it is often important that institutional capacity be in place, as well as the wherewithal to coordinate planning and implementation activities at and between each spatial level.

This study draws lessons from global best-case examples of transit-oriented metropolises that have direct relevance to cities in developing countries. It also reports the results of two in-depth case studies of rapidly growing and motorizing cities that introduced extended BRT systems: Ahmedabad, India and Bogota, Colombia. Two shorter case studies—of Guangzhou, China and Ho Chi Minh City, Vietnam—provide additional insights into factors that are critical to transforming cities with transit. All four cases represent cities that are aggressively investing in high-capacity transit systems at a time of rapid growth, meaning that these investments are in a position to significantly shape their urban futures. Factors that have both contributed to and inhibited sustainable patterns of growth are identified, and possible ways to overcome barriers are suggested.

The qualitative approaches used in conducting the case studies included informant interviews of public officials and other stakeholders, reviews of background reports and secondary materials, and site visits to BRT station areas. In addressing the degree to which BRT investments have shaped urban form and built environments, the case studies pay particular attention to the following concerns:

- the degree to which local authorities defined and articulated a land-use vision of the future (visioning the future)
- the degree to which implementation tools were introduced and procedural mechanisms put into place to translate visions of urban-regional futures into on-the-ground actions (tools and processes)
- the roles and contributions—past, present, and potentially future—of public transit investments and services in shaping and giving rise to urban form (public transit and urban development)
- the core lessons that are potentially transferable to other global city regions (core lessons).

Factors that may have hindered spatial integration are also identified. In several instances, matched pair analyses were conducted to investigate whether there were differences in land development between BRT station areas and otherwise similar control neighborhoods that were beyond the typical walking distance to a station.

The case studies also focus on the important issue of whether BRT investments and their corresponding urban development impacts improved access and living conditions for the underprivileged. Only if disadvantaged and marginalized populations are better off as a result of transit and land-use integration can such interventions be considered successful contributors to development.

In addition, the cases focus on BRT systems because BRT systems are being built at a rapid-fire pace throughout the developing world, due to their lower investment costs in comparison to metros and other rail options and their relatively short construction periods. Currently, more than 130 BRT systems exist worldwide, and at least as many are in various stages of planning, advanced engineering, and construction. In addition, BRT is probably the most suitable high-quality transit service for cities with populations of less than 500,000, which account for a large share of future global urban population growth.

The findings and recommendations of this study are applicable to other transit modes as well, however, because core relationships between transit and urban development hold regardless of the mode adopted. Although a metrorail investment in a busy urban district might prompt developers to build taller office buildings than a BRT investment, the fundamental relationship is the same: accessibility improvements conferred by transit encourage densification.

Structure of This Book

The rest of this book is organized as follows. Chapter 2 describes successful efforts by cities to integrate public transit and land development. These cities offer core lessons on how investment in transit can shape urban growth and how the built environment enhances demand for public transit.

Chapter 3 presents two in-depth cases in developing countries: Bogota, Colombia and Ahmedabad, India. Both cases show that BRT investments have significantly enhanced urban mobility across their metropolitan areas but that in the absence of proactive planning, market forces have often steered urban growth away from BRT corridors. These cases also reveal that planning for mobility took priority over concerted efforts to reshape the cities and achieve a long-term vision of urban form through BRT investments. In both cities, government agencies at all levels are beginning to realize the importance of integrating public transit with urban development as a means of enhancing their cities' economic competitiveness, improving environmental conditions, and increasing social equity. Chapter 3 also introduces two shorter case studies, Guangzhou, China and Ho Chi Minh City, Vietnam, which show other initiatives of transit and land-use integration.

Chapter 4 identifies key constraints in integrating transit and built environments in rapidly growing cities of the world, as well as recommendations on ways to overcome barriers and promote successful transit and land-use relationships. Topics addressed include short-term needs versus long-term visions, regional and institutional coordination for planning and implementation, and regulatory constraints for strategic development. Based on lessons from global best-case practices introduced in chapter 2, and the four case studies examined in chapter 3, the concluding chapter makes specific recommendations on how to overcome barriers and promote successful transit and land use relationships.

Notes

1. The terms *transit* and *public transport* are used interchangeably in this book. *Transit* is often used in the United States; *public transport* is more common throughout the rest of the world.
2. Other international development banks include the African Development Bank, the Asian Development Bank, the CAF Development Bank of Latin America, the European Bank for Reconstruction and Development,

the European Investment Bank, the Inter-American Development Bank, and the Islamic Development Bank.
3. In this context, *automobiles* refer to vehicles with engines, including cars, trucks, and motorcycles.

References

Acioly C., Jr. 2000. "Can Urban Management Deliver the Sustainable City?" In *Compact Cities: Sustainable Urban Forms for Developing Countries*, 3rd ed., ed. M. Jenks, and R. Burgess, 127–40. London: Routledge.

Angel, S., J. Parent, D. L. Civco, and A. M. Blei. 2011. *Making Room for a Planet of Cities*. Cambridge, MA: Lincoln Institute of Land Policy.

Bernick, M., and R. Cervero. 1997. *Transit Villages for the 21st Century*. New York: McGraw-Hill.

Bertaud, A. 2003. "Cleaning the Air in Atlanta: Transit and Smart Growth or Conventional Economic?" *Journal of Urban Economics* 54(3): 379–400.

Bournay, E. 2008. "Urban Density and Transport-Related Energy Consumption." http://www.grida.no/graphicslib/detail/urban-density-and-transport-related-energy-consumption_eda9.

Calthorpe, P. 1993. *The New American Metropolis: Ecology, Community, and the American Dream*. New York: Princeton Architectural Press.

Cervero, R. 1998. *The Transit Metropolis: A Global Inquiry*. Washington, DC: Island Press.

———. 2000. *Informal Transport in the Developing World*. Nairobi: United Nations Centre for Human Settlement.

Cervero, R., G. Arrington, J. Smith-Heimer, and R. Dunphy. 2005. "Transit Oriented Development in America: Experiences, Challenges, and Prospects." Report No. 102, Transit Cooperative Research Program, Washington, DC.

Cervero, R., and J. Day. 2008a. "Residential Relocation and Commuting Behavior in Shanghai, China: The Case for Transit-Oriented Development." Working Paper UCB-ITS-VWP-2008–4, Berkeley Center for Future Urban Transport, University of California, Berkeley, CA. http://escholarship.org/uc/item/0dk1s0q5.

———.2008b. "Suburbanization and Transit-Oriented Development in China." *Transport Policy* 15 (5): 315–23.

Cervero, R., and S. Seskin. 1995. "Transit and Urban Form." Report No. 6, National Academy of Science, Transportation Research Board, Washington, DC.

Chamon, M., P. Mauro, and Y. Okawa. 2008. "Mass Car Ownership in the Emerging Market Giants." *Economic Policy* 23 (54): 243–96.

Curtis, C., J. Renne, and L. Bertolini. 2009. *Transit Oriented Development: Making It Happen*. Surrey, United Kingdom: Ashgate.

Ewing, R., and R. Cervero. 2010. "Travel and the Built Environment." *Journal of the American Planning Association* 76 (3): 265–94.

Fraker, H. 2008. "Sustainable Neighborhood 'Eco-Blocks' in China." http://bie.berkeley.edu/ecoblocks.

———. 2009. "Sustainable Neighborhood 'Eco-Blocks' in China: Qingdao Sustainable Neighborhood Demonstration Project." Urban Sustainability Initiative, Berkeley Institute of the Environment, University of California, Berkeley, CA. http://bie. berkeley.edu/ecoblocks.

Fulton, L. and Cazzola, P. 2008. "Transport, Energy, and CO_2 in Asia: Where are We Going and How Do We Change It?" PowerPoint Presentation at "The Better Air Quality 2008 Workshop," Bangkok, Thailand.

Gakenheimer, R. 2011. "Land Use and Transport in Rapidly Motorizing Cities: Contexts of Controversy." In *Urban Transport in the Developing World*, ed. H. T. Dimitriou and R. Gakenheimer, 40–68. Northampton, MA: Edward Elgar.

Giuliano, G. 2004. "Land Use Impacts of Transportation Investments: Highways and Transit." In *Geography of Urban Transportation*, 3rd ed., ed. S. Hanson, and G. Giuliano, 237–73. New York: Guilford Press.

Gomez-Ibanez, J., and J. Meyer. 1993. *Going Private: The International Experience with Transport Privatization*. Washington, DC: Brookings Institution.

GTZ (Deutsche Gesellschaft für Technische Zusammenarbeit). 2004. *Land Use Planning and Urban Transport*. Eschborn, Germany: GTZ.

Guo, Z., A. Agrawal, J. Dill, M. Quirk, and M. Reese. 2011. "The Intersection of Urban Form and Mileage Fees: Findings from the Oregon Road User Fee Pilot Program." Report 10-04, Mineta Transportation Institute. http://transweb.sjsu.edu/PDFs/research/2909_10-04.pdf.

IBM. 2010. *The Globalization of Traffic Congestion: IBM 2010 Commuter Pain Survey*. Armonk, NY: IBM.

———. 2011. *Frustration Rising: IBM 2011 Commuter Pain Survey*. Armonk, NY.

Jacobs, G., A. Aeron-Thomas, and A. Astrop. 2000. "Estimating Global Road Fatalities." Transport Research Laboratory, Berkshire.

Lund, H., R. Cervero, and R. Willson. 2004. "Travel Characteristics of Transit-Oriented Development in California." Statewide Planning Studies, Final Report FTA Section 5313 (Caltrans Transportation Grant). California Department of Transportation, Sacramento.

Lund, H., R. Willson, and R. Cervero. 2006. "A Re-evaluation of Travel Behavior in California TODs." *Journal of Architecture and Planning Research* 23 (3): 247–63.

Mitric, S. 2011. "Urban Transport Projects: Pattern and Trends in Lending, 1999–2009." World Bank, Transport Research Support, Washington, DC.

NASA Earth Observatory. 2005. "Urban Growth in Jakarta, Indonesia." http://earthobservatory.nasa.gov/IOTD/view.php?id=5693.

———. 2009. *Tehran Urbanization.* http://earthobservatory.nasa.gov/IOTD/view.php?id=41308.

Newman, P., and J. Kenworthy. 1989. *Cities and Automobile Dependence: An International Sourcebook.* Aldershot, United Kingdom: Gower.

Reutersward, L. 2009. "Putting Africa on the Agenda." In *Cities: Part of the Solution.* Brussels: European Union Ministry of the Environment.

Romualdez, B. G. 2012. "Metro Manila's Deadly Air." *Philippine Star,* April 12. http://www.philstar.com/Article.aspx?articleId=796091and publicationSubCategoryId=66.

Schwela, D., and O. Zali. 1999. *Urban Traffic Pollution.* London: E & FN Spon.

Suzuki, H., A. Dastur, S. Moffatt, N. Yabuki, and H. Maruyama. 2010. *Eco^2 Cities: Ecological Cities as Economic Cities.* Washington, DC: World Bank.

UNEP (United Nations Environmental Programme). 2010. "Cleaner, More Efficient Vehicles: Global Fuel Economy Initiative." http://www.unep.org/transport/gfei/autotool/understanding_the_problem/Trends_and_scenarios.asp.

World Bank. 1996. *Sustainable Transport: Priorities for Policy Reform.* Washington, DC: World Bank.

———. 2002. *Cities on the Move: A World Bank Urban Transport Strategy Review.* Washington, DC: World Bank.

WRI (World Resource Institute). 2012. "Statement: Development Banks Announce 'Game Changer' for Sustainable Transport at Rio+20." http://www.wri.org/press/2012/06/statement-development-banks-announce-game-changer-sustainable-transport-rio20.

Zimmerman, S. 2008. "Land Use and Metros." Presentation at the World Bank workshop "Urban Rail Development," Beijing, June 27.

CHAPTER 2

Lessons from Sustainable Transit-Oriented Cities

Global experiences show that cities on sustainable pathways are able to successfully link public transit investments and urban development. This was a core message of the book, *The Transit Metropolis: A Global Inquiry* (Cervero 1998). This chapter builds upon that work, updating and extending half the cases from *The Transit Metropolis*. Several case cities were also added to highlight recent good practices in transit and land-use integration and to examine innovative land value capture financing methods.

Cities that have successfully integrated transit and urban development have done so in one of two ways. Adaptive cities altered their urban form—through higher densities and mixed land-use patterns, for example—to support what is inherently the most resourceful form of motorized mobility: high-capacity, high-quality transit services, such as metros and bus rapid transit (BRT). Other cities focused on adaptive transit, modifying transit in less traditional ways to allow it to better serve market-driven, largely low-density patterns of urban and suburban development.

This chapter first reviews the experiences of seven adaptive cities—cities that created a compact, mixed-use, walking-friendly built form that has enabled high-quality, high-capacity public transit services to thrive. The cities include two Scandinavian cities (Copenhagen and Stockholm); four Asian cities (Hong Kong SAR, China; Seoul; Singapore; and Tokyo); and one North American city (Washington, DC).

These seven cases are followed by a review of two cities with successful BRT systems, Curitiba, Brazil and Ottawa, Canada. Although Curitiba is included in this group, it has more attributes of an adaptive city (that is, high-rise, lineal patterns of development) than an automobile-centric city oriented to flexible, adaptive forms of transit. It is the common feature of BRT services that links this group. Because chapter 3 focuses on two BRT cities, Ahmedabad, India and Bogota, Colombia, the experiences of bus-based Curitiba and Ottawa are particularly germane to the themes of this book.

Most of the cases reviewed are from developed countries, whose experiences are not directly applicable or easily transferred to rapidly developing cities like Ahmedabad and Bogota. For this reason, the aim of this chapter is less to shape the precise practices of rapidly growing cities in developing countries, and more to impart key principles and lessons that can guide the planning and practices of cities currently planning for or investing in large-scale transit systems.

The cities reviewed differ immensely in geographic size, population, economic bases, socio-demographic makeup, and intensities of transit usage (see annex table 2A.1 for comparative background information on nine of these cities). They range from Denmark's capital, Copenhagen, with a metropolitan population of about 1.2 million, to the world's two largest megalopolises—metropolitan Tokyo and Seoul, each with more than 24 million inhabitants. The share of daily trips by transit ranges from 21 percent in Ottawa to more than 60 percent in Hong Kong SAR, China; Seoul, Republic of Korea; and Singapore. Such wide variation underscores the difficulties of generalizing and drawing lessons that are applicable to all settings and contexts. Clearly, creating sustainable cities of the future calls for adapting core lessons and insights gained from best-case practices to the political, cultural, and institutional realities of particular urban settings.

A signature feature of successful transit metropolises is that they are environmentally sustainable. Another is that compact urban forms are generally needed for high ridership levels, and thus positive environmental outcomes, to be attained. That is, mass transit needs mass. An increasingly critical argument is that transit-oriented sustainable urban forms are fully consistent with economic prosperity and productivity.

Global statistics, using some of the city-region cases in this report, shed light on these matters. The International Association of Public Transport (UITP) publishes the Mobility in Cities database, which provides background data on a number of international cities, including some of the case cities.

Vehicle kilometers traveled (VKT) per capita is widely viewed as the best aggregate metric for gauging sustainability in the urban transport sector. As VKT per capita increases, so does fossil fuel consumption; tailpipe emissions (for example, carbon dioxide [CO_2] and photochemical smog); and land consumption from roadway expansion. Figure 2.1 reveals a strong negative association between transit usage and VKT per capita. Cities such as Stockholm; Hong Kong SAR, China; and Curitiba, Brazil stand out for their comparatively small environmental footprints.

The positive association between population density and transit ridership is shown in figure 2.2. Although not sufficient, compact patterns of development are usually a necessary feature of a successful transit system, at least when measured on the basis of per capita transit ridership.

The ways in which relationships between transportation and urban form influence economic productivity have garnered increased policy attention in recent years. Some research finds that compact and highly accessible cities

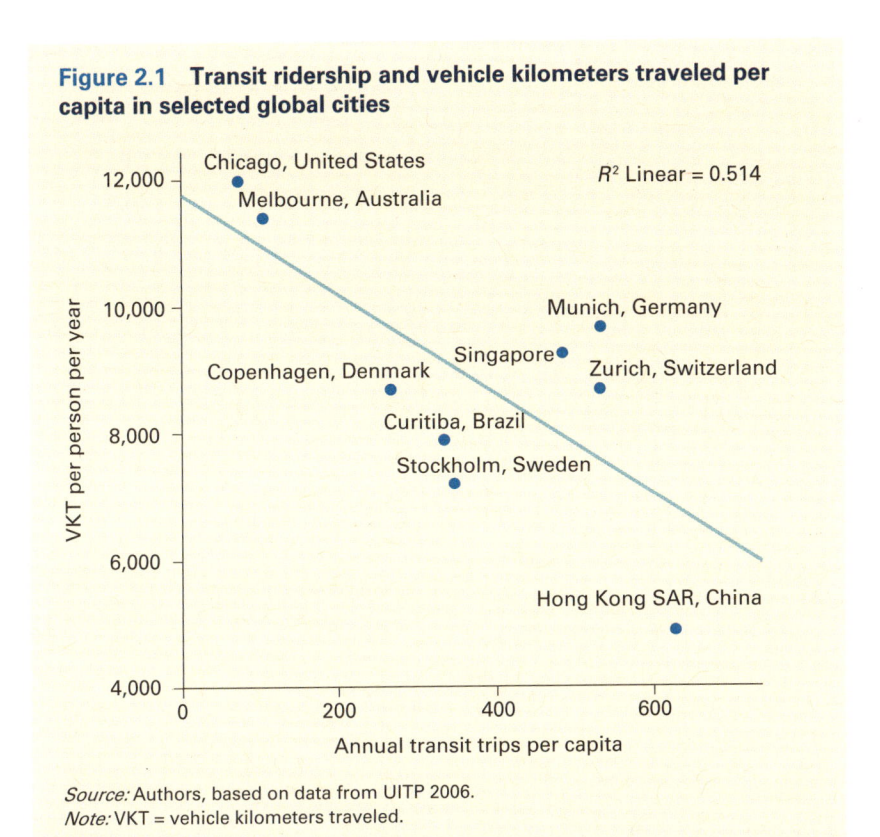

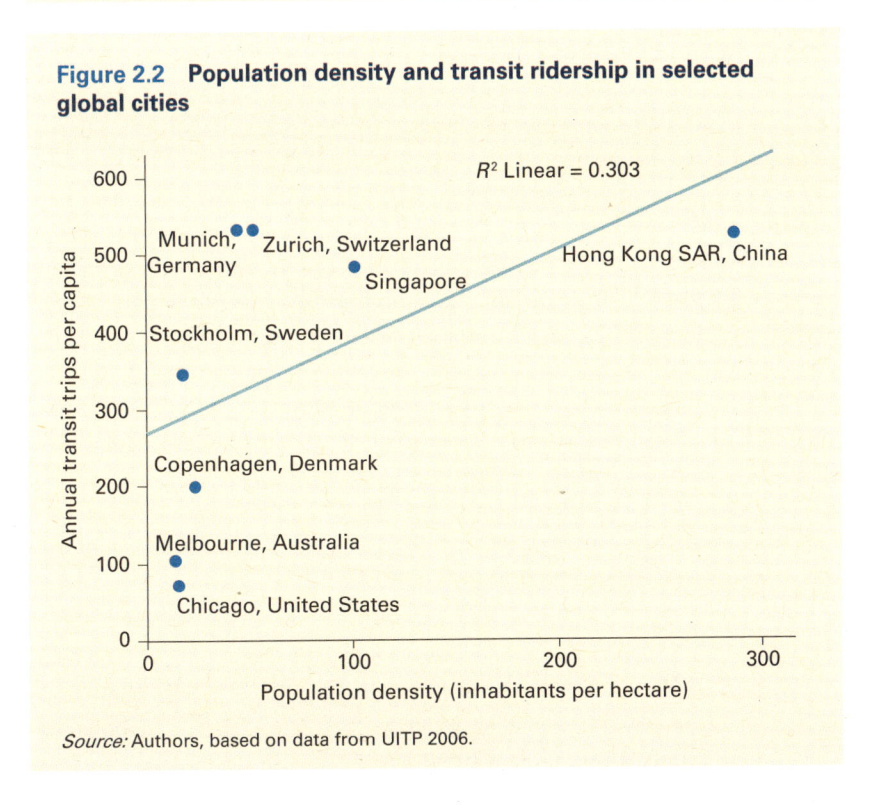

Figure 2.1 Transit ridership and vehicle kilometers traveled per capita in selected global cities

Source: Authors, based on data from UITP 2006.
Note: VKT = vehicle kilometers traveled.

Figure 2.2 Population density and transit ridership in selected global cities

Source: Authors, based on data from UITP 2006.

Table 2.1 Transit ridership, vehicle kilometers traveled, and GDP in selected cities

City	Transit trips/person/year	Vehicle kilometers traveled/person/year	GDP per capita ($)
Hong Kong SAR, China	627	4,880	27,600
Munich, Germany	534	9,670	45,800
Zurich, Switzerland	533	8,690	41,600
Singapore	484	9,240	28,900
Stockholm, Sweden	346	7,210	32,700
Curitiba, Brazil	334	7,900	6,800
Copenhagen, Denmark	268	8,700	34,100
Melbourne, Australia	105	11,400	22,800
Chicago, United States	73	12,000	40,000

Source: Authors, based on data from UITP 2006.

are associated with relatively high levels of labor productivity (Prud'homme and Lee 1999; Cervero 2001, 2009). Well-designed cities and efficient pricing of infrastructure that helps slow VKT growth can also promote economic growth, studies reveal. A report by the Center for Clean Air Policy (2011), for example, finds that states in the United States with lower VKT per capita tend to have higher gross domestic product (GDP) per capita. Although correlations do not prove causality and other researchers have reached opposite conclusions (QuantEcon 2009), most observers agree that the aim should be less about encouraging physical movement and more about designing communities and pricing resources to maximize economic and social interactions.

For the global cities studied in the UITP database, low VKT and high transit ridership are at least not associated with low economic performance (table 2.1). European cities with world-class transit systems, such as Munich and Zurich, for example, have high average GDP per capita, high transit ridership, and relatively modest VKT per capita. Zurich is one of the wealthiest cities in the world, ranking first in 2011, according to the City Mayor's database. Its high per capita level of transit ridership is matched by commercial real estate values that are among the highest in the world; its quality of life is rated the highest in the world (Mercer 2002); it has one of the lowest vehicle ownership rates in the developed world (40 percent of households have no cars); and its air quality is among the best of any European city (Cervero 1998; Mees 2009).

Transit and Land-Use Integration in Adaptive Cities

This section reviews experiences in seven adaptive cities: Copenhagen; Stockholm; Hong Kong SAR, China; Seoul; Singapore; Tokyo; and the Washington, DC metropolitan area, where metrorail investments were used

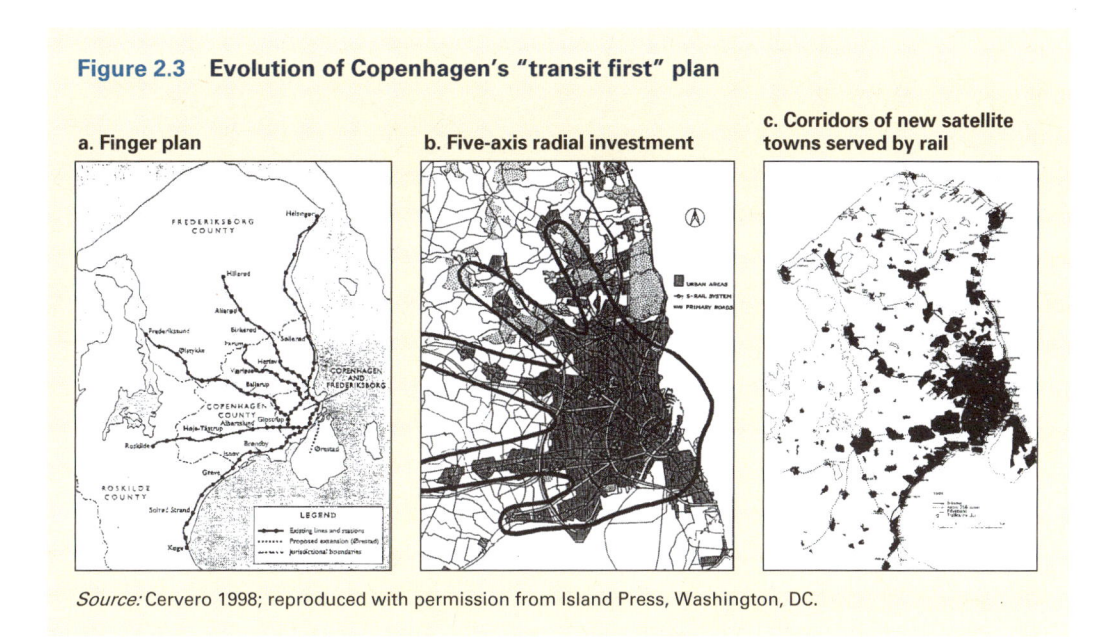

Figure 2.3 Evolution of Copenhagen's "transit first" plan

a. Finger plan

b. Five-axis radial investment

c. Corridors of new satellite towns served by rail

Source: Cervero 1998; reproduced with permission from Island Press, Washington, DC.

to create a more compact, mixed-use, pedestrian-friendly urban form. It highlights the planning, design, institutional, and financial approaches used to leverage transit-oriented station areas and corridors.

Copenhagen: Transit Oriented and Bike Friendly

A textbook example of long-range planning visions shaping rail investments, which in turn shaped urban growth, comes from Copenhagen, with its celebrated "finger plan." Early in the planning process, planners identified corridors for channeling overspill growth from the urban centers. Rail infrastructure was built, often in advance of demand, to steer growth along desired growth axes. Greenbelt wedges set aside as agricultural preserves, open space, and natural habitats were designated and major infrastructure directed away from districts with these features. The evolution of Copenhagen—from a finger plan to a directed rail-investment program along defined growth axes to a finger-like urbanization patterns—is shown in figure 2.3.

On the periphery of Copenhagen are new towns that are bike and pedestrian friendly. Suburban towns of 10,000–30,000 inhabitants, like Ballerup, Brønby, and Høje-Taastrup, are laced by greenways that connect neighborhoods, schools, retail centers, and pocket parks to inviting rail stops. About half of residents in these middle-class, master-planned new towns take a train to work, and four out of five walk, bike, or take a bus to their community's rail station.

Copenhagen planners have long embraced the notion that industrial progress should not encroach on the rights and needs of pedestrians and cyclists. They created one of the first and the longest car-free streets in Europe, Strøget, which, during summer, accommodates some 55,000 pedestrians, often shoulder to shoulder. Street life is not viewed only in terms of foot traffic but also with regard to stationary activities. Jan Gehl, a noted urban designer from Copenhagen, sold city leaders on the idea that great public spaces accommodate not only busy pedestrians but also casual sitting, relaxing, and milling about. Today, some 80,000 square meters of public squares—big and small, grand and modest—dot central Copenhagen.

One of the chief ways of meeting the needs of cyclists has been the expropriation of car lanes and curbside parking for their exclusive use. Between 1980 and 2005, Copenhagen's inventory of bike lanes increased from 210 to 410 kilometers within an area of about 90 square kilometers. Over the same period, the number of bike trips rose 80 percent. By 2005, 36 percent of journeys to work in Copenhagen were by bicycle, the highest mode split of any capital city in Europe. The city's master plan, Eco-Metropolis for 2015, commits Copenhagen to become "the world's best city for bicycling" (City of Copenhagen 2008). Copenhagen has set an ambitious goal of 50 percent of its citizens biking to work or school by 2015. New, separated cycle-tracks are being added in hopes of achieving this goal.

To further boost cycling, Copenhagen introduced a short-term bike lease program, called City Bikes, in 1995. More than 2,000 white bikes have been placed at some 140 bike stands throughout the city. In addition to improving rail access, the program reduced on-vehicle carriage of bikes, freeing up train capacity for passengers. City Bikes is overseen by a local nonprofit organization that hires hundreds of "rehabilitees" (prisoners who are being rehabilitated) to maintain the bikes. The organization reports that 55 percent of the rehabilitees get jobs after participating in the program (Foundation City Bikes 2009). Statistics reveal how well articulated Copenhagen's "access shed" is for transit riding. A 2002 survey of 15 suburban rail stations found that people walked 38–100 percent of access trips up to 1 kilometer; for trips 1–2 kilometers away, cycling accounted for 40 percent of access trips. Beyond 2 kilometers, buses handled two-thirds of access trips. Even 4 kilometers from stations, twice as many access trips were by bicycle as by car. Danish designers have found that acceptable walking and cycling distances can be stretched considerably by creating attractive, visually stimulating, and safe travel corridors. Partly by doing so, Copenhagen succeeded in reducing CO_2 emissions per capita by 25 percent between 1990 and 2008 (City of Copenhagen 2010).

A transit-oriented built form that is pedestrian and bike friendly is not the only factor accounting for Copenhagen's low annual VKT per capita of 8,700 (see table 2.1). Also critical have been national policies that aim to moderate car ownership and usage. Every four years since World War II, the national government has issued policy guidelines aimed at shaping the land-constrained country's physical development. Over the years, a series of national directives have called for targeting Greater Copenhagen's future growth around rail transit stations. National infrastructure funds are tied to compliance with these directives. Although they do not carry the force of law, Denmark's national directives clearly imply that localities are to make good faith efforts in encouraging transit-oriented development (TOD). The nation's Ministry of Environment has veto power over proposed local development projects. These veto powers have been exercised sparingly over the years, in large part because most localities strongly support sustainable patterns of development.

In addition to national directives that mandate that major trip generators be sited near rail stops, Denmark adds taxes and fees that typically triple the retail price of a new car. At 250 motor vehicles per 1,000 inhabitants, Copenhagen's vehicle ratio is about half that of large German cities like Hamburg and Frankfurt.

Local policies also restrict car travel. Central-city road capacity in Copenhagen has been kept constant since 1970; outside the core city, additional road capacity must be matched by at least as many square meters of additional bike lanes and bus lanes. Parking has also been restricted, particularly near rail stops. The outsourcing of parking to peripheral areas has led to a 2–3 percent annual reduction in core-area parking. Central-city bus services have been enhanced by a system of reserved lanes and signal prioritization.

Also strengthening Copenhagen's standing as a transit metropolis has been the expansion of rail services. The city has built new rail "fingers," notably, an automated, fully grade-separated line to the new-town of Orestad, south of the center city (figure 2.4).

Rail services preceded development in Orestad, a clear case of building transit first to guide development. From the start, Orestad was a true mixed-use community, designed as a place to live, work, shop, learn, and play. Particular attention was paid to the livability of the new community. Housing was built close to parks and canals and connected by plazas and pathways. Cafes and squares were sited to attract customers who arrive by foot. Neighborhood parks were designed to meet the diverse recreational needs of residents. In contrast to the drab, standardized appearance of Copenhagen's early-generation TODs, Orestad also features a variety of architectural styles carefully planned to interact and blend with one another. Many of Orestad's signature buildings were designed by world-class architects, and several have won prestigious design awards. Orestad's diversity is underscored by one of the largest car-free housing developments anywhere, called Urbanplanen.

Another rail line being built in the region follows a circular route, providing "cross-finger" connections. This Cityringen metro line will serve a number of districts outside the city proper not served by the S-Train commuter rail system. The sale of land whose value has appreciated in anticipation of new rail services has helped finance new investments like Cityringen, the Orestad line, and Copenhagen's first light rail line, Letbanen, being built parallel to the region's third ring road.

Copenhagen planners have also taken advantage of new technologies to enhance the transit riding experience. In 2009, the city introduced a

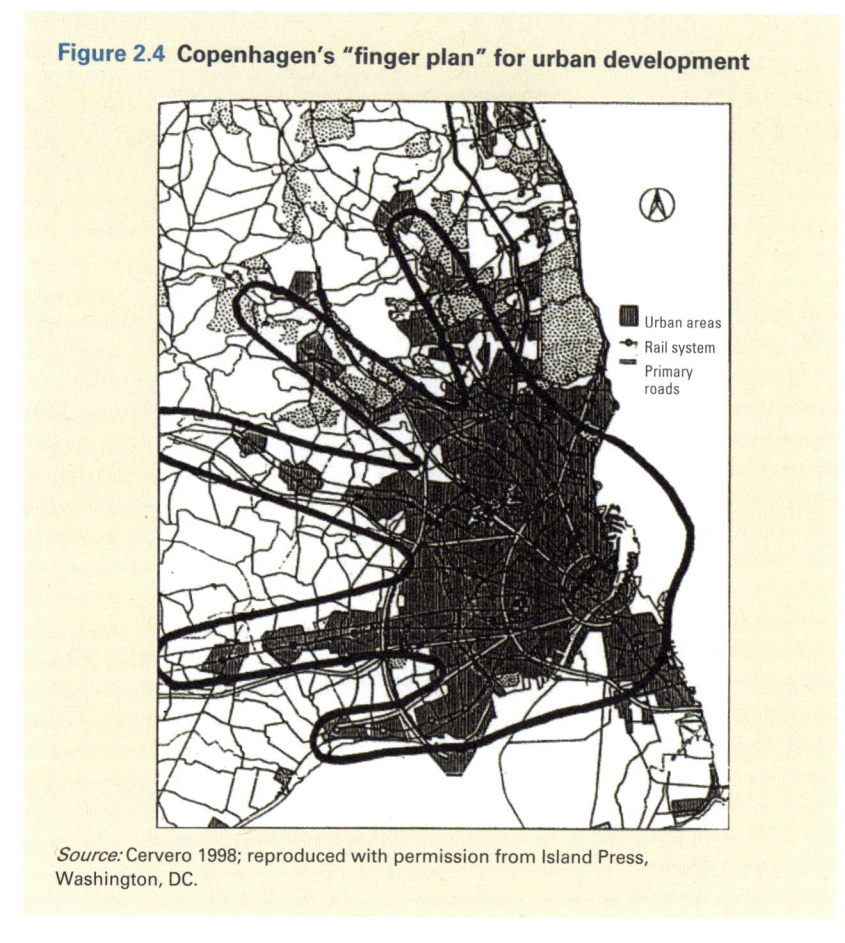

Figure 2.4 Copenhagen's "finger plan" for urban development

Source: Cervero 1998; reproduced with permission from Island Press, Washington, DC.

new state-of-the-art mobile ticket for transit trips. Customers are now able to buy and display tickets on their mobile phones for transit rides on the metro, suburban commuter rail lines, and city buses.

Stockholm: First-Generation Transit Necklace, Second-Generation Urban Regeneration

The last half century of strategic regional planning has given rise to regional settlement and commuting patterns in Greater Stockholm that have substantially reduced dependency on automobiles in middle-income suburbs. Stockholm's investment in radial rail lines has given rise to a "string of pearls" urban form and a balanced use of land for work and housing. By consciously establishing a balance between jobs and housing along rail-served axial corridors, Stockholm planners produced directional flow balances in commuting periods. During peak hours, 55 percent of commuters are typically traveling in one direction on trains and 45 percent are heading in the other direction.

Stockholm's transit mode share is nearly twice that found in larger rail-served European cities, such as Berlin; it is even higher than inner London's market share. Perhaps most impressive, Stockholm is one of the few places where automobile use appears to be receding. Between 1980 and 1990, Stockholm was the only city among a sample of 37 cities that registered a per capita decline in automobile use—a drop of 229 annual kilometers of travel per person (Kenworthy and Laube 1999). Its VKT per capita remains among the lowest in the world (see table 2.1). An independent analysis by Siemens AG/McKinsey (2008) finds Stockholm's per capita CO_2 emissions from transportation lower than four other rail-served and considerably larger global cities (London, New York, Rome, and Tokyo).

These statistics do not mean that Stockholm is "anti car." In fact, Stockholm has a relatively high level of car ownership (555 cars per 1,000 inhabitants) (European Commission 2012). In a well-designed transit metropolis like Stockholm, residents simply drive less; they are more judicious and discriminate in their use of the cars more than car owners in other cities. Most Stockholmers use public transport to get to work, selectively using cars where they have natural advantages, such as for grocery shopping or weekend excursions.

Stockholm is credited with spearheading TOD in the age of the motorway, in the form of master plans for new towns like Vällingby, where the rail stop sits squarely in the town center. Upon exiting the station, passengers step into a car-free public square surrounded by shops, restaurants, schools, and community facilities. The civic square, adorned with benches, water fountains, and greenery, is the community's central gathering spot—a place to relax, socialize, and hold special events, such as public celebrations, parades, and demonstrations. Sometimes the square doubles as a place for farmers to sell their produce or street artists to perform, changing chameleon-like from an open-air market one day to a concert venue the next. The assortment of flower stalls, sidewalk cafes, newsstands, and outdoor vendors dotting the square, combined with the musings and conversations of residents sitting in the square, retirees playing chess, and everyday encounters among friends, adds color and breathes life into the community. A community's rail station and its surroundings are thus more than a jumping off point to catch a train—they should also be the kinds of places people are naturally drawn to. If done well, TODs are "places to be," not "places to pass through" (Bertolini and Spit 1998).

Development of Hammarby Sjöstad. The first generation of TOD in metropolitan Stockholm was on former greenfields, such as Vällingby and Kista. More recently, a push has been made to redevelop brownfields. The most notable example is Hammarby Sjöstad, an eco-community that has taken form along a recently built inner-ring tramway.

The development of Hammarby Sjöstad marked an abrupt shift in Stockholm's urban planning practice. For decades, new towns had been built on peripheral greenfield sites. Hammarby Sjöstad is one of several "new-towns/in-towns" created based on Stockholm's 1999 city plan, which set forth a vision of "building the city inward."

Consisting of some 160 hectares of brownfield redevelopment, Hammarby Sjöstad stands as Stockholm's largest urban regeneration project to date. Because the project focuses on a new inner-city transit line and is designed for energy self-sufficiency and minimal waste, it has been called a "green TOD" (Cervero and Sullivan 2011). Just as the greenfield town of Vällingby pioneered TOD, Hammarby Sjöstad is a paragon of TOD with green urbanism and green architecture (table 2.2).

The community's signature transit element is a new tramway, Tvärbanan, which runs through the heart of the community along a 3-kilometer boulevard (Hammarby Allé and Lugnets Allé). In TOD fashion, taller buildings (mostly six to eight stories) cluster along the transit spine, and building heights taper with distance from the rail-served corridor. Trams run every seven minutes in peak hours and provide five-minute connections to Stockholm's metro underground network and commuter trains. Rail stations are well designed and fully weather protected, and they provide real-time arrival information. The city's buses run on biogas produced by local wastewater processing.

Parks, walkways, and green spaces are also prominent throughout Hammarby Sjöstad. Where possible, the natural landscape has been preserved. Bike lanes run along major boulevards, ample bike parking can be found at every building, and bike and pedestrian bridges cross waterways. Design features that are integral to TOD, like buildings that go up to the sidewalk line (that is, no set-backs), offer comfortable and secure walking corridors with clear sight lines. They also bring destinations together and, by creating side friction (parallel movements that prompt vehicles to slow down and encourage pedestrian activities), slow traffic.

The presence of three car-sharing companies, which together provide access to 37 low-emission vehicles, has further reduced the need to own a car in Hammarby Sjöstad. The area was designed with just 0.25 parking spaces per dwelling unit (though this rate has inched up some in recent years). All commercial parking is for a fee, and rates discourage long-term parking. The neighborhood sits just outside Stockholm's congestion toll boundary, adding another incentive to use public transport, walk, or bike when heading to the central city.

Hammarby Sjöstad's green urbanism is found in energy production, waste and water management, and building designs. The annual energy use of buildings in Hammarby Sjöstad is set at 60 kilowatt hours, a third less than for the city as a whole. All windows are triple-glazed and walls thoroughly insulated. Other conservation measures include extra heat insulation, energy-efficient windows, on-demand ventilation, individual metering of heating and hot water in apartments, electrically efficient installations, lighting control, solar panels, fuel cells, reduced water flow, and low-flush toilets.

The ecological feature of Hammarby Sjöstad that has garnered the most attention is the fully integrated closed-loop eco-cycle model. This clever system recycles waste and maximizes the reuse of waste energy and materials for heating, transportation, cooking, and electricity.

Table 2.2 Green transit-oriented development attributes of Hammarby Sjöstad, Sweden

Built environment	Green transportation		Green urbanism	
	Infrastructure	Programs and policies	Energy	Open space, water, and stormwater
Brownfield Infill Former army barracks: • High density along light rail boulevard (8 stories) • TOD: Mixed use with ground-floor retail and a wide range of goods and services	"Tvärbanan" light rail line: 3 stops in district: • 5 minutes to major station • 10–30 minutes to all parts of Center City • 7-min peak headway 2 bus lines Ferry Bike lanes and pedestrian bridges Ample bike parking at every building Car-sharing for 3 companies, 37 vehicles Near congestion toll boundary Pedestrian-friendly design/ complete streets	Transit-Boulevard is focus of activity/ commerce Grid streets increase connectivity/ calm traffic Convenient bike parking/ storage at every building	Waste converted to energy: • Food waste and wastewater sludge converted to biogas and used for heating • Combustible waste burned for energy and heat • Paper recycled Heat recaptured for reuse Combined heat and power plant Low-energy construction and energy saving measures: • Efficient appliances • Maximum insulation and triple-glazed windows	Stormwater treatment: • Rainwater collection • Maximum permeable surfaces • Purify runoff through soil filtration Ample open space: • Inner courtyards • Parks • Playgrounds • Green median • Borders large nature reserve with ski slopes Preservation of existing trees and open space Reduced water flow faucets and low-flush toliets

Source: Cervero and Sullivan 2011.

Also impressive is the community's approach to water management. All storm water, rainwater, and snowmelt is collected; purified locally through sand fiber, stormwater basins, and green roofs; and released in purified form into a lake. A preserved oak forest, ample green surfaces, and planted trees help collect rainwater to ensure cleaner air and provide a counterbalance to the dense urban landscape.

Hammarby Sjöstad is well on its way to becoming a low-carbon ecocommunity. Relative to conventional development, the project reduced air, soil, and water emissions and pollution by 40–46 percent; nonrenewable energy use by 30–47 percent; and water consumption by 41–46 percent (Cervero and Sullivan 2011). Similar to the rest of Stockholm, 95 percent of all waste produced by Hammarby Sjöstad's household is reclaimed.

Table 2.3 Mode splits for journeys in various parts of Stockholm County (percent)

Mode of transportation	Inner city	Southern suburbs	Western suburbs	Hammarby Sjöstad
Car	17	39	43	21
Public transit	36	28	23	52
Bike/walk	47	32	34	27

Source: Authors, based on data from Grontmij 2008.

Environmental benefits have accrued from Hammarby Sjöstad's relatively high share of nonmotorized (walking and bicycling) trips. In 2002, the project's mode splits were public transit 52 percent, walking/cycling 27 percent, and private cars 21 percent (table 2.3)—a much more ecological split than in suburban neighborhoods of Stockholm with similar incomes (Grontmij 2008). Noncar travel shares are thought to be considerably higher today. Car ownership has also fallen, from 66 percent of households in 2005 to 62 percent in 2007, in line with averages for the denser, core part of Stockholm (Grontmij 2008). Residents' carbon footprint from transportation in 2002 was considerably lower than comparison communities (438 versus 913 kilograms of CO_2 equivalent/apartment/year) (Grontmij 2008). Stockholm's goal is to become fossil fuel free by 2050.

Another barometer of Hammarby Sjöstad's environmental benefits is the community's relatively healthy local economy. Median household income was higher and the unemployment rate lower than the city of Stockholm as a whole in 2006, and land prices and rents have risen more rapidly over the past decade than most other parts of the Stockholm region (Grontmij 2008).

Transport demand management and pedestrian- and transit-oriented projects. Congestion pricing is an important component of creating a functional and livable core city. Stockholm's electronic road pricing (ERP) scheme, introduced in 2004 on a trial basis, charges motorists for entering the central city on weekdays, using a graduated price scheme. Buses, taxis, eco-fuel cars, and drivers coming and going from the isolated island of Lidingo are exempted.

As traffic conditions and the quality of public transit services improved, citizens' support grew steadily (Eliasson and others 2009). In a referendum in 2007, 53 percent of Stockholm residents voted to make the road pricing trial permanent. During the first two years of the permanent scheme, peak-period traffic volumes within the pricing zone fell 25 percent (removing 1 million vehicles from the road a day), CO_2 emissions fell 14 percent, and daily toll revenues reached about $300,000 (Eliasson and others 2009).

Some revenues from congestion tolls have gone to enhance transit services; most have been used to upgrade road facilities, including the South City tunnel project (Sodra Lanken), which removes through-traffic from central-city surface streets, and a western bypass project. Revenues are also going toward a major inner-city land reclamation project in the Slussen area. Guided by a master plan by noted architect Norman Foster, Slussen—which has been called a tangled mass of highway overpasses—is to become a pedestrian- and transit-oriented central-city infill project. Slussen will feature attractive public spaces and water terraces that link pedestrians on a historic route into the old city.

Also in the works are makeovers of Stockholm's first-generation transit villages. Vällingby's upgrading is being called one of Sweden's largest suburban renewal projects. Skarholmen, Spanga, and Kista Science City are also being renovated as second-generation TODs.

Hong Kong SAR, China: Profitable Transit

Any visitor to Hong Kong SAR, China, instantly recognizes that public transit is the lifeblood of the city. The city boasts a wide array of transit services, including a high-capacity railway network, surface-street trams, ferries, and an assortment of buses and minibuses. In late 2007, the city's main passenger rail operator, Mass Transit Railway Corporation (MTRC), merged with the former Kowloon-Canton Railway Corporation, forming a 168-kilometer network of high-capacity, grade-separated services on the island of Hong Kong; the Kowloon peninsula; the Northern Territories (to the Chinese border); and, through a recent extension, to the new international airport. In 2000, more than 90 percent of all motorized trips were by public transit, the highest market share in the world (Lam and Bell 2003; Cervero and Murakami 2009).

The combination of high urban densities and high-quality public transit services has not only produced one of the highest levels of transit usage in the world (570 annual public transport trips per capita), it has also substantially driven down the cost of motorized travel. In 2002, more than half of all motorized trips made by city residents were half an hour or less (ARUP 2003). Motorized travel consumes, on average, about 5 percent of the city's GDP. This figure contrasts sharply with more automobile-oriented global cities, such as Houston, Texas, and Melbourne, Australia, where more than one-seventh of GDP goes to transportation (IAPT 2002). Hong Kong SAR, China residents enjoy substantial travel cost savings even in comparison with much larger global cities with extensive railway networks, like London and Paris.

Hong Kong SAR, China is one of the few places in the world where public transit makes a profit. It does so because the city's rail operator, MTRC, has adopted the "Rail+Property" (R+P) program (Cervero and Murakami 2009). R+P is one of the best examples anywhere of transit value capture in action. Given the high premium placed on access to fast, efficient, and reliable public transit services in a dense, congested city, the price of land near railway stations is generally higher than elsewhere, sometimes by several orders of magnitude. MTRC has used its ability to purchase the development rights for the land around stations to recoup the cost of investing in rail transit and turn a profit. The railway has also played a vital city-shaping role. In 2002, about 2.8 million people, 41 percent of the population, lived within 500 meters of a railway station (Tang and others 2004).

The profit motive accounts for MTRC's active involvement in land development. As a private corporation that sells equity shares on the Hong Kong stock market, MTRC operates on commercial principles, financing and operating railway services that are self-supporting and yield a net return on investment. The full costs of public transit investments, operations, and maintenance are covered by supplementing fare and other revenues with income from ancillary real estate development, such as the sale of development rights, joint ventures with private real estate developers, and the operation of retail outlets in and around subway stations. The local government is MTRC's majority stockholder, ensuring that the company weighs the broader public interest in its day-to-day decisions. At the same time, the ownership of 23 percent of MTRC's shares by private investors exerts market discipline, prompting the company to be entrepreneurial.

Between 2001 and 2005, property development produced 52 percent of MTRC's revenues. By contrast, railway income, made up mostly of fare-box receipts, generated 28 percent of total income. MTRC's involvement in all property-related activities—development, investment, and management—produced 62 percent of total income, more than twice as much as fares. An example of an R+P project that has yielded both high rates of financial returns and high ridership (and thus fare-box income) is Maritime Square at the Tsing Yi Station (figure 2.5).

Timing is crucial in MTRC's recapturing of the value added by rail service. MTRC purchases development rights from the local government at a "before rail" price and sells these rights to a selected developer (among a list of qualified bidders) at an "after rail" price. The difference between land values with and without rail services is substantial, easily covering the cost of railway investments. When bargaining with developers, MTRC also negotiates a share of future property development profits or a co-ownership position from the highest bidder. Thus, MTRC receives a "front end" payment for land and a "back end" share of revenues and assets in kind.

MTRC has hardly been the sole financial beneficiary of R+P. Society at large has also reaped substantial rewards. Between 1980 and 2005, it is estimated that Hong Kong SAR, China received nearly $140 billion (in current dollars) in net financial returns. This estimate is based on the difference between earned income ($171.8 billion from land premiums, market capitalization, shareholder cash dividends, and initial public offer proceeds) and the value of injected equity capital ($32.2 billion from land grants). Thus, the government has enjoyed huge financial returns and seeded the

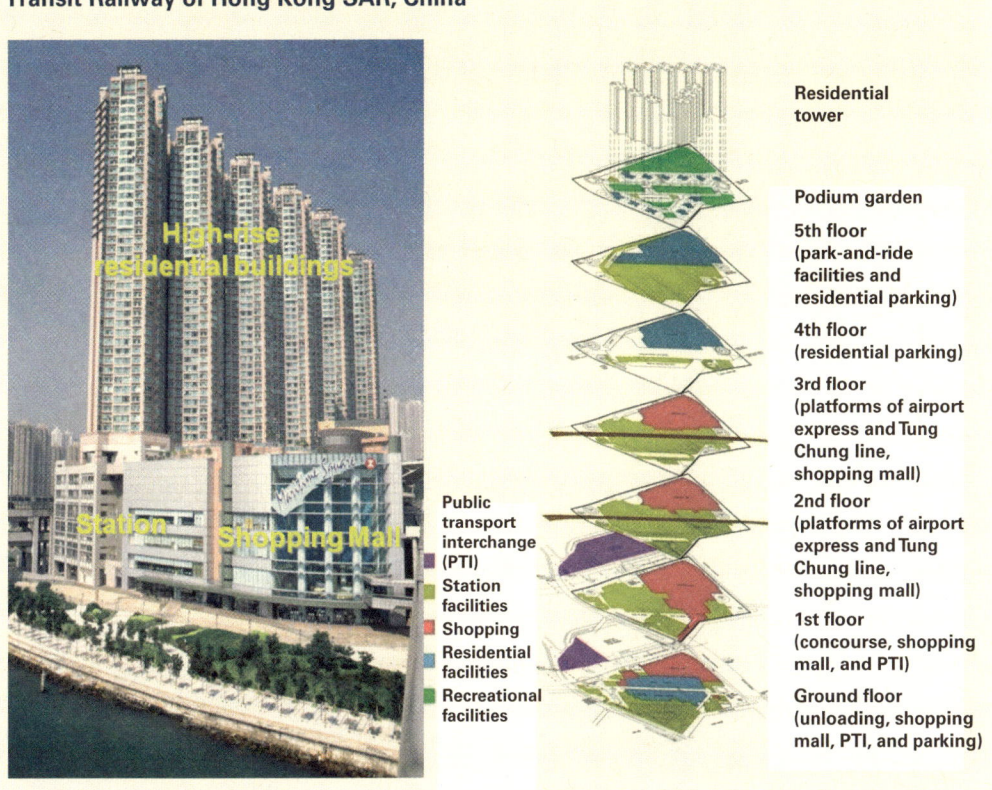

Figure 2.5 The Maritime Square residential-retail project developed by the Mass Transit Railway of Hong Kong SAR, China

Source: Courtesy of MTR Corporation Ltd.
Note: Situated above the Tsing Yi Station between the center of the city and the new international airport, Maritime Square features a hierarchy of integrated uses: a shopping mall extends from the ground floor to the third level; the station concourse sits on the first floor, with rail lines and platforms above and ancillary/logistical functions (such as public transit/bus interchange and parking) at or below; above the fourth and fifth floor residential parking lies a podium garden, and above that are luxury residential towers.

construction of a world-class railway network without having to advance any cash to MTRC. Moreover, the $140 billion figure is only the direct financial benefit. The indirect benefits—for example, reduced sprawl, air pollution, and energy consumption and higher ridership through increased densities— have increased net societal returns well beyond $140 billion.

Hong Kong SAR, China has long had tall towers perched above railway stations. But density alone does not make a good TOD. Often missing was a high-quality pedestrian environment and a sense of place. Most first-generation R+P projects featured indistinguishable apartment towers that funneled pedestrians onto busy streets and left them to their own devices to find a subway entrance. Growing discontent over sterile station-area environments and older buildings' sagging real estate market performance prompted MTRC to pay more attention to principles of good town planning and urban design.

In 2000, MTRC created a town planning division within the corporation to pursue land development strategies that met corporate financial objectives while also enhancing station-area environments. Before 2000, R+P projects followed the existing development pattern rather than anticipated development; yet, with an in-house town planning department, MTRC became more proactive. The company is now ahead of market demand, building high-quality, pedestrian-friendly TODs to steer growth. Research shows that the design of high-quality walking environments has increased financial returns per square meter for R+P projects (Cervero and Murakami 2009). Pedestrian-friendly R+P projects have contributed to sustainable urbanism as well as sustainable finance, as these benefits have been capitalized into land prices.

Seoul: Bus Rapid Transit and Urban Land Reclamation

At the turn of the 21st century, Seoul embarked on a bold experiment in urban regeneration, principally involving the reclamation of urban space given to the automobile in the post–Korean War era. Through the leadership of Myung-Bak Lee, the former mayor of Seoul and the current president of the Republic of Korea, the city has sought to strike a balance between transit infrastructure as a provider of mobility and public space as an urban amenity. In good part, this effort has been prompted by the desire to make Seoul globally competitive with the likes of Hong Kong SAR, China, Shanghai, and other East Asian heavyweights of by emphasizing quality of life every bit as much as mobility and large-scale infrastructure development.

Like many modern metropolises in East Asia, over the past several decades Seoul has followed a pattern of American-style sprawl, fueled by steady economic growth and the concomitant meteoric rise in private automobile ownership. However, population densities in Seoul (10.4 million inhabitants spread over a land area of 605 square kilometers) have historically been and remain high by global standards. The city of Seoul itself, along with the port city of Incheon and surrounding Kyunggi Province, constitute the Seoul Metropolitan Area (also called the Seoul National Capital Area), with more than 23 million inhabitants—the world's second-largest urban agglomeration. In 2006, Seoul and Incheon combined had the sixth-highest population density in the world (16,700 people per square kilometers). Because of such high densities, the Seoul metropolitan government has over the years aggressively sought to decentralize growth, mainly in the form of building master-planned new towns sited on the region's periphery.

A severe housing shortage and rising housing rents (fueled largely by land speculation) during the 1980s prompted the Korean government to build new towns quickly, as a mass-produced commodity. Twenty-six new towns have been built in the greater Seoul Metropolitan Area over the past three decades. Most were built in a modernist Le Corbusier style, as mid- to high-rise "towers in the park."

The shortage of central-city land combined with the presence of a protective greenbelt that surrounds the city of Seoul resulted in most new towns being built in the region's far-flung fringes (Jun and Hur 2001).

New-town development achieved its goal of stabilizing housing prices, but it did so at a price: congestion on radial links to the urban center worsened, tailpipe emissions and fuel consumption rose, and demand for expensive highway infrastructure mushroomed. Between 1990 and 1996, the average commuting distance of new-town residents increased 70 percent (Jun 2000). Longer trips combined with increased car ownership inevitably translated into steadily worsening traffic congestion: average speeds during evening hours in the Seoul Metropolitan Area fell from 24 kilometers an hour in 1998 to 17 kilometers an hour in 2003. Daily commuting expenses rose sharply, as well: one study estimated the out-of-pocket cost (ignoring the value of time and externalities) incurred by new-town residents living outside of Seoul's greenbelt at $12 a day (Jun and Bae 2000).

By the late 1990s, rumblings could be heard within public policy circles that the region's new towns were a failed experiment, exacerbating traffic congestion and reducing environmental quality. Some feared that such factors, along with the productivity losses from long commutes, were becoming a drag on economic growth, prompting companies and their workers to relocate elsewhere in the country and possibly even abroad. The idea of reurbanizing Seoul's central areas through "new-towns/in-towns" began to surface.

Myung-Bak Lee led the charge of reinvesting in the central city and regenerating Seoul. In 2001, Lee ran for mayor of Seoul, largely on a platform of reinvigorating the central city as means of creating a more sustainable yet productive city. Lee campaigned on the premise that Seoul could achieve a better balance between function and the environment by reordering public priorities so as to emphasize quality of place. Before becoming mayor, Lee found and led the Hyundai Group for three decades, Korea's largest builder of public works and infrastructure projects, including highways.

Lee won a decisive victory. Upon assuming office, in early 2002, he moved quickly on his campaign promises. His vision called not only for expanding public transit services but also for reducing the ecological footprint of private cars by reclaiming urban space consumed by roads and highways, especially space used to funnel new-town inhabitants in and out of the central city. Why scar the interior of the city, he reasoned, to funnel suburbanites to office jobs in the core? A major culprit was the network of elevated freeways that converged on central Seoul—facilities that severed longstanding neighborhoods, formed barriers and created visual blight, cast shadows, and sprayed noise, fumes, and vibrations on surrounding areas. Although freeways provided important mobility benefits, Lee recognized that those benefits had to be weighed against their nuisance effects, particularly in today's amenity-conscious workplace.

Figure 2.6 **Transformation of Seoul's Cheong Gye Cheon from an elevated freeway to an urban greenway**

a. Elevated freeway

b. Urban greenway

Source: Seoul Metropolitan Government 2003.

The removal of a six-kilometer elevated freeway in the heart of Seoul, Cheong Gye Cheon (CGC), and the restoration of an urban stream and pedestrian-friendly greenway was a natural choice to launch Lee's vision of a more sustainable urban landscape for the city. Change was swift. By February 2003, a plan for the freeway removal was completed; five months later, the freeway had been completely dismantled. Some two years later, in September 2005, the restored CGC stream and linear greenway was opened to the public, following a major public celebration and ribbon cutting by Mayor Lee (figure 2.6). The entire cost of the freeway demolition and stream restoration was $313 million.

Equally important in symbolic terms was the mayor's decision to convert a massive 1.3 hectare surface-street intersection to an oval-shaped grass park in front of Seoul's City Hall, the nerve center of the city. The huge swath of real estate devoted to car maneuvers in front of City Hall, an architectural icon and one of the busiest locations in the city, created an extremely pedestrian-hostile environment. Today, the green oval is one of the city's most popular gathering places.

Mayor Lee made his policy intentions clear when publicly stating that the transformation of space for cars to space for people represented "a new paradigm for urban management in the new century" (Seoul Metropolitan Government 2003, p. 1). His views were partly shaped by what was happening in several Latin American cities at the time, especially Curitiba, Brazil, which he visited at the invitation of Jaime Lerner, former mayor of Curitiba. Mayor Lee defended the roadway removal projects on the grounds that "we want to make a city where people come first, not cars." The diminution of roadway capacity represents, in many ways, a recasting of public priorities. In Seoul's case, it marked a shift from building infrastructure that enhances automobility to infrastructure that enhances public amenities and the quality of urban living. A longer-term objective was to encourage more households to settle in the central city and in redevelopment districts, thus reversing the centrifugal flow of residents to Seoul's outskirts and beyond—in effect, creating a new form of urban development.

In and of itself, the withdrawal of road capacity in an increasingly automobile-dependent society will do little to enhance the quality of urban living. Mayor Lee understood that public transit had to be substantially expanded and upgraded to absorb the traffic (169,000 cars a day on the CGC freeway) displaced by large-scale reductions in roadway capacity. The city did so partly by extending subway lines. More important was the 2004 opening of seven new lines of exclusive median-lane buses (stretching 84 kilometers, later expanded to 162 kilometers) and 294 kilometers of dedicated curbside bus lanes. Figure 2.7 shows the staged expansion of BRT services in Seoul.

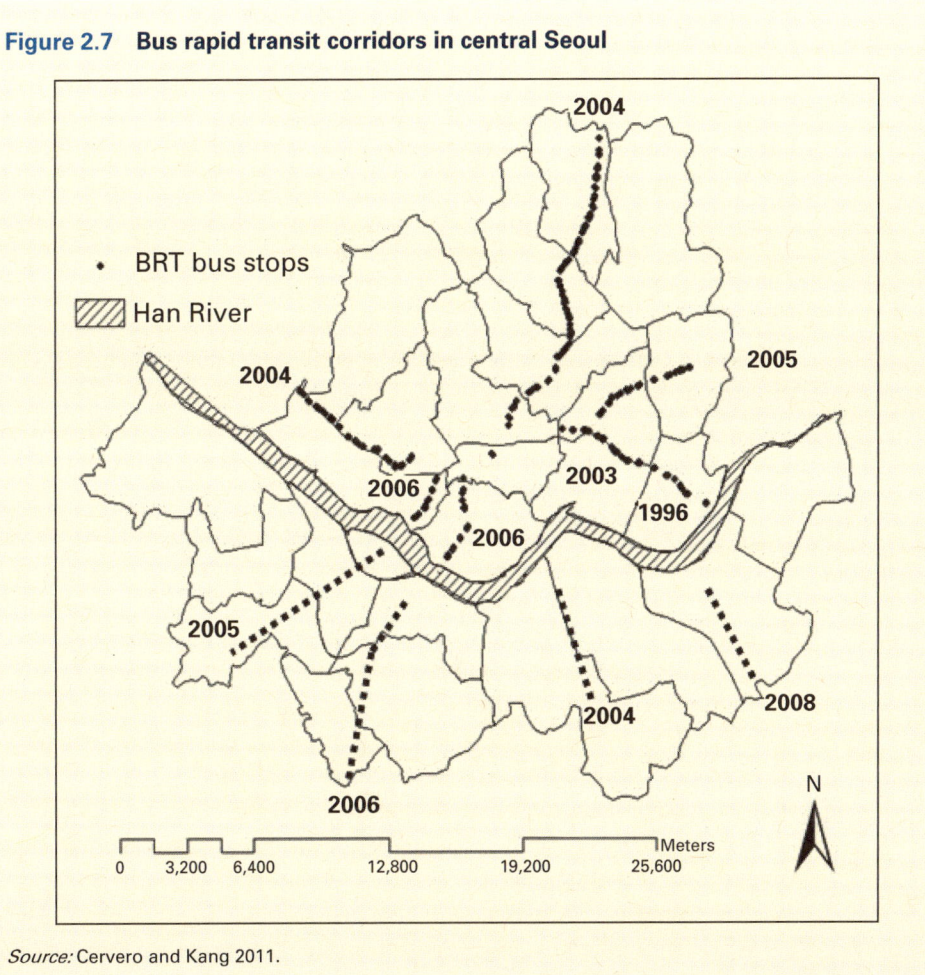

Figure 2.7 Bus rapid transit corridors in central Seoul

Source: Cervero and Kang 2011.

Seoul's BRT investments have paid off handsomely. Bus operating speeds have increased from an average of 11 kilometers to more than 21 kilometers per hour, and speeds have increased in some passenger-car lanes (table 2.4). BRT buses, moreover, carry more than six times as many passengers per hour as buses operating on regular mixed-traffic lanes. And because they are less subject to the vagaries of ambient traffic flows, buses operating in dedicated lanes have become more reliable: the travel-time variation of Seoul's BRT buses is, on average, five times less than that of buses operating on nonexclusive lanes (Seoul Development Institute 2005). Protected lanes have also reduced the number of accidents, which declined 27 percent one year after BRT services were introduced. Because of these service enhancements and safety improvements, ridership on BRT buses increased 60 percent faster than on non–BRT buses between 2004 and 2005.

BRT was just one of several transit transformations introduced in Seoul. In the early 2000s, skyrocketing operating deficits prompted the metropolitan government to create a semipublic transit organization that set and enforced rules and standards on bus routes, schedules, and private operating practices. Many routes were reorganized into a timed-transfer and pulse-scheduling arrangement. All bus services were classified into one of four types of services: red (long-distance and intercity services), blue (trunk services), green (feeder services), and yellow (circular services). Red long-distance intercity lines link satellite cities with one another and downtown Seoul. Blue trunk lines connect the subcore and central-city Seoul. Green feeder buses mainly funnel passengers to subway stations and express bus stops. Yellow circular lines orbit the urban core.

Also introduced at the time of land reclamation was a sophisticated smart fare card that has allowed for efficient distance-based pricing and integrated bus-rail fares. A real-time traffic information system with message boards and in-vehicle navigation aids was installed to guide traffic flows and alert motorists to downstream hot spots. Curbside parking was substantially curtailed to help expedite traffic flows. More draconian was the introduction of a scheme that requires motorists to leave their cars at home once every 10 days (based on the last number of their license plate).

Land market responses to the BRT investments as well as projects like the CGC freeway-to-greenway conversion suggest that the net impacts have been positive (Kang and Cervero 2009; Cervero and Kang 2011). In a crowded, congested, and land-constrained city like Seoul, increased accessibility prompted property owners and developers to intensify land uses along BRT corridors, mainly by converting single-family residences to multifamily units, apartments, and mixed-use projects.

Land markets capitalized these accessibility gains, particularly in parcels used for condominiums and higher-density residential uses. Land price premiums of about 5–10 percent have been recorded for residences within 300 meters of BRT stops (Cervero and Kang 2011). For retail shops and other nonresidential uses, premiums were more varied, ranging from 3

Table 2.4 Operating speeds of cars and buses in Seoul before and after opening of exclusive median-lane bus lanes
(kilometers per hour)

Road	Before (June 2004)	After (August 2004)	Percentage change
A			
Bus (exclusive lane)	11.0	20.3	85.0
Car (other lane)	18.5	19.9	7.6
B			
Bus (exclusive lane)	13.1	22.5	72.0
Car (other lane)	20.3	21.0	3.4
C			
Bus (exclusive lane)	13.0	17.2	32.0
Car (other lane)	18.0	19.1	6.1

Source: Seoul Development Institute 2005.
Note: Seven new lines of exclusive median-lane buses were opened in 2004.

percent to 26 percent over a smaller impact zone of 150 meters from the nearest BRT stop.

Greenways supported by expanded transit services further boosted land prices and development activities along high-amenity corridors. Housing prices within 3 kilometers of the elevated freeway fell, reflecting a disamenity; once the corridor was transformed to a greenway, prices of homes within 2 kilometers rose as much as 8 percent (Kang and Cervero 2009) (figure 2.8).

Commercial parcels also increased following the freeway-to-greenway conversion, as did the concentration of high-value-added industries that hire white-collar professionals and "creative class" workers (Kang and Cervero 2009). Given these changes in prices, one could argue that residents of Seoul valued the quality of the urban space more highly than a freeway. Quality of place won out over automobility as a desirable urban attribute.

In addition to the attractions of greenery and open space, part of the land-value gains conferred by the freeway-to-greenway conversion likely also reflected indirect environmental benefits. Air pollution levels along the CGC corridor have fallen since the stream restoration and greenway conversion. Concentrations of fine-grained particulate matter (PM_{10}) along the corridor were 13 percent higher than Seoul's regional average before the conversion; after the conversion, they were 4 percent below the region's average (Seoul Development Institute 2005). Concentrations of nitrogen dioxide (NO_2), a precursor to the formation of photochemical smog, fell from 2 percent above the regional average when the freeway was in operation to 17 percent below the regional average after the greenway was in place.

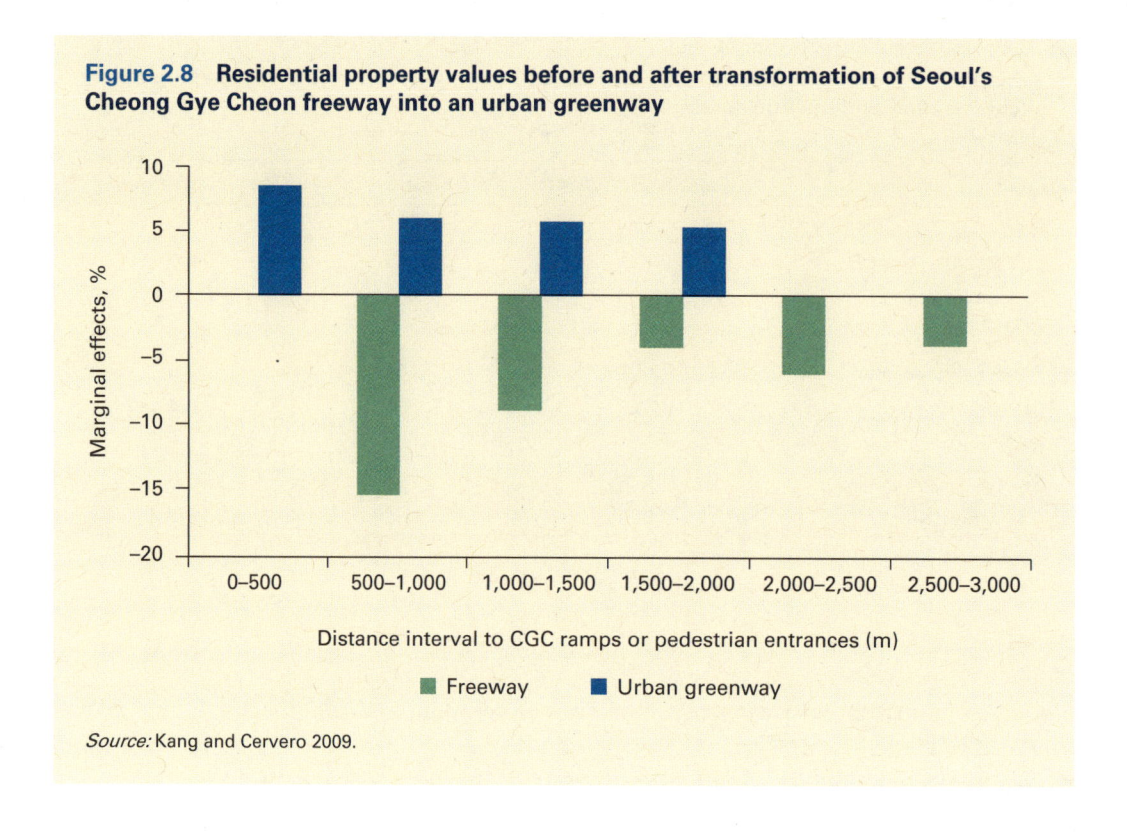

Figure 2.8 Residential property values before and after transformation of Seoul's Cheong Gye Cheon freeway into an urban greenway

Source: Kang and Cervero 2009.

Many urban centers suffer a heat-island effect, with temperatures higher than surrounding suburban and rural areas because of greater surface area coverage. Seoul is no exception. The spillover "cooling" benefits from the freeway-to-greenway conversion are revealed by a heat-island study that finds that ambient temperatures along the central-city stream were 3.3°C lower and temperatures along the greenway 5.9°C lower than along a parallel surface arterial five blocks away (Hwang 2006).

The longer-term consequences of Seoul's bold experiment with urban land reclamation are yet to be seen. The hope and expectation of many urban planners and green politicans is that reclamation will slow the pace of new-town development, reduce the spatial mismatch between development north (primarily employment) and south (primarily housing) of the Han River, and spur redevelopment of former industrial land. More balanced infill development, planners hope, will make Seoul an attractive global city that appeals to international finance and businesses as well as tourists, professionals, and foreign investors.

Singapore: Transit-Oriented Development Empowered by Transportation Demand Management

The city-state of Singapore is internationally renowned for its successful integration of transit and regional development, placing the urbanized island of 5.1 million inhabitants on a sustainable pathway both economically and

Figure 2.9 Singapore's Constellation Plan

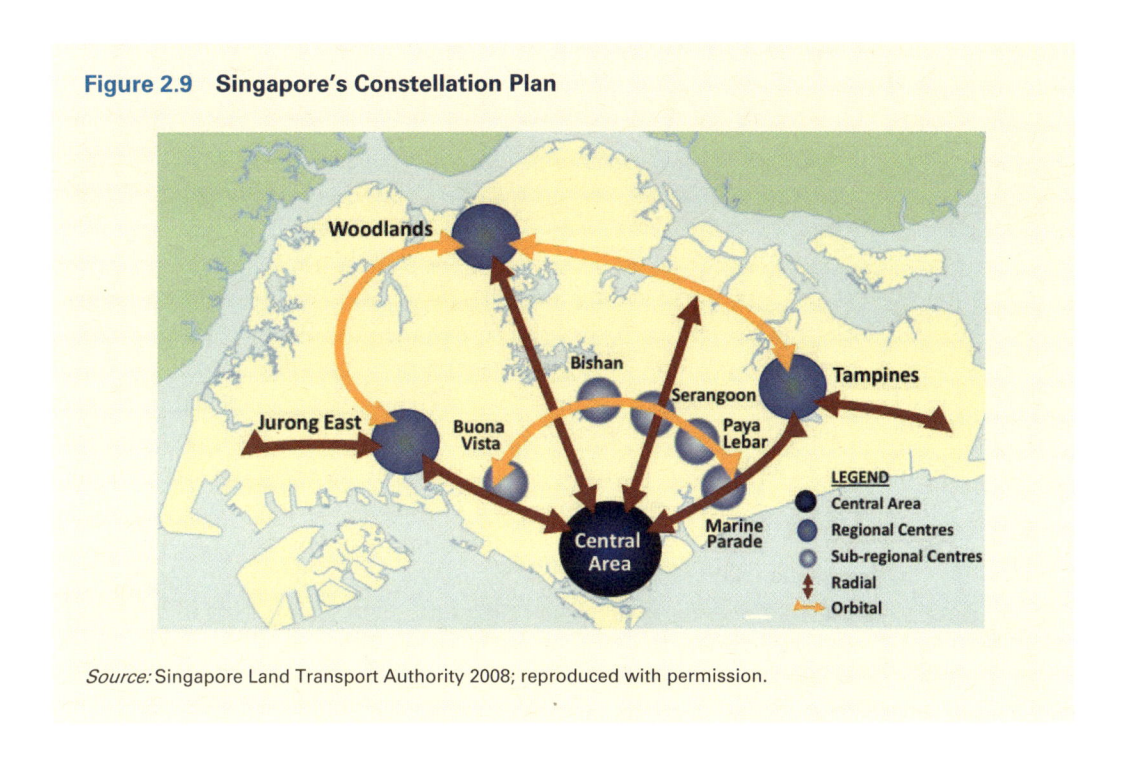

Source: Singapore Land Transport Authority 2008; reproduced with permission.

environmentally. Its transformation over the post–World War II period from a backwater port awash in third-world poverty to a dynamic, modern, industrialized city-state has been remarkable.

As part of a national economic development strategy, Singapore has embraced Scandinavian planning principles that call for radial corridors that interconnect the central core with master-planned new towns. Its structure plan, called the Constellation Plan, looks like a constellation of satellite "planets," or new towns, that surround the central core, interspersed by protective greenbelts and interlaced by high-capacity, high-performance rail transit. Radial rail links interconnect Singapore's high-rise urban core with the hierarchy of subcenters, and a looping mix of heavy and light rail lines connects the subcenters (figure 2.9).

Like Stockholm and Copenhagen, this rail-served settlement pattern has produced tremendous transportation benefits. VKT per capita is among the lowest of any urbanized region in the world with per capita GDP of more than $25,000, and the annual number of transit trips per capita is high (484 in 2006) (UITP 2006).

Singapore adopted the approach of building new towns that are not independent, self-contained units but rather nodes with specialized functions that interact with and depend on one another. Some satellite centers are primarily industrial estates, others are predominantly dormitory communities; most are mixed-use enclaves. About three-quarters of residents of master-planned new towns work outside their town. Most, however, commute within the radial corridor that connects their town to Singapore's central business district. Travel is thus predominantly within, not between, rail-served corridors. The dispersal of mixed land uses along corridors has created two-way travel flows and spread travel demand more evenly throughout the day.

Singapore's progressive "transit first" policies complement its transit-oriented Constellation Plan. The city has introduced a three-tier fiscal program that comes as close to "getting the prices right" within the urban transport sector as any city in the world. The first tier of charges is subscription fees for owning a car. Made up of high registration fees, import duties for automobile purchases, and a licensing surcharge based on a quota system (a certificate of entitlement that is indexed to congestion levels), these charges principally cover the fixed costs associated with providing basic levels of road infrastructure and parking facilities. The second tier of charges is use related, in the form of fuel taxes and parking fees. These charges cover the incremental costs for scaling road capacity to traffic volumes and maintaining roadway infrastructure. The third set of charges—in the form of real-time ERP—forces motorists to internalize the externalities they impose when using their cars during peak hours. Fees fluctuate according to congestion levels, forcing motorists to bear some of the costs they impose on others in the form of time delays and air pollution. Within a month of initiating ERP in 1998, traffic along a main thoroughfare fell 15 percent and average rush hour speeds rose from 36 to 58 kilometers per hour. Vehicle quotas, congestion prices, and an assortment of fees and surtaxes (which add as much as 150 percent to a car's open market value) have reduced the annual growth of Singapore's vehicle population from 6 percent in 1997 to less than 3 percent in 2010—a remarkable achievement for a city in which per capita incomes have risen faster over the past two decades than virtually anywhere in the world.

Charging motorists more to own and use cars is but one form of transportation demand management (TDM) found in Singapore. As in Europe, car sharing has gained a foothold in Singapore, the only Asian city where this is the case. Singapore also has an off-peak vehicle licensing scheme that allows vehicles holding such licenses to be used only during the morning and evening off-peak periods Mondays through Saturday and any time Sunday.

Although higher prices and TDM have boosted transit usage, their influences are being eclipsed by rising income, which continues to push up Singapore's rates of car ownership and motorization. Singapore has among the most affordable housing (thanks to government provisions of mass-produced units), freeing up personal income for the second most costly durable good purchased by households, the private car. In the early 1990s, the ratio of the average housing price to average annual household income (2.3) was far lower than the ratio of the average price of a new car to income (3.7). Over the 1974–95 period, the price elasticity for car ownership was –0.45, compared with an income elasticity of 1.00, according to one study (Chu, Koh, and Tse 2004). Even if automobile prices increase at twice the rate of household incomes, such elasticities suggest that motorization rates will continue to rise in Singapore.

Rising congestion is reflected by statistics on the density of cars on land-constrained Singapore's fairly fixed supply of road supply. In 1995 (the year the vehicle quota system was introduced), the number of vehicles per kilometer of road was 180; by 2010, the figure had risen to 250. Car ownership increased by only 11 percent between 2000 and 2005; between 2005 and 2010, it increased 39 percent (Singapore Government n.d.).

In the face of this rapid rise in car ownership, Singapore is turning to higher congestion tolls as a way to temper motorization. The logic of raising congestion tolls is expressed in the long-term master plan: "Although congestion charges such as ERP encourage motorists to consider whether and when to drive, ownership costs are sunk costs and may in fact result in motorists driving more rather than less. Hence, as we expand the electronic road pricing (ERP) system, we will continue to shift the focus of our demand management strategies from ownership taxes to usage charges" (Singapore Land Transport Authority 2008, p. 57).

Singapore's centralized form of governance has allowed land development and transit services, which are overseen by different authorities (the Urban Redevelopment Authority and the Land Transport Authority), to be closely coordinated, both institutionally and financially. Revenues generated from high vehicle ownership and usage charges, for instance, go to the general treasury, which channels them into vastly enhanced and expanded transit services as well as the construction of the armature of rail TODs (for example, sidewalk networks, civic squares, bus staging areas). Because of the island-state's world-class transit service offerings and TOD built form, congestion tolls are politically possible, as for a significant share of trips, travel times are lower using public transit than private cars. Of 8.9 million daily motorized trips made in Singapore in 2010, 4.5 million were by rail or bus transit (Singapore MRT 2011). Long-range planning goals call for raising this share to two-thirds.

The role of rail transit in capturing larger shares of motorized trips has increased, and it is slated to continue to do so in coming years. The length of Singapore's world-class rapid transit system more than doubled, to 138 kilometers in 2011 from 67 kilometers in 1990, leading to a doubling of ridership, to nearly 2 million riders a day, from a little under 1 million in 1998. In 1999, Singapore added automated light rail services to the mix, with trackage increasing from 8 kilometers in 1999 to 29 kilometers in 2010. Bus ridership in 2011 was only 1.5 times higher than total rail ridership, down from 3 times higher than rail in 1998. Singapore's latest land transport master plan, released in 2008, embraces "making public transport a choice mode" and "managing road usage" as strategic thrusts toward retaining its status as a world-class transit metropolis.

Tokyo: Public-Private Urban Regeneration

Tokyo's position as a global transit metropolis mimics that of Hong Kong SAR, China, and Stockholm, albeit in different ways. As in Hong Kong SAR, China, the private sector has historically linked transit investments and urban development through value capture mechanisms; as in Stockholm, the focus of the transit/land-use nexus has been on urban regeneration rather than new-town development in recent years, albeit more for market than urban policy reasons.

Tokyo's railway network—owned and operated by a mix of public, private, and quasi-private entities—is by far the world's largest. Most of the region's extensive network of suburban railway lines was built by private companies that received government concessions and exclusive rights to design, build, and operate rail services. Tokyo's railway companies have historically leveraged real estate development to both pay for infrastructure and produce profits for shareholders. They have opened convenience stores and shopping malls within and adjacent to stations.

What most distinguishes Tokyo's railway companies is their construction of large-scale new towns on once virgin lands (Cervero 1998). West of central Tokyo, where many of the region's most up-market suburbs are located, entire communities are the domains of powerful conglomerates that are best known for their department store chains—Keio, Odakyu, Seibu, and Tokyu—but which first and foremost are in the business of railway and real estate development. All started as private railway companies that over time branched into businesses closely related to the railway industry, including real estate, retailing, bus operations, and electric power generation. Such business expansion made good economic sense; placing shopping malls, apartments, and entertainment complexes near stations generated rail traffic, and railways brought customers to these establishments. During the 1980s, at the height of railway/new-town co-development and a surge in Japanese real estate prices, railway companies were earning investment returns on ancillary real estate projects in the range of 50–70 percent, with profit margins from real estate far outstripping profits from transit services (figure 2.10).

Tokyu Corporation is Greater Tokyo's largest private railway enterprise. It was among the first companies to advance the business model of railway/new-town co-development. From 1960 to 1984, Tokyu Corporation's 23-kilometer rail line transformed a vast, hilly, scarcely inhabited area into a planned community, Tama Den-en Toshi (Tama Garden City), of a half million residents. Tokyu used land consolidation techniques to assemble farmland at cheap prices in advance of rail construction and to finance neighborhood infrastructure. Under this approach, landowners formed a cooperative that consolidated (often irregularly shaped) properties and returned them as smaller but fully serviced (usually rectangular) parcels. Roads, drainage, sewerage, parks, and other infrastructure were funded through the sale of the "extra" reserved land contributed by cooperative members. Land consolidation relieved railway companies such as

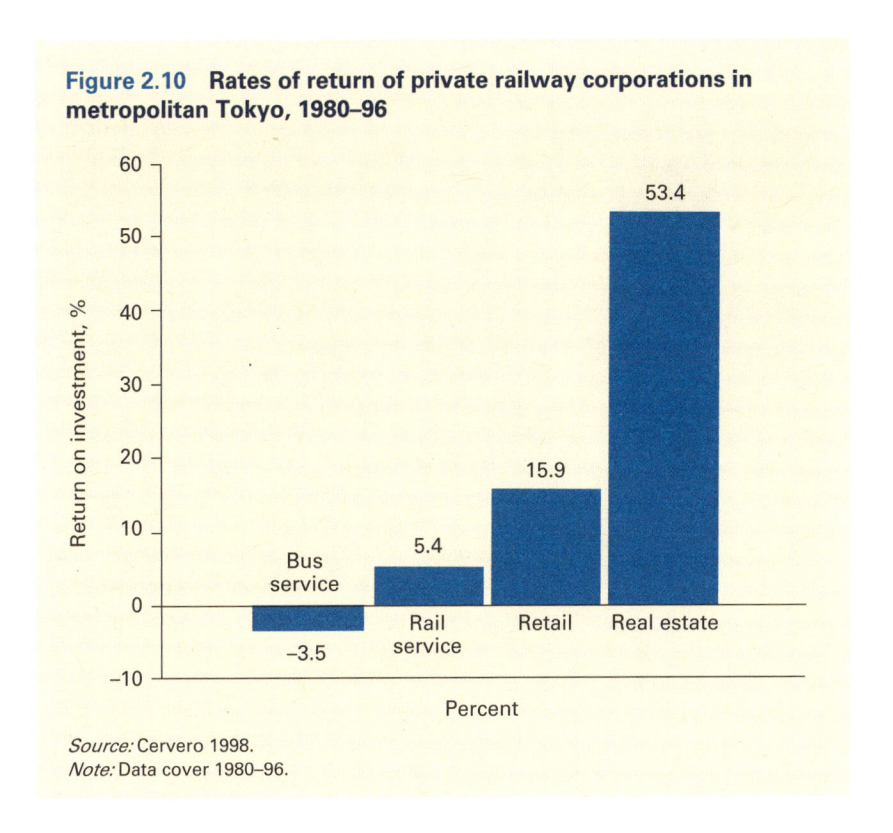

Figure 2.10 Rates of return of private railway corporations in metropolitan Tokyo, 1980–96

- Bus service: −3.5
- Rail service: 5.4
- Retail: 15.9
- Real estate: 53.4

Source: Cervero 1998.
Note: Data cover 1980–96.

Tokyu from the up-front burden and risks of acquiring land and financing infrastructure.

A new era for Tokyo's private railway companies began in the 1990s, when the bursting of Japan's real estate price bubble saw the market valuations of rail companies' landholdings fall. Powerful demographic trends, such as declining birth rates and an aging population, combined with the slowing of the economy, reduced the demand for new-town construction. To spread the risks of a shakier real estate market, private railway companies partnered with third parties to pursue large-scale development projects. Recent real estate projects of Tokyu Corporation, for example, have relied on Real Estate Investment Trust (REIT) funding.

Changing traffic conditions have also had a hand in changing the portfolios of Tokyo's private railways. Greater Tokyo's rail-served new towns and subcenters featured housing and retail services, but most white-collar jobs remained in the urban core (Cervero 1998; Sorensen 2001). The result was tidal radial patterns of commuting, which exacerbated traffic congestion in the urban core. Long commutes combined with crowded trains and roadways helped trigger a return-to-the-city movement. Several large-scale redevelopment projects are now underway as joint ventures between private railways and real estate companies, targeted at young professionals, empty-nesters, and other less traditional niche markets drawn to central-city living. In a break from tradition, when buildings above subway stations

Figure 2.11 Street life near Shinjuku metrorail station, Tokyo

Photo by Robert Cervero.

were exclusively office or commercial projects, major subway stations now feature high-end housing and consumer services. Residential and commercial districts around several central-city stations, notably Akihabara, Shibuya, Shinagawa, and Shinjuku, are now abuzz with activity 24/7 (24 hours a day, 7 days a week) (figure 2.11).

Tokyo's two former public railways, JR East and Tokyo Metro, are also pursuing the redevelopment and infilling of strategic central-city land parcels. In the case of JR East, mounting fiscal losses incurred by the former Japan National Railway (with an accumulated debt of $300 billion) led to privatization in 1987. At the time, the national government gave JR East large developable land parcels around terminal stations, prime for commercial redevelopment. Borrowing from the practices of the Tokyu Corporation and other private railway consortia, JR East and Tokyo Metro aggressively transformed these properties into high-rise commercial ventures. In 2006, real estate yielded returns on investment of more than 40 percent for both former public railways.

JR East's showcase real estate project is Tokyo Station City, developed jointly with other private interests. Tokyo Station City features high-rise, class-A office buildings; retail centers; and hotels (figure 2.12). It is well suited for large-scale redevelopment, thanks to the large amount of buildable space above depots as well as high pedestrian traffic volumes. On a typical weekday in 2005, about half a million passengers passed through Tokyo station (JR East 2005).

Like MTRC in Hong Kong SAR, China, Tokyo's private railways are clearly responding to market price signals, as indicated by an analysis of

Figure 2.12 Tokyo Station City

Source: Japan Railway Corporation East (http://www.jreast.co.jp; reproduced with permission).
Note: This high-rise commercial project mixes the old and new, with the restored historical station (lower left) flanked by towering office, retail, and hotel structures.

2005 residential land prices along 16 mostly private railway corridors as a function of distance to central Tokyo. Within and along the Yamanote loop, where most large-scale redevelopment projects have been built on land owned by private railway companies, residential prices are generally twice what they are 15–20 kilometers from the center. Since 2000, the only area where residential land has gained value has been around terminal stations on the Yamanote loop.

It is at intermodal rail stops served by high-speed rail—notably, the Tokaido Shinkansen line—where urban development activities in Greater Tokyo have been most prominent. Around the newly opened Shinagawa Shinkansen station in central Tokyo, for example, the metropolitan government, the national government, the privatized Central Japan Railway Company, and private real estate developers joined forces to co-develop prestigious office towers and shopping malls. The project featured high-quality public green plazas and well-designed pedestrian circulation systems as a lure to firms and workers that place a premium on livability and are drawn to urban amenities when deciding where to open a business or to work.

These joint transit–commercial redevelopment efforts aim not only to increase the number of business passengers on the Tokaido Shinkansen line, but also to raise the potential of land value capture around the terminal

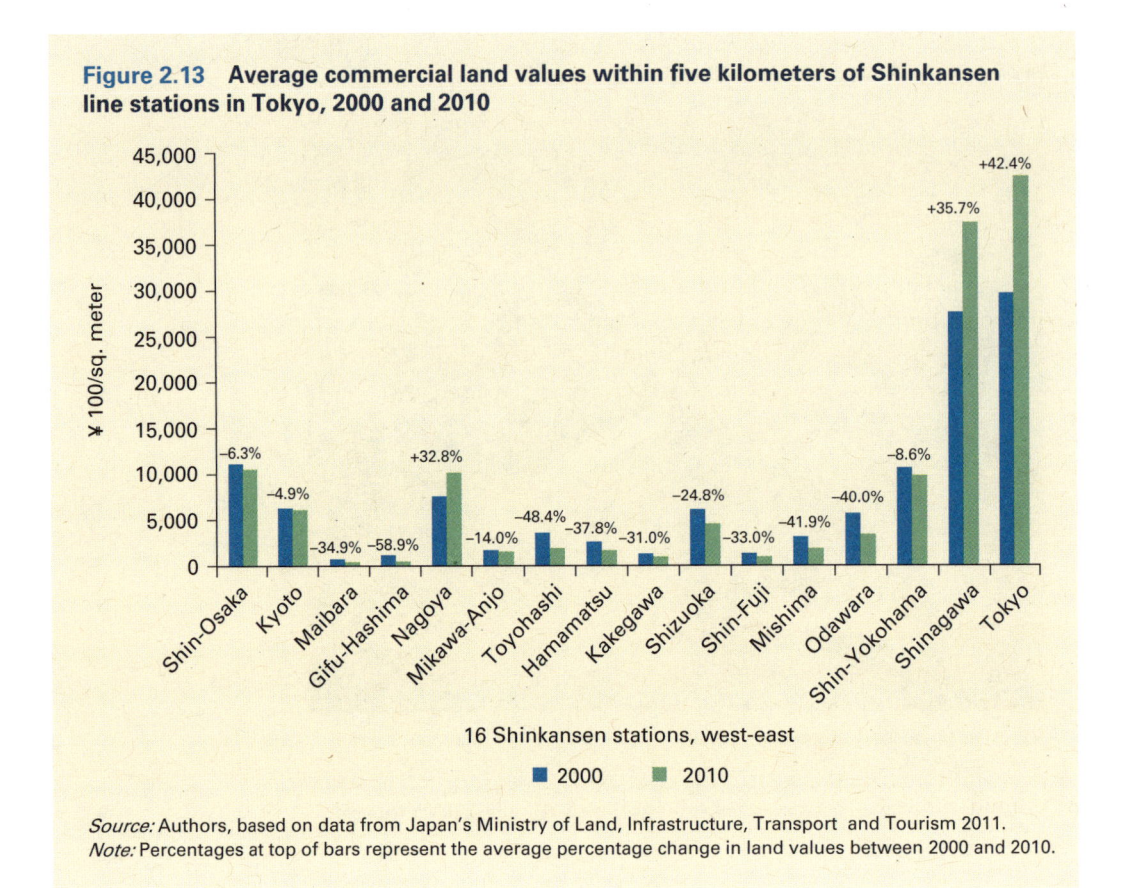

Figure 2.13 Average commercial land values within five kilometers of Shinkansen line stations in Tokyo, 2000 and 2010

Source: Authors, based on data from Japan's Ministry of Land, Infrastructure, Transport and Tourism 2011.
Note: Percentages at top of bars represent the average percentage change in land values between 2000 and 2010.

stations. Nagoya, Shinagawa, and Tokyo and have considerably increased commercial land values within 5 kilometers of Shinkansen stations where large-scale redevelopment projects were delivered through public-private partnerships (figure 2.13). Compared with many private intercity railway corporations in Osaka and Tokyo, the former Japanese National Railways was historically reticent to capture land development benefits around the Nagoya Shinkansen stations. However, in response to Japan's urban regeneration boom in the past decade, real estate revenue streams of the privatized Central Japan Railway Company (JR Central) soared—from ¥24.3 billion ($0.21 billion) in fiscal 1999 to ¥66.7 billion ($0.74 billion) in fiscal 2009—largely from the new commercial property packages redeveloped around the Nagoya Shinkansen station (JR Central 2011).[1]

Washington, DC, and Arlington County, Virginia: A Transit-Development Success Story

More growth has occurred near metropolitan Washington, DC's heavy rail system in the past quarter century than anywhere in the United States. From 1980 to 1990, 40 percent of the region's office and retail space was built within walking distance of a Metrorail station (Cervero and others 2004).

The fact that the timing of the railway investment (late 1970s through 1980s) coincided with a rapid period of growth (more jobs were added in metropolitan Washington, DC than anywhere in the United States) helped steer new development to rail-served corridors. Combined with height limit restrictions within the District of Columbia and federal policy that mandates that government offices be located near rail stations, these factors encouraged TOD.

The recipient of most spillover growth from Washington, DC has been Arlington County, Virginia, just across the Potomac River (Cervero and others 2004). This 26-square-mile county just south of the nation's capital has experienced a tremendous increase in building activity since the opening of Washington Metrorail in 1978. More than 25 million square feet of office space, 4 million square feet of retail space, 25,000 mixed-income dwelling units, and 6,500 hotel rooms were built over the past three decades.

Much of this growth has been wrapped around Metrorail stations, guided by a "necklace-of-pearls" vision articulated in the "bull's eye" concept plan adopted in the late 1960s (figure 2.14). Of the nearly 190,000 people living in Arlington County, 26 percent reside within a Metrorail-served corridor (roughly a quarter mile walk shed from the station), even though these corridors represent only 8 percent of county land area. If the development added to these two corridors had been built at suburban density standards, as in neighboring Fairfax County, Virginia, seven times as much land area would have been required.

The transformation of once rural Arlington County into a showcase of compact, mixed-use TOD has been the product of ambitious, laser-focused station-area planning and investment. Before Metrorail, planners in Arlington County understood that high-performance transit provided an unprecedented opportunity to shape growth. They introduced various strategies—targeted infrastructure improvements, incentive zoning, development proffers, and permissive and as-of-right zoning—to entice private investment around stations. After preparing countywide and station-area plans on desired land-use outcomes, density and set-back configurations, and circulation systems, they changed zoning classifications, allowing developments that complied with these classifications to proceed unencumbered. The ability of complying developers to create TODs "as-of-right" (which ensures the issuance of development permits as long as projects adhere to the requirements of local plans) was particularly important. It allowed developers to line up capital, secure loans, incur up-front costs, and phase in construction without fear that the local government might change its mind regarding permitted uses, building densities, and the like.

Another key factor that gave rise to TODs was the decision not to set Arlington County's Metrorail rail corridor in the median of Interstate 66. Instead, county officials persuaded the region's transit authority to align the corridor in traditional urban centers to help jump-start the process of

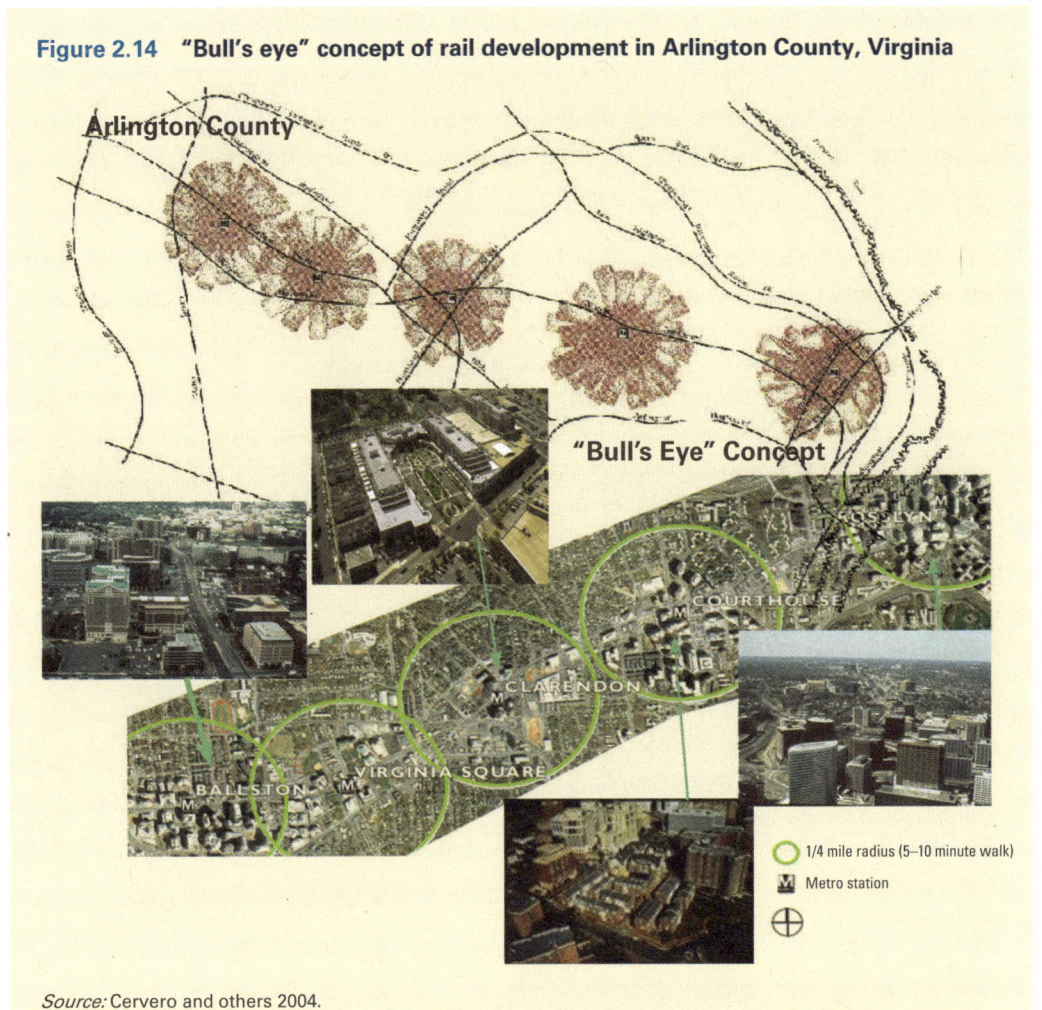

Figure 2.14 "Bull's eye" concept of rail development in Arlington County, Virginia

Source: Cervero and others 2004.
Note: The bull's eye concept targets urban growth along the Rosslyn-Ballston corridor. Over the entire corridor, most land uses and urban activities found throughout the greater metropolitan area are clustered within a five-minute walk of one of the five stations. Rosslyn is predominantly an office center; Courthouse functions as a government center; Clarendon features retail and commercial uses; Virginia Square has museums and performing arts centers; and Ballston has offices, hotels, stores, condominiums, and government buildings. Collectively, the mix of land uses along the Rosslyn-Ballston corridor ensures that during peak hours, Metrorail trains are full in both directions, as passengers travel up and down the corridor.

urban regeneration, even though doing so substantially increased construction costs.

Arlington County's transit ridership statistics reveal the payoff of concentrated growth along rail corridors. The county boasts one of the highest percentages of transit use in the Washington region, with 39.3 percent of Metrorail corridor residents commuting to work by public transit—twice the share among county residents who live outside the Metrorail corridors. At several apartments and condominium buildings near the Rosslyn and Ballston stations, about two-thirds of employed residents take public transit to work.

An important outcome of promoting mixed-use development along rail corridors has been balanced jobs and housing growth, which in turn has produced balanced two-way travel flows. Counts of station entries and exits in Arlington County are nearly equal during both peak and off-peak hours. As a result, trains and buses are largely full in both directions. The presence of so much retail, entertainment, and hotel activity along the county's Metrorail corridors has filled trains and buses during midday and on weekends. Arlington County averages more passengers at its stations in off-peak hours than other jurisdictions in the region except downtown Washington, DC. Balanced mixed-use development has translated into as close to a 24/7 ridership profile as any U.S. setting outside a central business district.

Part of the credit for the transit-oriented growth of Arlington County is the entrepreneurial leanings of the region's rail authority. Over the past two decades, the Washington Metropolitan Area Transit Authority (WMATA)—an independent regional transportation authority responsible for designing, building, and operating the region's rail transit and public bus services—has aggressively sought to recapture value through joint development activities. Metrorail's joint development program of air-rights leases and station connection fees generate about 2 percent of the system's annual revenues; increased ridership—and thus fare-box intake—at least doubles this percentage (Cervero and others 2004).

Proactivism accounts for much of WMATA's joint development success. A vital step in WMATA pursuing value capture was the creation of a real estate development department within the agency at the very beginning, before the construction and opening of railway services. By hiring seasoned real estate professionals to staff and manage this department, WMATA positioned itself to seek out remunerative joint development possibilities. Private-sector experiences helped create a more entrepreneurial approach to land development than is found at most U.S. transit agencies. Staff members were given the financial resources to purchase land around planned rail stations on the open market, often before formal plans were announced and thus at fairly reasonable prices. Rather than waiting and reacting to developer proposals, WMATA's real estate office actively sought out mutually advantageous joint development opportunities. With financial and institutional support from board members, WMATA's real estate office has over time amassed an impressive portfolio of landholdings, much of it purchased on the open market. To date, WMATA had undertaken more than 30 development projects at a value of more than $2 billion on land the agency owns.

Over time, WMATA has refined its joint development activities. Station sites are carefully screened according to a set of criteria that gauge development potential. For sites selected, a request for proposals is issued to solicit developer interests. Through negotiations, a developer team is chosen and contracts specifying the financial terms of the deal are drawn up. With the help of a private real estate firm, WMATA now rates potential sites according to the likely degree of private sector interests and development constraints.

Because joint development is controlled by a transit agency, it is the form of value capture that has the greatest potential for financing rail investments in much of the world. It requires, however, an institutional capacity to expand beyond the traditional mission of transit agencies (that is, building and operating transit services) to venture into other entrepreneurial realms, such as real estate development and co-development. As suggested by experiences in metropolitan Washington, institutional reforms are often a necessary part of any successful transit value capture scheme.

Integrating Transit and Land-Use Planning through Adaptive Transit and Bus Rapid Transit

The two cases reviewed in this section—Curitiba and Ottawa—are given the "adaptive transit" moniker mainly because they turned to an inherently flexible technology—the rubber-tire bus—as high-capacity transit carriers. Both cities feature high-rise, mixed-use development around a number of BRT stations but also retain many lower-density neighborhoods that are served by feeder lines. Thus, they rely on adaptive bus-based transit to provide a versatile mix of transit services while also supporting rail-like TOD.

Curitiba, Brazil: The Lineal Bus Rapid Transit Metropolis

Curitiba is internationally renowned as one of the world's most sustainable, well-planned cities, in large part because of its success at integrating BRT investments and urban development. The city's experiences underscore the environmental benefits of balancing urban growth along bus-served linear axes and aggressively pursuing a "transit first" policy. By emphasizing planning for people rather than cars, Curitiba has evolved along well-defined radial axes that are intensively served by dedicated busways. Along some corridors, streams of double-articulated (that is, two accordion section) buses haul 16,000 passengers an hour, comparable to the number much pricier metrorail systems carry. The city's system of 390 routes served by 2,000 vehicles carries 2.1 million passengers a day, twice as many as in 1990. To ensure a transit-oriented built form, Curitiba's government mandates that all medium- and large-scale urban development be sited along a BRT corridor. Orchestrating regional growth is the Institute for Research and Urban Planning (IPPUC), an independent entity charged with ensuring integration of all elements of urban growth.

A design element used to enhance accessibility in Curitiba is the "trinary"—three parallel roadways with compatible land uses and building heights that taper with distance from the BRT corridor (figure 2.15). Zoning ordinance and urban design standards promote ridership productivity and environmental quality. The first two floors of the busway that do not count against permissible plot ratios (building height/land area) are devoted

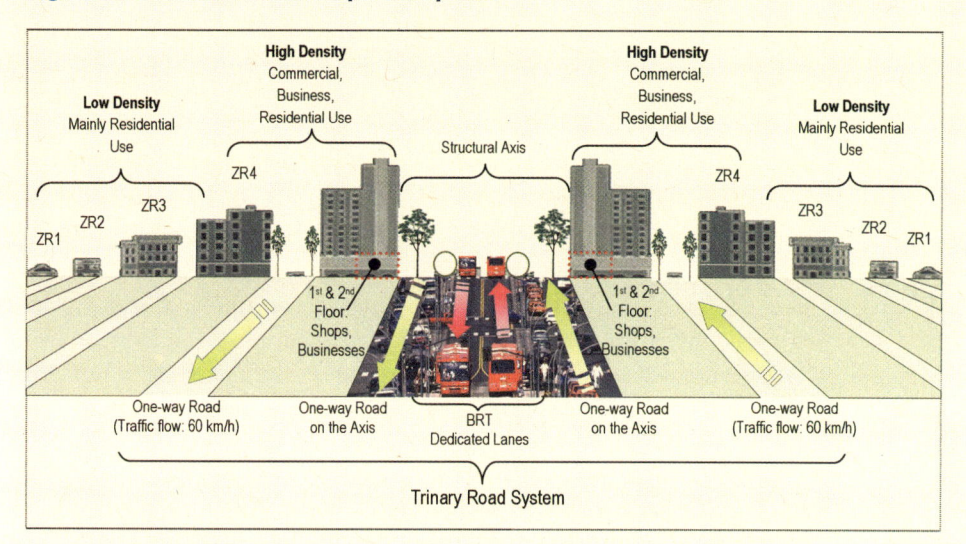

Figure 2.15 Curitiba's trinary road system

Source: Suzuki and others 2010; reproduced with permission of the Transportation Research Board.
Note: Bi-articulated buses operate alongside sidewalks and slow-speed frontage roads. Ground-floor retail on the lower floor of buildings and upper-level office and residential space—set back several meters to allow sunlight to reach the street level—creates a rich mix of land uses along trinary corridors. The inclusion of mixed land uses and affordable housing allows developers to increase building heights, adding density to the corridor. Streetscaping enhancements have created a pleasant pedestrian milieu. Frequent-stop, bi-articulated buses operate on the mainline of the trinary corridor; limited-stop "speedy" buses flank parallel one-way roads. People traveling longer distances often opt for the limited-stop buses, whereas people traveling shorter distances or going to destinations bypassed by the speedy buses usually patronize the mainline frequent-stop services. The market has responded to this rich, differentiated mix of bus-based services along the corridor with high-rise development, supported by zoning and public improvements like sidewalks and landscaping.

to retail uses. Above the second floor, buildings must be set back at least five meters from the property line, to allow sun to cast on the transitway. The inclusion of upper-level housing entitles property owners to density bonuses, which has led to vertical mixing of uses within buildings. An important benefit of mixed land uses and transit service levels along these corridors, in addition to extraordinarily high ridership rates, has been balanced bidirectional flows, ensuring efficient use of bus capacity, just as in Stockholm and Arlington County, Virginia. The influences of the trinary structure on channeling trips are revealed by 2009 origin-destination statistics, which indicate that 78 percent of passengers boarding at the terminus of the north-south corridor are destined to a bus stop on the same corridor (Duarte and Ultramari 2012).

Curitiba is one of Brazil's wealthiest cities, yet it averages considerably more transit trips per capita than Rio de Janeiro and São Paulo, which are much larger. Its share of motorized trips by transit (45 percent) is the highest in Latin America (Santos 2011). High transit use has appreciably shrunk the city's environmental footprint. Curitiba's annual congestion cost per capita of $0.67 is a fraction of São Paulo's ($7.34) (Suzuki and others 2010). The city also boasts the cleanest air of any Brazilian city with more than 1 million inhabitants, despite being a provincial capital with a sizable industrial sector. The strong, workable nexus that exists between Curitiba's bus-based transit system and its mixed-use linear settlement pattern deserves most of the credit.

Sustained political commitment has been an important part of Curitiba's success. The harmonization of transit and land use took place over 40 years of political continuity, marked by a progression of forward-looking, like-minded mayors who built on the work of their predecessors. A cogent long-term vision and the presence of a politically insulated regional planning organization, the IPPUC, to implement the vision have been crucial in allowing the city to chart a sustainable urban pathway.

In recent years, Curitiba has begun to experience the limits of rubber-tire technologies. With buses operating on 30-second intervals on main routes during peak hours, bunching problems have disrupted and slowed services. Veritable "elephant trains" of buses have increased operating costs and precluded the kinds of economies of scale enjoyed by trains operated by a single driver. Extreme overcrowding has prompted many middle-class car-owning travelers to switch to driving. In the words of one urban planner, "Many Curitibanos view [BRT] as noisy, crowded and unsafe. Undermining the thinking behind the master plan, even those who live alongside the high-density rapid-bus corridors are buying cars" (Lubow 2007, p. M8). A long-discussed light rail line, to replace overcrowded buses, has yet to gain momentum, mainly because of cost concerns.

The Green Line is the city's first new BRT corridor in years, an 18-kilometer corridor that was converted from a federal highway. Like Bogota's celebrated BRT, the Green Line has passing lanes, which greatly increase capacity by supporting express services.

Meanwhile, recent legislation has taken bold steps to alter zoning and land use along the Green Line to promote TOD. Formerly a national highway dotted with truck stops and lumberyards, this hodgepodge of industrial uses is slated to become a pedestrian-friendly, mixed-use corridor that can accommodate up to half a million new residents.

As important to the enrichment of services in Curitiba is an evolved view of BRT corridors as rights of way that also accommodate linear parks (strips of long park areas located to next to railways, bus lines, roads, canals, or rivers) and bike paths. A law passed in 2010 promotes the preservation of green space along the corridor by giving developers increased building rights if they purchase or preserve land along the corridor as parks.

Ottawa: North America's First High-End Bus Rapid Transit

North America's best example of BRT–based TOD comes from Canada's capital, Ottawa. Borrowing a chapter from Scandinavian metropolises like Copenhagen and Stockholm, Ottawa's leaders began with a concept plan that defined desired growth axes and then strategically invested in a high-quality, high-capacity transitway to drive growth along these corridors

Figure 2.16 Transitway development in Ottawa, Canada

a. Urban form vision of desired growth axes

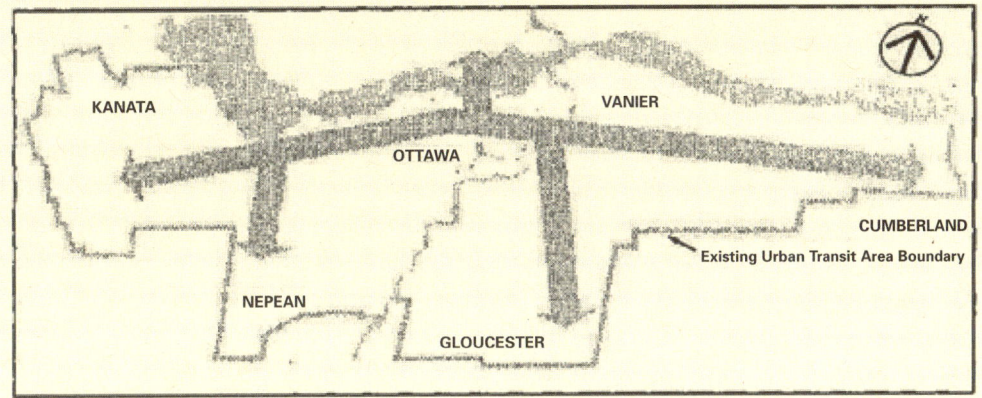

b. Transitway investment to drive growth along desired growth axes

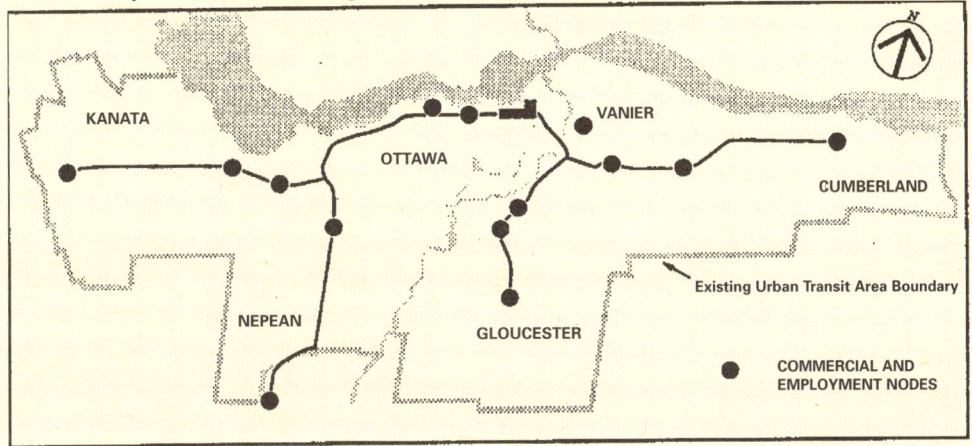

Source: Cervero 1998; reproduced with permission from Island Press, Washington, DC.

(figure 2.16). As a result of supportive zoning and world-class bus services, growth gravitated to bus corridors between 1985 and 2000.

Institutional factors partly account for Ottawa's success in implementing a long-range vision. A regional planning body, the Regional Council, was formed in 1969 to carry out comprehensive planning, invest in major infrastructure, and provide regional services such as air quality management. A checks-and-balances system is in place in which localities oversee land-use decisions, which the regional authority can override if it considers them incompatible with the regional plan. In practice, the regional authority rarely overrules the wishes of municipalities.

Based on broad-based citizen input, in 1974, the Regional Council endorsed a multicentered urban structure: downtown Ottawa would retain its position as the dominant commercial, employment, and cultural center of the region, and it would be surrounded by a hierarchy of primary and secondary urban centers, interconnected by high-quality transit. Market-driven (predominantly low-density) patterns of development would be permitted outside these centers.

The chief instrument for achieving this desired physical form was the busway. With a vision in place and the agreement to build a busway to make the vision a reality, the Regional Council turned its attention to land-use management. TOD policies were introduced that called for substantial increases in the share of regional jobs located near Transitway stations. The long-term goal called for 40 percent of the region's jobs to be within walking distance (400 meters) of the Transitway. The two principal suburban catchments for job growth, the Orléans and Kanata urban centers, were slated to host more than 10,000 new jobs. The official plan also required that regional shopping centers with more than 375,000 square feet (34,840 square meters) of gross leasable space be sited near the Transitway or future extensions.

Ottawa officials also adopted a "transit first" policy early in their BRT planning: improvements to the existing transit system and the development of rapid transit were to take precedence over all forms of road construction and widening. The regional plan specifically called for creating rapid transit services. No commitments were made on preferred routing or transit technologies.

Ottawa opted for a busway at a time when every other medium-size North American metropolis investing in new transit systems selected the eminently more popular light rail transit technology. Similar in size to Ottawa, Calgary and Edmonton both constructed regional light rail systems in the 1970s and 1980s; Vancouver, Canada's third-largest metropolis, built an elevated "advanced" light rail system, called SkyTrain. The decision to go with a busway made the Ottawa-Carleton region a maverick of sorts, but in dollars and cents it made good sense, as busways were shown to be 30 percent less expensive to build and 20 percent less expensive to operate than a light rail. Because of the busway's relatively high operating speeds, the region has been able to get by with 150 fewer buses than it would have needed to carry the same number of passengers on surface streets. These savings exceeded the $275 million capital outlay for the first 20 kilometers of the busway.

Perhaps most important, a busway was better suited to the region's future land-use vision of concentrated workplaces and retail destinations encircled by largely low-density, single-family detached housing. From a travel standpoint, such a settlement pattern translates into "many-to-few" trip origins and destinations. A point-to-point rail system, planners reasoned, was incompatible with this spatial pattern of trips. Rather, they reasoned, the geometry of a flexible busway system that allowed trunkline buses to morph into neighborhood feeders was much more compatible with the geography of future travel. As in all good transit metropolises, a close

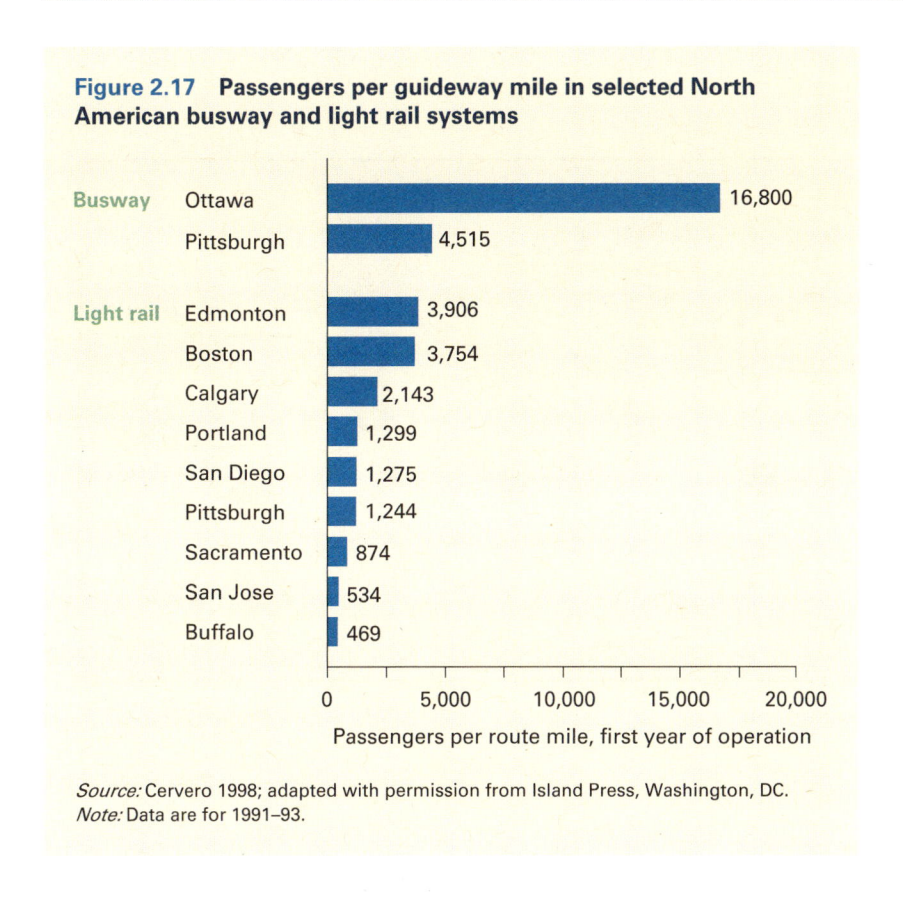

Figure 2.17 Passengers per guideway mile in selected North American busway and light rail systems

Busway	Ottawa	16,800
	Pittsburgh	4,515
Light rail	Edmonton	3,906
	Boston	3,754
	Calgary	2,143
	Portland	1,299
	San Diego	1,275
	Pittsburgh	1,244
	Sacramento	874
	San Jose	534
	Buffalo	469

Passengers per route mile, first year of operation

Source: Cervero 1998; adapted with permission from Island Press, Washington, DC.
Note: Data are for 1991–93.

correspondence between the physical design of transit and spatial pattern of trip making was achieved.

Within the first year of operation, Ottawa's busway outperformed all other North American busway and light rail systems built in the early 1990s by nearly four to one on a passenger per guideway-mile basis (figure 2.17). With more than 140 public transit trips per person per year, Ottawa has one of the highest transit utilization rates in North America, even when compared with much larger rail-served cities like Chicago and Philadelphia.

As with successful transit metropolises in Scandinavia and elsewhere, Ottawa's TOD vision was buttressed by a series of TDM measures that aimed to level the playing field by either regulating car use or passing on price signals to motorists that began to reflect broader societal costs. Most notable were parking policies. When the Transitway opened in 1983, the federal government began eliminating free parking for its employees and reducing the number of downtown parking spaces. By 1984, downtown Ottawa had 15 percent fewer parking spaces than in 1975, despite a near doubling of office space. The federal government also introduced flexible working schedules for its employees, producing a more even distribution of transit usage over the course of the day. Supportive parking policies were also introduced at busway stations. OC Transpo (the Ottawa-Carleton

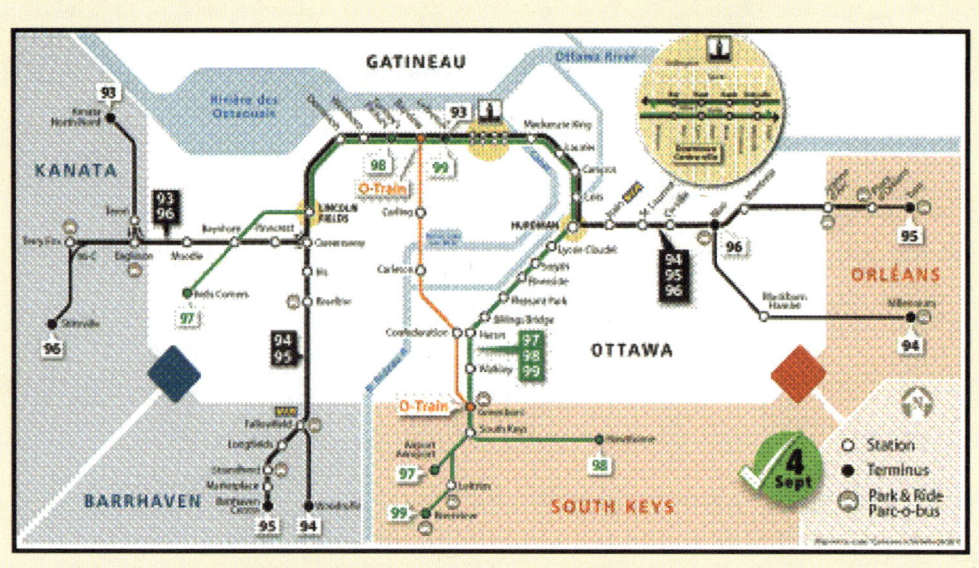

Figure 2.18 Ottawa's Transitway network, including O-Train light rail line linked to busway

Source: Municipality of Ottawa 2008.
Note: Current plans call for replacing the downtown surface-street busway segment, shown in the circular insert, with an underground light rail system tied to the O-Train light rail line to the south.

Regional Transit Commission) restricted park-and-ride facilities to the busway's terminuses to encourage the use of feeder and express services as well as to increase the development potential of selected stations. Other requirements included zoning targets of placing 40 percent of future job growth and all regional trip generators of more than 100,000 square meters within 400 meters of a busway stop.

In addition to "sticks," various pro-transit "carrots" were concurrently introduced, including one of the first bus-based, real-time passenger information systems anywhere; targets for transit mode splits for cordon lines throughout the region (which govern where service improvements are directed); and eco-passes, which provide regular transit users with deep fare discounts. In 1982–85, the city adopted a set of TOD design guidelines that call for, among other things, building setbacks to create human-scale development; public art to enliven station areas; and short street blocks, cut-through walkways, and easy way-finding to enhance the quality of pedestrian environments linked to busway stations (Municipality of Ottawa 2007).

Like Curitiba, Ottawa has experienced some of the growing pains, and limitations, of a highly successful BRT system. Historically, more than 60 percent of regional buses on the Transitway passed through a downtown one-way, surface-level couplet (two one-way streets that run parallel to each other) causing peak-period traffic snarls and the bunching of buses. With passenger throughput having reached the capacity of a surface transit system, a decision was made to convert the downtown busway into a light-rail subway alignment.

The Downtown Tunnel, expected to cost about $1.4 billion, is the single costliest transit investment under consideration in Ottawa. It would extend the O-Train light rail, which began operation in 2001 as a pilot project to evaluate the benefits of converting Ottawa's Transitways to light rails, north through downtown (figure 2.18). Local officials are quick to point out that BRT is not being abandoned but simply converted to light rail transit along the highest-capacity downtown Transitway corridor. Indeed, new or expanded BRT Transitways are planned in the east, west, and south portions of metropolitan Ottawa.

Ottawa's past three decades of "transit first" policies continue to pay off in terms of high ridership levels. Transit use has increased steadily since 1998, by about 3.5 percent a year. From 70 million passengers in 1998, annual ridership reached about 100 million in 2010. Ottawa's transit mode share has remained steady, at nearly 15 percent of daily trips, despite declining mode shares in almost all other Canadian cities (Municipality of Ottawa 2008).

Conclusion

A number of lessons can be drawn from international best-case experiences that have direct relevance to cities in developing countries and elsewhere that are investing in BRT and other high-capacity transit systems. Chapter 4 highlights these lessons.

One overarching principle followed by all cities is that successful transit and land-use integration requires a cogent vision of the future city. Visions of how the city will ideally grow and the role of transportation investments and policy in achieving this urban-form vision were well articulated in all cases. Moreover, land-use visions shaped transportation decisions far more than vice versa, reflecting the core notion that transportation is a means, not an end unto itself. For adaptive cities, the vision of compact, mixed-use, often lineal corridors produced "necklace-of-pearls"–style built forms and induced sustainable mobility choices. For adaptive transit, policy focused on investing in flexible, lower-cost transit systems, like BRT, which can better serve market-driven patterns of development. It is this unwavering commitment to linking transit investments and urban development in mutually beneficial and reinforcing ways that distinguishes these successful global cases.

Applying such principles and practices to rapidly growing and motorizing cities in developing countries is a challenge. Chapter 3 describes how four cities—Ahmedabad, India; Bogota, Colombia; Guangzhou, China; and Ho Chi Minh City, Vietnam—are meeting this challenge.

Annex Table 2A.1 Modes of transportation in selected cities

City (Region)	Population: City	Population: Metropolitan area	Population density (residents per square kilometer): City	Population density: Metropolitan area	GDP per capita (US dollars)	Area (square kilometers): City	Area: Metropolitan area	Car ownership (cars owned per 1,000 residents)	Transit ridership (annual riders per capita)	Mode of transportation in city (percent): Public transit	Private automobile	Bicycle	Walking
Copenhagen, Denmark	662,600 (2011)	1,199,300 (2011)	5,407	2,452	68,000 (2010)	123	456	184	228	27	40	33	—
Curitiba, Brazil	1,764,500 (2010)	3,210,000 (2010)	4,062	211	8,000 (2007)	430	15,417	400	355	45	—	—	—
Hong Kong SAR, China	7,061,200 (2010)	7,061,200 (2010)	6,480	6,480	45,736 (2008)	1,104	1,104	82	574	88	11	1	—
Ottawa, Canada	883,400 (2011)	1,236,300 (2011)	317	197	73,500 (2008)	2,778	5,716	557	142	21	68	2	9
Singapore	5,076,700 (2010)	5,076,700 (2010)	7,315	7,315	63,867 (2010)	694	—	100	263	63	27	0	10
Seoul, Republic of Korea	10,646,000 (2010)	23,616,000 (2010)	17,000	12,446	27,809 (2008)	605	1,897	214	1,028	69	26	5	—
Stockholm, Sweden	1,372,565 (2010)	2,064,000 (2010)	3,597	317	70,950 (2008)	382	6,519	373	213	45	52	3	—
Tokyo, Japan	13,185,500 (2011)	36,682,500 (2011)	6,027	2,629	40,337 (2008)	2,188	13,752	308	1,107	51	12	14	22
Washington, DC Metro Area	618,000 (2011)	5,580,000 (2011)	3,886	372	76,200 (2008)	177	14,412	680	63	37	48	3	12

Source: Authors' compilation based on Cervero 1998; Pucher and Buehler 2005; PricewaterhouseCoopers 2009; Singapore Land Transport Authority 2010; Santos 2011; http://en.wikipedia.org; http://international.stockholm.se/Future-Stockholm/Urban-development/; http://www.kk.dk/sitecore/content/Subsites/CityOfCopenhagen/SubsiteFrontpage/Press/FactsOnCopenhagen/Statistics/Income/HouseholdsFamilyType.aspx;http://www.kk.dk/sitecore/content/Subsites/CityOfCopenhagen/SubsiteFrontpage/Press/FactsOnCopenhagen/Statistics/CarsforprivateUse/CarsForPrivateUse.aspx; http://ltaacademy.gov.sg/doc/J11Nov-p60PassengerTransportModeShares.pdf;http://www.ottawa.ca/visitors/about/economy_en.html; http://en.wikipedia.org/wiki/List_of_cities_by_GDP; http://www.mwcog.org/uploads/committee-documents/Zl1fWFIW20111110130359.pdf; and http://ltaacademy.gov.sg/doc/J11Nov-p60PassengerTransportModeShares.pdf.

Note: Figures in parentheses show the year of the data. — = Not available.

Note

1. Conversion calculated based on exchange rate of $1= ¥ 114.37 in 1999 and ¥ 93.52 in 2009.

References

ARUP. 2003. "Travel Characteristics Survey 2002: Final Report." Hong Kong Special Administrative Region, Transport Department, Hong Kong SAR, China.

Bertolini, L., and T. Spit. 1998. *Cities on Rails: The Redevelopment of Railway Station Areas.* London: E & FN Spon.

Center for Clean Air Policy (CCAP). 2011. "Growing Wealthier: Smart Growth, Climate Change and Prosperity." CCAP, Washington, DC.

Cervero, R. 1998. *The Transit Metropolis: A Global Inquiry.* Washington, DC: Island Press.

———. 2001. "Efficient Urbanization: Economic Performance and the Shape of the Metropolis." *Urban Studies* 38 (10): 1651–71.

———. 2009. "Transport Infrastructure and Global Competitiveness: Balancing Mobility and Livability." *Annals of the American Academy of Political and Social Science* 626: 210–25.

Cervero, R., and C. Kang. 2011. "Bus Rapid Transit Impacts on Land Uses and Land Values in Seoul, Korea." *Transport Policy* 18: 102–16.

Cervero, R., and J. Murakami. 2009. "Rail + Property Development in Hong Kong: Experiences and Extensions." *Urban Studies* 46 (10): 2019–43.

Cervero, R., S. Murphy, C. Ferrell, N. Goguts, Y. Tsai, G. Arrington, J. Boroski, J. Smith-Heimer, R. Golem, P. Peninger, E. Nakajima, E. Chui, R. Dunphy, M. Myers, S. McKay, and N. Witenstein. 2004. *Transit Oriented Development in America: Experiences, Challenges, and Prospects.* Washington, DC: National Academies Press.

Cervero, R., and C. Sullivan. 2011. "Green TODs: Marrying Transit-Oriented Development and Green Urbanism." *International Journal of Sustainable Development and World Ecology* 18 (3): 210–18.

Chu, S., W. Koh, and T. Tse. 2004. "Expectations Formation and Forecasting of Vehicle Demand: An Empirical Study of the Vehicle Quota Auctions in Singapore." *Transportation Research* Part A, 38 (5): 367–81.

City of Copenhagen. 2008. *Eco-Metropolis: Our Vision for Copenhagen 2015.*

———. City Mayors database. n.d. http://www.citymayors.com/economics/richest_cities.html. 2010. *Copenhagen Traffic Strategy.*

Duarte, F., and C. Ultramari. 2012. "Making Public Transport and Housing Match: Accomplishments and Failures of Curitiba's BRT." *Journal of Urban Planning and Development* 38 (2): 183–94.

Eliasson, J., L. Hultkrantz, L. Nerhagen, and L. S. Rosqvist. 2009. "The Stockholm Congestion-Charging Trial 2006: Overview of Effects." *Transportation Research* Part A, 43 (3): 240–50.

European Commission. 2012. *Eurostat*. Brussels.

Foundation City Bikes. 2009. "Copenhagen City Bike."

Grontmij, A. B. 2008. "Report Summary: Follow-up of Environmental Impact in Hammarby Sjöstad." Stockholm.

Hwang, K. 2006. *Cheong Gye Cheon Restoration and City Regeneration: Cheong Gye Cheon, Urban Revitalization and Future Vision*. Seoul: Seoul Metropolitan Government.

IAPT (International Association of Public Transport). 2002. Mobility in Cities Database. http://uitp.org/publications/Mobility-in-Cities-Database.cfm.

JR (Japanese Railway) East. 2005. "Tokyo: JR East." http://www.jreast.co.jp/e/index.html.

JR (Japanese Railway) Central. 2011. Databook 2010. Tokyo.

Jun, M. J. 2000. "Commuting Pattern of New Town Residents in the Seoul Metropolitan Area." *Journal of Korean Regional Development Association* 12 (2): 157–70.

Jun, M. J., and C. Bae. 2000. "Estimating Commuting Costs of Seoul's Greenbelt." *International Regional Science Review* 23 (3): 300–15.

Jun, M. J., and J. W. Hur. 2001. "Commuting Cost of Leap-Frog Newtown Development in Korea." *Cities* 18 (3): 151–58.

Kang, C., and R. Cervero. 2009. "From Elevated Freeway to Urban Greenway: Land Value Impacts of Seoul, Korea's CGC Project." *Urban Studies* 46 (13): 2771–94.

Kenworthy, J., and L. Laube. 1999. *An International Sourcebook of Automobile Dependence in Cities: 1960–1990*. Boulder, CO: University of Colorado Press.

Lam, W., and M. Bell. 2003. *Advanced Modeling for Transit Operations and Service Planning*. Oxford: Elsevier.

Levinson, H., S. Zimmerman, J. Clinter, S. Rutherford, R. Smith, J. Cracknell, and Richard Soberman. 2003. "Bus Rapid Transit, Vol. 1: Case Studies in Bus Rapid Transit." Report 90, Transit Cooperative Research Program, Washington, DC.

Lubow, A. 2007. "The Road to Curitiba." *New York Times Magazine*, May 20.

Mees, P. 2009. *Transport for Suburbia: Beyond the Automobile Age*. Oxford: Earthscan.

Mercer, W. M. 2002. *Worldwide Quality-of-Life Survey*. New York: Arthur D. Little.

Ministry of Land, Infrastructure, Transport and Tourism (MLIT). www.mlit.go.jp.

Municipality of Ottawa. 2007. *Land Use/Transit-Oriented Development: Ottawa's Transit-Oriented Development Guidelines*. Ottawa: Municipality of Ottawa.

———. 2008. "Transportation Master Plan." Publication 19-82, Municipality of Ottawa.

Perloff, H. 1975. *Modernizing the Central City: New Towns Intown . . . and Beyond*. Cambridge, MA: Ballinger Publishing Company.

PricewaterhouseCoopers. 2009. *Global City GDP Rankings: 2008 to 2025*. London: Pricewaterhouse Coopers. https://www.ukmediacentre.pwc.com/Media-Library/Global-city-GDP-rankings-2008-2025-61a.aspx.

Prud'homme, R., and G. Lee. 1999. "Sprawl, Speed and the Efficiency of Cities." *Urban Studies* 36 (11): 1849–58.

Pucher, J. and Buehler, R. 2005 "Making Cycling Irresistible: Lessons from the Netherlands, Denmark, and Germany." *Transport Reviews* 28 (4): 495–528.

QuantEcon, Inc. 2009. "Driving the Economy: Automotive Travel, Economic Growth, and the Risks of Global Warming Regulations." Cascade Policy Institute, Portland, OR.

Santos, E. 2011. *Pioneer in BRT and Urban Planning*. Saarbrücken, Germany: Lambert Academic Press.

Seoul Development Institute. 2005. *Toward Better Public Transport*. Seoul: Seoul Metropolitan Government.

Seoul Metropolitan Government. 2003. *CGC Restoration Project*. Seoul: Seoul Metropolitan Government.

Siemens AG/McKinsey and Company. 2008. *Building Competitive Cities*. Stuttgart, Germany.

Singapore Government. n.d. http://www.singstat.gov.sg.

Singapore Land Transport Authority. 2008. *Long Term Master Plan: A People-Centered Land Transport System*. Singapore.

———. 2010 *Singapore Land Transport: Statistics in Brief*. Singapore. http://www.lta.gov.sg/content/dam/ltaweb/corp/PublicationsResearch/files/FactsandFigures/LTA_2010.pdf.

Singapore MRT. 2011. *SMRT Annual Report 2011*. Singapore.

Sorensen, A. 2001. "Subcentres and Satellite Cities: Tokyo's 20th Century Experience of Planned Polycentrism." *International Planning Studies* 6 (1): 9–32.

Suzuki, H., A. Dastur, S. Moffatt, N. Yabuki, and H. Maryyama. 2010. *Eco^2 Cities: Ecological Cities as Economic Cities*. Washington, DC: World Bank.

Tang, B. S., Y. H. Chiang, A. N. Baldwin, and C. W. Yeung. 2004. *Study of the Integrated Rail-Property Development Model in Hong Kong.* Hong Kong Polytechnic University, Hong Kong SAR, China.

UITP (International Association of Public Transport). 2006. Mobility in Cities Database. Brussels.

CHAPTER 3

Integrating Transit and Urban Development in Cities in the Developing World

Although transit and land-use integration has gained tremendous attention in policy circles, it rarely occurs in practice, particularly in rapidly growing cities in developing countries. This situation is all the more alarming given the brisk pace at which bus rapid transit (BRT) systems are being built in hopes of placing rapidly growing cities on a more sustainable mobility pathway.

This chapter reviews challenges that selected cities in the developing world have faced in integrating transit and urban development. It examines experiences in four cities, all of which are rapidly urbanizing and motorizing and all of which are committed to expanding public transit services in the quest to become more sustainable.

The cities selected as in-depth cases—Ahmedabad, India and Bogota, Colombia—were chosen for several reasons. First, both cities have invested in extensive BRT systems. Second, the two cities are at different stages of urbanization, Ahmedabad at a preliminary stage and Bogota at a more advanced stage. Third, the two cities have very different experiences with BRT operations. Differences in the length of time their systems have existed (Ahmedabad's system became operational in late 2009, whereas Bogota launched its system in 2000), political and institutional structures, and planning cultures provide insights into the challenges of linking transit and urban development.

These two study cases are analyzed using a common framework, in an effort to understand the interaction of transit and land development under a similar microscopic lens. Both case analyses focus on public-sector initiatives and actions, such as the designs of transit investments and services, planning strategies, regulations, taxation policies, and development incentives. Of particular interest is how such factors combined with BRT investments influence urban development patterns. The chapter also examines other factors that influence the integration of transit and urban development, such as the institutional and regulatory contexts of decision-making and funding mechanisms.

In the assessment of these cases, transit oriented development (TOD) is set as a viable model for creating sustainable urban futures. When combined with TOD, transportation demand management (TDM) is also viewed as a promising way to achieve desirable mobility outcomes, such as increased transit ridership. Improved connectivity—defined here as the strategic linkages between urban locations with different land uses and functions through high-quality transit services, including linkages between social housing and public transport—is also a key component of successful integration.

The chapter also presents two shorter case studies: Guangzhou, China and Ho Chi Minh City, Vietnam. These cases, prepared using secondary sources, are included to showcase their proactive approaches to particular aspects of integrating BRT systems with the built environment. The Guangzhou case illustrates the positive impacts of high-capacity BRT on vibrant corridor development in high-density built-up areas. The Ho Chi Minh City case highlights an inclusive planning process, using design *charettes*, that are facilitating cross-sector coordination.

Ahmedabad: A City at a Critical Juncture

Today, Ahmedabad finds itself at a critical juncture. The city, in the Indian state of Gujarat, is emerging as a thriving economic hub in India. Located in the Delhi-Mumbai Industrial Corridor, Ahmedabad is the fifth most populous city in the country, with a population of 5.5 million. It is also one of the fastest-growing cities in the world; its population is expected to reach 10 million over the next 20 years, placing it among the world's megacities (CoE UT CEPT 2011; Forbes 2010). The city's expansive infrastructure, strong industrial base, commercial tradition, and strategic location continue to attract significant numbers of businesses, investments, and new residents. Like other large cities in India, Ahmedabad is grappling with the challenges of rapid urban expansion, mounting motorization and congestion, and uncoordinated public and private land and transportation development.

Janmarg, India's first BRT system, began operations in 2009.[1] It has significantly improved the mobility of Ahmedabad's citizens. It has gained fame as an exemplary BRT system for developing countries, receiving national and international awards.[2]

However, because Janmarg has been framed and envisioned as a mobility improvement rather than an instrument for guiding urban growth, the city has yet to exploit the huge potential of BRT investment to promote sustainable forms of urban development. Such achievement would significantly improve economic competitiveness, quality of life, and social inclusiveness in the city over the long term.

The Janmarg Bus Rapid Transit System

In 2005, the Ahmedabad Municipal Corporation (AMC) made the Janmarg BRT its highest-priority transit investment in its "Accessible Ahmedabad" vision, a linchpin in achieving its longer-term goal of enhancing accessibility for all.[3] This vision of an accessible city focuses primarily on the introduction of rapid buses as opposed to orienting land-use activities to the busway. Improved accessibility is to be achieved by moving people around the city more swiftly, not by bringing urban activities closer together.

The decision to build Janmarg coincided with the national government's announcement of a reform-linked urban investment financing program, the Jawaharlal Nehru Urban Renewal Mission (JnNURM), initiated in 2005. The JnNURM provides matching grants to local governments, on the condition that cities prepare a city development plan articulating their long-term visions, a detailed project report, and an implementation schedule for the proposed urban reforms.

The following year, the national government adopted the National Urban Transport Policy, which included integrated urban transport and land-use planning as its first objective. To promote this policy, the national government encouraged cities to undertake public transport projects, particularly BRT, together with nonmotorized transport investments by linking JnNURM's funding with the principles embodied in the National Urban Transport Policy. Ahmedabad's Janmarg was the first BRT project to receive JnNURM funding, which accelerated its implementation.[4]

When complete, Janmarg's busway system will span some 220 kilometers. Phase I of the project led to a 45-kilometer network (figure 3.1). Phase II, currently under construction, adds another 58.0 kilometers; Phase III proposes adding an additional 40.2 kilometers. The rest of the system will be constructed in subsequent phases.

Accessibility is an important plan component for Janmarg. For Phase I corridors, 20 percent of the city's population lives within walking distance of the 1-kilometer buffer zone. This figure is expected to increase to about 73 percent when the 143-kilometer system is built, after completion of Phase III. In order to reach the largest number of people possible, Ahmedabad planners carefully selected routes in the fastest-growing areas of the city, emphasizing high-quality operations (for example, dedicated bus lanes, full-service bus stations, and pay-and-park systems) in the planning and design processes. The BRT routes were also selected to connect busy places but avoid congested roads. To achieve these goals, planners gave priority to widening roads, providing new road linkages, and adding grade separations (bridges and underpasses) for both rail and intersecting roadways. Janmarg Phase I, which began construction in October 2007, was opened to the public at the end of October 2009, serving the eastern and western portions of Ahmedabad (see the red circular network in figure 3.1). Its three operational routes pass through the city's densest areas. It is operated as a "closed

Figure 3.1 Phases I, II, and III of Ahmedabad's Janmarg bus rapid transit system

Source: CoE UT CEPT 2012.

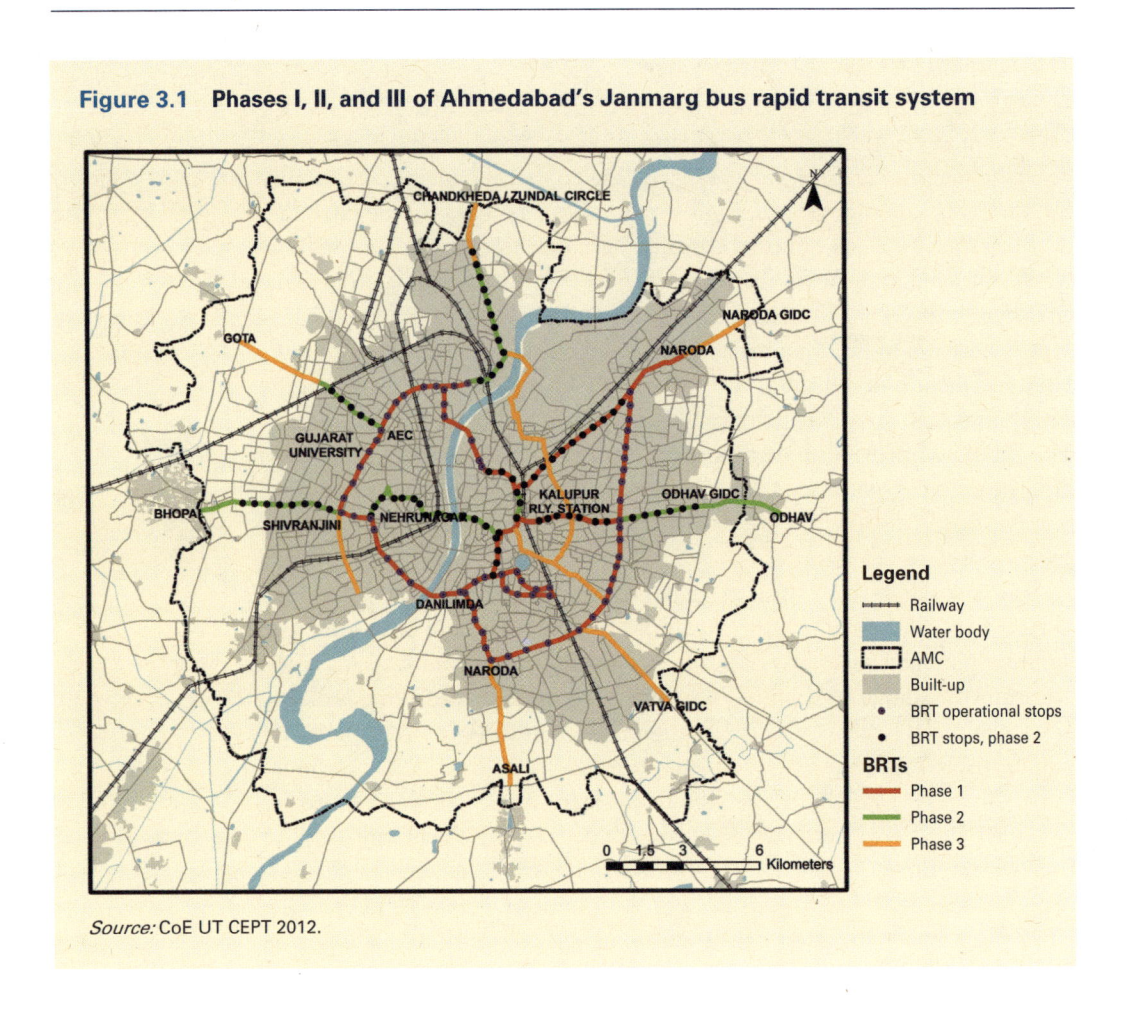

system" with dedicated bus lanes, meaning no buses leave the lanes and become feeders on local streets.

Janmarg is heavily utilized. Daily ridership increased by a factor of 10 in two years, from 13,000 in October 2009 to 135,000 in November 2011. During peak periods, buses operate with average headways (intervals between buses) of 2.5 minutes, travel at 25 kilometers per hour, and average 95 percent on-time departure. Fares are affordable: the distance-based fare structure ranges from Rs 2 ($0.02) for a 1.5-kilometer trip to Rs 5 ($0.09) for a 5.0-kilometer trip. Citizens appreciate the improved citywide mobility provided by the accessible, affordable, and safe Janmarg, consistently giving the system an 8.5 out of 10 rating in monthly user satisfaction surveys.[5] The system also provided opportunities to improve open space around station areas (figure 3.2).

Effective system design and speedy construction were possible thanks to a supportive institutional framework that enabled collaborative planning and decision making by all relevant institutions. Under an AMC initiative, participation by the Gujarat state government in decision making as well as funding was particularly effective in seamlessly implementing the project.

Figure 3.2 Before and after Janmarg at the Anjal station area

a. Before

b. After

Source: CoE UT CEPT 2009.

Janmarg's steering committee also included other key urban development players, such as state government departments, the Gujarat Urban Development Corporation, the Gujarat Infrastructure Development Board, AMC's various departments, and the Ahmedabad Urban Development Authority (AUDA).[6] Each institution had a different role to play in Janmarg's construction, based on its comparative strengths and advantages. For instance, transportation planners and engineers from the Centre for Environmental Planning and Technology University carried out system design, and the AMC supervised construction work by private contractors.

Today, Janmarg is operated and managed by Ahmedabad Janmarg Ltd. (AJL), which is wholly owned by the AMC. Bus operators are selected through a transparent public bidding process, and tenders are evaluated on a per kilometer basis. Under a public-private partnership (PPP) scheme, the private sector also provides other services, including automatic ticketing, passenger information systems, and maintenance of the BRT corridor, stations, and parking facilities. AJL's revenue comes from the Urban Transport Fund (UTF), which includes fare-box payments, parking charges, advertising, and proceeds from the sale of additional floor area ratio (FAR) along BRT corridors. Janmarg can use this fund to finance transit improvements and operational deficits.

Development along the Janmarg Corridor

Ahmedabad has experienced a flurry of new property development in recent years. Much of it, however, has been away from Janmarg corridors. The eventual impact of the Janmarg BRT on urban form is still unclear, because the system only opened in 2009 and many more kilometers of services are yet to be built. As the city has focused mainly on improving mobility rather than shaping urban growth, development has been left mainly to market forces. There has been little proactive planning to incentivize or encourage private growth near Janmarg stations.

The built-up area of Ahmedabad is currently expanding toward the city periphery, with more development along the roads networked citywide, which are also used and planned for BRT corridors.[7] However, the current BRT system primarily serves built-up areas—where land for new development and densification is limited—whereas corridors planned for future phases extend beyond the built-up areas, suggesting a greater potential for shaping urban growth in coming years.

Corridor assessments reveal that the initial market response has been a reaction to development opportunities along the planned and constructed segments of the Janmarg system. New developments along the corridors are most evident in economically vibrant areas, such as the corridors of Dudeshwar–Delhi Darwaza and the Kalupur Narod. The first corridor is close to the Sabarmati Riverfront Development Project, whose 10.4-kilometer stretch along the river is undergoing redevelopment with sidewalks, parks, and gardens to make the area more accessible to the public (box 3.1). The Kalupur Narod corridor is also being upgraded, following the redevelopment of textile mill sites that had been closed for decades.

Brownfield development of closed state-owned textile mills—once the economic backbone of the city called the "Manchester of the East"—has also been apparent. Although many mills were forced to shut down during the 1970s and 1980s, most remained unredeveloped until recently, partly because of the repealed Urban Land Ceiling Act (ULCA) which involves many creditors and lengthy procedures.[8] Currently, these sites are being handed over to the AMC and private developers after the arbitration process.[9] Land parcels occupy premier locations throughout the city, many of them near Janmarg stations on the eastern side of Ahmedabad, on the east side bank of the Sabarmati River (figure 3.3).

Not surprisingly, private developers have aggressively sought to maximize profits over the past half decade, taking advantage of the city's economic boom. Many have accelerated property development in response to the increasing demand for housing, capitalizing on both greenfield and brownfield opportunities. However, few private developers coordinate their projects with public plans or give much thought to TOD integration with land parcels located near Janmarg stations. According to private developers, prices of land near the stations have nearly doubled between 2006 and 2011. To date, however, private developers have been the only

Box 3.1 Ahmedabad's Sabarmati Riverfront Development Project

Initiated in 1997, the Sabarmati Riverfront Development Project is a notable Ahmedabad success story. The 10-kilometer riverfront had long faced problems, such as illegal settlements, environmental degradation, and water pollution. The project revitalized the riverfront neighborhoods for business and residential uses, installed public amenities, connected the east and west sides of the river and relocated riverfront residents in degraded houses to 4,000 units of new social housing prepared by the city. The project's success has instilled the local government and citizens with pride and confidence.

Figure B3.1.1 International kite festival at the riverfront, 2006

Source: Sabarmati Riverfront Development Corporation, Ltd. 2010.

beneficiary, profiting from the increased land value created by government investment.

Factors Working in Ahmedabad's Favor

Ahmedabad's experiences managing urban growth and promoting economic development have been remarkable, especially compared with other large cities in India. The city is often rated as one of India's best-planned cities.[10] Its achievements are the result of a planning culture that embraces innovative tools and financing schemes, as well as good governance that enables smooth planning implementation. Several elements, discussed below, represent opportunities to develop transit and land in a more coordinated way.

Linking transit and public housing in development. Informal housing in Ahmedabad has been increasing for three decades, rising from 17.2 percent

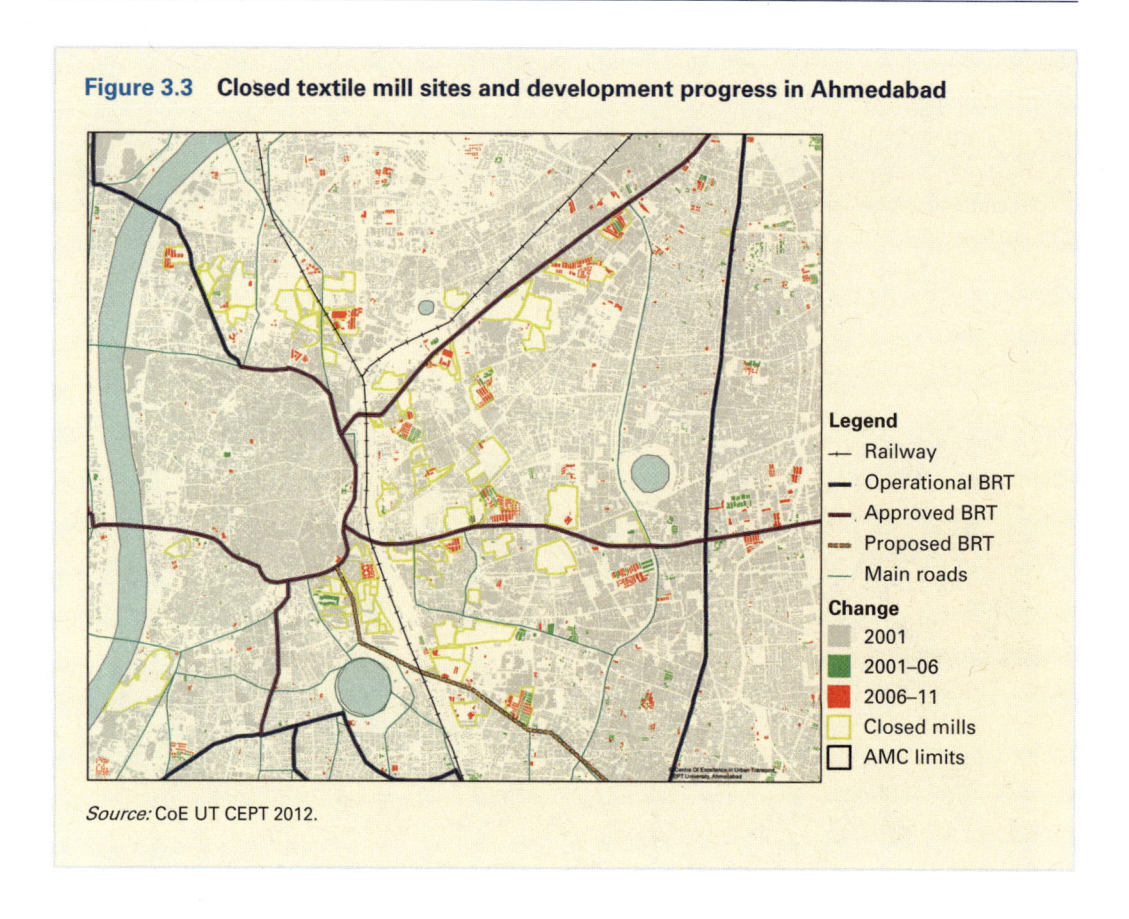

Figure 3.3 Closed textile mill sites and development progress in Ahmedabad

Source: CoE UT CEPT 2012.

of total housing in the 1960s to 22.8 percent in the 1970s, and then to 25.6 percent in the 1990s (Bhatt 2003). During the late 1990s, an estimated 40 percent of households were living in informal housing and *chawl* houses (Bhatt 2003). Originally built to accommodate textile mill workers, *chawl* houses are dilapidated structures rented to low-income households. In the late 1990s, they accounted for about 18 percent of the city's housing stock. Informal settlements are apparent along the riverfront, on public lands, and on any available vacant spaces. Together with a lack of adequate and affordable housing for the city's marginalized residents, residential demand for the growing population as a whole is becoming a progressively pressing issue.

The AMC is addressing such housing issues by developing former textile mill sites. After these sites are redistributed to the public and private sector, redevelopment plans will focus on social housing and commercial development. The planned housing is especially crucial because low-income residents, particularly residents affected by public infrastructure development projects, including Janmarg, are prioritized for relocation into these developments. Welfare facilities, including schools and medical clinics, are also being developed. Incoming households will improve livelihoods through better housing conditions and access to services, including proximity to

Janmarg. Private developers will also benefit, as they are free to use their allocation for the construction of commercial or residential buildings, made more lucrative by their premier location in the city center and proximity to public transport.[11]

To date, capacity to accommodate marginalized residents on former textile redevelopment sites has been limited, partly because of the FAR constraint (capped at 2.25). Development that accommodates the growing demand for housing and commercial space could be encouraged by allowing higher FARs to increase the maximum building volume or by requiring private developers to reserve a certain percentage of units, often 25 percent, as "affordable social housing" units for low-income residents who are eligible for government rental assistance, with the remaining housing units priced at market rates.[12]

Financing scheme that captures land value. Ahmedabad has traditionally taken a progressive approach toward municipal and infrastructure financing. It has introduced a number of innovative financing schemes including India's first municipal bond, various PPP arrangements, and the Town Planning Scheme system.

From a TOD perspective, the sale of additional FAR and the "guidance value" property tax system are particularly notable. In 2002, a law allowing the sale of additional FAR for properties abutting streets 18 meters wide or wider, including all BRT corridors, was passed. The current permissible FAR is 1.80, which can be increased to 2.25. In 2011, the city earned about $26 million from the sale of FAR bonuses, which represented 4.5 percent of the city's total revenues and 5.0 percent of its total investment budget. Currently, the city is discussing raising the FAR along transit corridors. The guidance value property tax levying system captures the increased land value created by public investment. The amount levied changes once every three years based on location, land use, and occupation of the owner/renter.

Strong urban planning tradition. Ahmedabad stands apart from other Indian cities for its strong tradition of urban planning. Institutionally, the AMC collaborates closely with the AUDA, which manages urban planning and development, formulates development plans, controls development activity, and provides physical and social infrastructure in the metropolitan region. AUDA delegates AMC to assume the same responsibilities and functions in the city area in close coordination with AUDA. The existence of the AUDA provides an efficient mechanism for coordinating regional growth and ensures consistency in urban planning practice and implementation across different administrations in the metropolitan region.

Planning and development follow a two-level process. The first level is the Development Plan, a macro strategy defining the direction of growth and envisioning citywide infrastructure. The second level is the Town Planning Scheme, which covers smaller geographic territories within the city, as delineated in the Development Plan. Ahmedabad has used the Town

Planning Scheme since 1915; about 75 percent of the city (about 300 square kilometers of urban development) was developed based on the scheme.

The Town Planning Scheme has allowed a rational pattern of land development to unfold. It has enabled local authorities to establish agricultural plots suitable for urban uses by altering the shapes of, sizes of, and access to specific land parcels. For example, a parcel of land could be differentiated for the use of roads (up to 20 percent of total parcel use); other public purposes (parks, playgrounds, and so forth, up to 15 percent); and low-income housing (up to 10 percent) (box 3.2).

The Town Planning Scheme is particularly important because it makes development an almost self-financing activity. The system aims to adjust irregular-shaped land parcels into a more productive shape upon development while investing in infrastructure, including roads, public parks, water lines, and a sewerage system. Although the original landowners lose some portion of their land in the adjustment process (by selling it to the public as part of the infrastructure fund or donating it for public use), they may benefit from higher land values in the area as a result of better infrastructure and land configuration. Throughout the process, landowners are not required to invest additional money, as relinquishing part of their original land parcel effectively covers the land readjustment and infrastructure investment cost.

The Town Planning Scheme process has also helped nurture an inclusive culture of plan making and implementation, as it includes intensive stakeholder participation and consultation in several stages. The first draft is unveiled at a landowners meeting, which is followed by three or four rounds of individual hearings with each landowner regarding physical and financial proposals before finalizing the land use.

Collaborative planning culture. Ahmedabad has strong political leadership and efficient horizontally and vertically coordinated government administrations, including the local and regional administrative bodies of the AMC and AUDA. In addition, institutions of higher learning and think tanks, such as the Centre for Environmental Planning and Technology University, are invited to take part in planning processes whenever necessary. This collaborative and inclusive planning culture was particularly apparent in the BRT planning and implementation phases. Citizens were also invited to comment and provide feedback on the Janmarg system at the initial stage of operation.

With a people-oriented and business-friendly city administration, governments in the Ahmedabad metropolitan area, especially the AMC, have nurtured a strong trust-based relationship with the business community and citizens. In fact, businesses as well as citizens have supported development efforts that might have faced opposition in some circumstances, such as the Sabarmati Riverfront Development Project, which involved resettling of some 4,000 households. The city's efforts to improve the livelihoods of

Box 3.2 Ahmedabad's Town Planning Scheme

Ahmedabad's Town Planning Scheme includes the following elements:

- reconstitution of landholdings
- appropriation of land for public uses without acquisition (up to 50 percent)
- local road networks (up to 20 percent)
- local social and physical infrastructure (up to 5 percent)
- land bank for urban poor (up to 10 percent)
- land appropriation as an adjusted compensation against increased land value (as a result of infrastructure investment)
- land bank for financing of infrastructure (15 percent).

Figure B3.2.1 Land adjustment in Ahmedabad

a. Before adjustment
(unarranged land parcels)

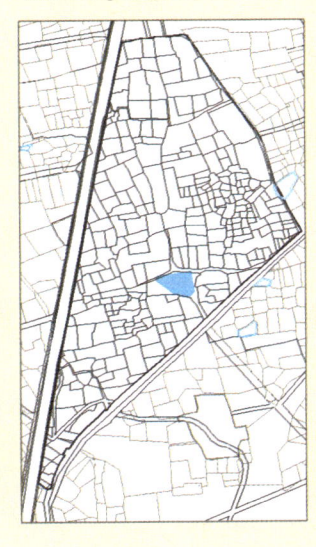

b. After adjustment
(arranged land parcels)

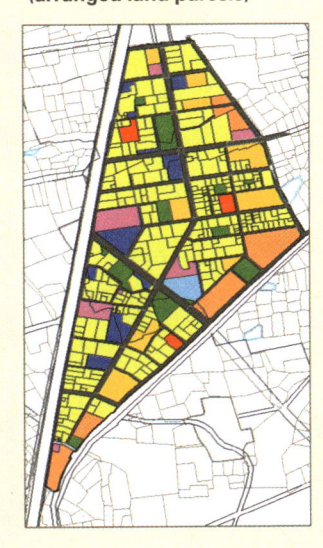

Source: Ahmedabad Urban Development Authority n.d.

the underprivileged population are also well accepted, as their plans are often shared publicly.[13]

Overcoming Obstacles to Sustainability

A number of challenges hamper the opportunity to promote TOD in Ahmedabad. These challenges concern land-use strategies and tools, land fragmentation and building deterioration, and the design of transit improvements and urban development.

Uniformly low floor area ratios and lack of strategically articulated densification. Low and fairly uniform FARs (of 1.8–2.25) limit growth around transit nodes. According to Ahmedabad's planners, allocating moderate FARs citywide is intended to disperse travel demand and thus decongest the city. The local government is also cautious about modifying the FAR for fear of possible accusations of land-related corruption. The maximum FAR in Ahmedabad (2.25) is modest compared with FARs in other Asian cities, such as Tokyo (20); Hong Kong SAR, China (12); and Seoul (10). As a result, strategic locations such as transit nodes and Janmarg stations are not much denser than other parts of the city. Although some efforts have been established between the strategic nodes and FAR modification, progress has been limited, in contrast to Janmarg construction and provision of services.

If FARs remain low and relatively uniform, a more automobile-oriented built form is almost inevitable. Given the current cap, most new development will be pushed out to the periphery, increasing the share of trips by motorized vehicles. Coupled with economic development and income growth, the share of future trips by small, atomized vehicles (such as two-wheelers and three-wheelers) is likely to grow as well. Low-density growth will more likely promote private automobile use than public transit use. In the near term, the city may experience less traffic congestion, as a result of evenly dispersed urbanization, but over the long term this pattern of development creates an urban form that is less conducive to high-capacity transit and more dependent on private automobile use, leading to more traffic congestion and air pollution.

Keeping FARs low also prevents property owners and developers from redeveloping their deteriorated low-rise properties into newer, taller buildings. Without redevelopment, the stock of degraded, uninhabitable buildings will deteriorate even further. These unfavorable conditions are particularly evident around Janmarg station areas and corridors, which are already surrounded by older, low-rise buildings situated on small parcels.

Together with a low FAR ceiling, the lack of a strategic development plan thwarts efficient and sustainable development. Although the region seems to be committed to creating a few satellite centers as part of the planned metrorail investment, little systematic effort or planning appears to be placed for creating third-tier centers along Janmarg's corridors. In contrast, as noted in chapter 2, hierarchical centers are a pivotal component of Singapore's successful integration of transit and development, supplemented by integrated intermodal services, including rail, bus, paratransit, and pedestrian ways. Development along Janmarg's corridors is left mostly to private developers, without guidelines or rules to maximize the use of urban space proximity of the transit stations and corridors.

The lack of strategic development is also apparent in the redevelopment of closed textile mill sites. Although these land parcels are located near Janmarg's stations and corridors, development is not sufficiently integrated. Public and private land developers are concentrating solely on redeveloping their allocations, without institutional or design coordination with surrounding counterparts. TOD guidelines, which typically provide principles for increased density and mixed land-use development, are lacking.

To strategically increase building volume and mixed land use around key nodes, such as areas around Janmarg stations or planned metro stations, the AMC needs to consider adopting a more flexible density control policy. Together with TOD principles and other urban development measures, such a policy could better promote the redevelopment of inner city areas and more efficiently plan subcenters.

Small parcels, informal land transactions, and degraded buildings. A host of issues, including the prevalence of small land parcels, the informality of land transactions, and the city's degraded building stock, is suppressing efforts to encourage BRT–based TOD. These problems stem in large part from various land-use regulations. The Rent Control Act of 1949, which aimed to protect tenants from eviction by landlords, resulted in dilapidated rental housing, as owners had little incentive to maintain the units or redevelop the land. The now-repealed Urban Land Ceiling Act of 1976 significantly contributed to the expansion of built-up areas outside the AMC, while promoting smaller development within the city's boundary. The Land Acquisition Act of 1984, used to acquire and develop lands by the public, unintentionally supports informal transactions because the large time gap between notice and payment, during which the land is often underpriced, discourages formal sales.

Together with the national government, the city needs to proactively address these issues if TOD is to be leveraged aggressively. In other countries, including Germany, Japan, and the Republic of Korea, land-adjustment schemes similar to the Town Planning Scheme have been used to revitalize long-distressed urban districts. In contrast, to date, Ahmedabad has applied the Town Planning Scheme only to convert rural land to urban uses.

Design shortcomings. Janmarg is designed as a closed system, requiring users to access stations situated in the medians of roads by foot, bicycle, car, two-wheeler, or other mode of public transit. Good design—for example, direct line-of-site access and clear way-finding—is needed to encourage people to choose Janmarg over other modes. The city has plans to include pay-and-park systems, bike lanes, and pedways, but more can be done. Currently, cycle tracks parallel the BRT lanes but do not allow for modal interaction; these tracks function more as an adjunct than as a feeder to Janmarg. There are no bicycle parking spaces. There is also no well-designed network of pedestrian ways and sidewalks that feed into stations; places where pedestrian ways do exist are sometimes occupied by motorcycles and other fast-moving vehicles. Local buses run by the Ahmedabad Municipal Transport Services (AMTS) function as feeders to other destinations in the region, but they are not well connected to the BRT system.[14] Ahmedabad could learn from some of Bogota's experiences building green feeder networks that support non-motorized transport, described later in this chapter.

Greater emphasis should be placed on increasing connectivity between surrounding land uses and Janmarg stations. Prioritizing design considerations during initial planning stages, when mobility investments and land development take place, would increase walkability around stations and Janmarg ridership. To date, little consideration has been given to placemaking. Many key redevelopment sites, such as former textile mill parcels, are undergoing redevelopment without much regard to urban design, aesthetics, or environmental quality. Station areas lack a distinguishing identity, accessibility is poor, and opportunities for mixed land uses have been completely missed.

Development of new, automobile-dependent towns. The New West, a newtown in western Ahmedabad City, accommodates global corporations and attracts upper-class residents. The district's built environment is distinct from the rest of the city, symbolized by tall, modern buildings in superblocks with few pedestrian ways in between. The road network was designed to accommodate smooth operation of private automobiles. Most buildings have at least one parking lot to accommodate residents and commuters.

Although this district should be connected to extended BRT services or the planned metro, the area is currently completely disconnected from any public transport; all residents and commuters must therefore depend on automobiles. Increasing FARs and mixed land uses at an early stage of New West's development, coupled with vastly improved transit services and pedestrian connections, would, with time, make the area far less automobile oriented and more transit oriented.

Embracing Opportunities for Sustainable Growth

Ahmedabad's major challenge to achieving smart, sustainable growth that is sensitive to community needs, is balancing rapid population and industrial expansion with available funding. The city's progressive planning culture, innovative development tools, and business-friendly mindset provide the necessary support to meet these challenges.

Janmarg's expansion and the new metro present significant opportunities for Ahmedabad to develop as a sustainable metropolis supported by transit. The city's current megaplans and projects, along with redevelopment opportunities at closed textile mill sites, could trigger locally tailored TOD.

One example of such an opportunity is the new metro development that plans to link Ahmedabad City and Gandhinagar City, the state capital, located in the north. This project provides an excellent opportunity for shaping Ahmedabad and surrounding regions with a strategic planning vision and implementation processes, especially as the planned rail line will pass through the city's landmark Sabarmati Riverfront Development Project. Successful integration of transit and land use through the development of the riverfront and mobility projects could serve as an iconic model for guiding future metropolitan development.

The Town Planning Scheme used in the greenfield development process could be proactively adjusted in the process of promoting TOD. Because the city's land parcels are small, particularly in the inner city, they require an additional land consolidation process. With almost a century of experience with the Town Planning Scheme in new development, the city could apply its knowledge and techniques to currently urbanized areas, as promoting building density in the already built-up area cannot be achieved without this capacity. The collaborative planning culture between governmental agencies and departments, as well as between the government and its citizens, is a great asset that could address current challenges facing transit and land-use planning.

Proactively exploring opportunities to capture increased land value as a result of transit development is a key element of successful long-term urban management. Captured value could be used to recover various costs of transit investment, social housing, infrastructure, and other developments, including physical designs for TDM. It could also help cover expenses for operations and maintenance of public transit. As TOD projects require significant financial resources, as evidenced by all three phases of Janmarg's construction and expansion, such effort becomes crucial as future megatransit projects—like the planned metro—require much greater resources.

At a smaller scale, city officials are considering raising the FAR of proposed metro and BRT corridors to 3.5. Doing so would allow the public sector to capture land value increases. At the same time, the city should strategically assign FARs to reflect the intensity of transit services as well as factors of economic, cultural, and environmental importance. The "Rail+Property" real estate development undertaken by private railway companies in Hong Kong SAR, China and Tokyo are examples that cities like Ahmedabad should consider emulating (see chapter 2 for details).

Advancing urban development in close coordination with improvements in land use and public transit would help Ahmedabad become a sustainable city. Many growing cities, including other cities in India, are developing or planning BRT systems and metros. Lessons learned from the proactive and strategic integration of transit and land use in Ahmedabad will be of critical importance for growing and expanding cities worldwide (Ahmedabad and its BRT system at a glance are shown in box 3.3).

Bogota: Beyond TransMilenio

Bogota, the capital of Colombia, has gained an international reputation as a very progressive city, pushing the sustainability envelope by focusing on mobility to enhance its economic efficiency, improve environmental conditions, and promote social equity. This city with 7.6 million people has some of the most progressive public investment initiatives in developing countries, including the first-class TransMilenio BRT; integrated TDM measures; the transit-linked social housing Metrovivienda program; the Alameda

Box 3.3 Ahmedabad and its bus rapid transit system at a glance

Table B3.3.1 Population statistics for Ahmedabad, India

Item	Figure
Population 2011 (million)	
City	5.5
Metropolitan region	6.3
Area (square kilometers)	
City	449
Metropolitan area	1,295
Population density (people/square kilometer)	
City	12,249
Metropolitan area	4,866
Annual population growth rate 2001–11 (percent)	
City	2.03
Metropolitan region	1.68

Source: World Bank study team and Ahmedabad Urban Development.

Figure B3.3.1 Map of Ahmedabad, India

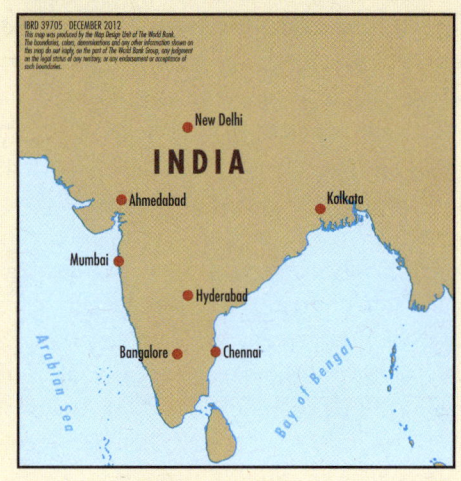

Source: World Bank.

Table B3.3.2 Capacity and infrastructure of the Janmarg bus rapid transit system

Feature	Figure
Daily carrying capacity	135,000 trips (as of November 2011)
Covered population	20 percent within 1 kilometers of Phase I buffer zone (expected to increase to 73 percent at end of Phase III)
Phase I	45 kilometers
Phase II (planned)	58 kilometers
Phase III (planned)	40.2 kilometers

Source: World Bank study team.

Figure B3.3.2 Janmarg bus

Photo by Hiroaki Suzuki.

Porvenir, the world's longest pedestrian way; and other public projects that incorporate good urban design and innovative financing schemes.

TransMilenio is recognized as the "gold standard" of BRT systems. Daily ridership totals more than 1.5 million, accounting for 74 percent of total public transit trips in the city, and two-thirds of the city's population lives within a kilometer of trunk and feeder lane buffer zone. Delegations of officials and dignitaries from around the world visit Bogota to marvel at this system.

A little more than a decade after the TransMilenio's construction, Bogota is facing a new set of challenges, caused by uncoordinated urban expansion (sprawl), traffic congestion, and deteriorating TransMilenio services that are not keeping up with demand. With an additional 2.5 million people projected in the region over the next four decades, policy makers and planners are increasingly looking at longer-term development and redevelopment of the urban fabric in order to achieve regional sustainability.

The first two implementation phases paid little attention to the value of strategically integrating TransMilenio with land use. However, both the national government and the city have recently begun to stress the importance of public transit such as TransMilenio, and its planned new metro in achieving a more sustainable urban future.

The TransMilenio Bus Transit System

In March 1998, the City of Bogota approved the TransMilenio as a part of its *Por la Bogota que Queremos* ("For the Bogota we all want") development plan. This plan included a long-awaited project intended to improve mobility and relieve traffic chaos, which was creating increasingly long commutes and fueling air pollution from vehicular emissions.

Initial stages of the system aimed to construct 388 kilometers of BRT in 22 corridors in the city, to be carried out in five phases between 1998 and 2016. Short- and mid-term implementation of the TransMilenio under Phase I and II projects were the main focus at that time. Details on future plans were to be determined when local and national budgets became available. Phase I of the project began in late 1998 and Phase II in 2006.[15]

Phase I opened in December 2000, 34 months after project conception. Totaling 42 kilometers, it introduced two main lines, Av. Caracas and Calle 80. Phase II added another 42 kilometers. Phase III, currently under construction, will add another 28 kilometers, making the system 112 kilometers long (figure 3.4).

To complement and further expand the reach of this service, the BRT system adopted a trunk-feeder model by establishing segregated busways on the city's major arterial roads and feeder buses that operate on existing roads in neighborhoods, starting at the trunk-line end stations. The feeder system adds 200 kilometers of coverage. As a large portion of the TransMilenio's service is targeted to low-income populations, its feeder buses operate in low-income neighborhoods on the urban periphery.

The TransMilenio system was built quickly, not only to respond to the mounting congestion crisis, but also to complete a portion of the system within the mayoral term that ran between 1998 and 2001. To minimize construction time, the system used Calle 80 and Av. Caracas as initial corridors. Calle 80 was selected because it was already undergoing reconstruction that included exclusive right-of-way infrastructure for buses. Both Calle 80 and Av. Caracas had been consistently mentioned in 30 years of transportation studies as first-priority corridors for future mass transit in Bogota.

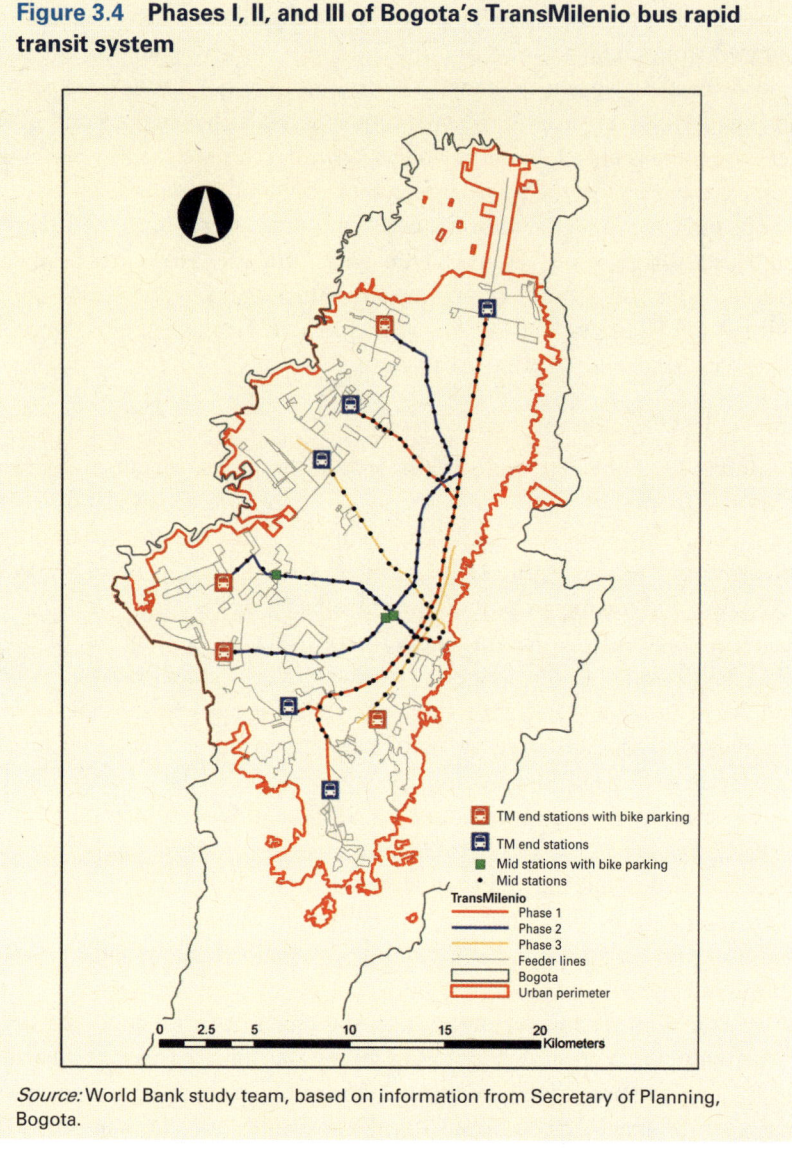

Figure 3.4 Phases I, II, and III of Bogota's TransMilenio bus rapid transit system

Source: World Bank study team, based on information from Secretary of Planning, Bogota.

The city conducted a thorough transportation planning study, including reconfirmation of these past study results, to determine the Phase I (short-term) and Phase II (mid-term) system routes. It then began redesigning Calle 80 to fit the envisioned TransMilenio system and began planning and designing Av. Caracas. Bus lanes and stations were located in the median of arterials to allow for rapid operation of buses. Large stations and overtaking lanes increased the capacity and the speed of the BRT system. This design, however, focused on mobility, overlooking broader urban development goals, such as strategic spatial guides or land-use plans to redistribute growth for improving existing environments.

New Developmental Challenges along the TransMilenio Corridor

Deteriorated main routes and worsening traffic congestion have overshadowed the TransMilenio's successes. The decline in service quality reflects both the system's popularity and the lack of attention to user needs. Between 2007 and 2008, for example, ridership increased 10.3 percent (135,292 passengers), while the number of buses increased just 2.2 percent (Hidalgo and EMBARQ 2010). In addition, the capacity of the main corridors was not expanded before 2011. As a result, buses on the busiest lines are usually overcrowded, forcing passengers to wait a long time. Meanwhile, traffic congestion in Bogota has worsened: private car ownership increased from 104 vehicles per 1,000 people in 2003 to 163 in 2008—a 12.3 percent annual increase—with almost no increase in roadway capacity (SDP 2010).

The cumulative effects have been deteriorating transit services. TransMilenio's average travel speed in the Av. Caracas corridor declined from 28 kilometers per hour in 2001 to 23 kilometers per hour in 2011, according to the Mobility Office. Declines in the quality of service have become so problematic that many people who are able to travel by alternate means, often by private vehicle, choose to do so.

The capacity to serve high volumes of riders in dense traffic corridors is thus facing physical and technical limitations, which has further impeded efforts to create higher-density mixed-use land projects around stations. In response, Bogota is starting to consider improving overall transit services, including the construction of a new metro.

Since TransMilenio's first construction phase, Bogota's real estate market has undergone a boom. Building densities across the city have increased, primarily in areas far from TransMilenio's main lines as well as around end stations and some peripheral feeder lines (box 3.4).

Changes in building density of this kind were expected, given that the system was designed to improve mobility, without much coordination with land use, leaving development mainly to market forces. Private developers were, for the most part, less interested in improving or redeveloping mid-station areas, partly because this land was already occupied. Instead, they aggressively developed commercial and residential buildings on the city's periphery or around end stations, where there was more vacant land. This development pattern is particularly evident in the relationship between land-use change and the phases of BRT construction (see box 3.4). For example, far less land densification occurred following Phase I construction than in subsequent phases, because TransMilenio's first lines were built along corridors that were already developed. New construction occurred only in the few large land parcels that were vacant along Calle 80. Meanwhile, areas with old, sometimes decrepit two- to three-story buildings near mid-stations were left untouched.

Densification of the built environment, mainly for residential and commercial use, along the Phase II corridor and feeder areas combined was higher by 8.0 percent than Phase I and Phase III areas by 5.5 percent and 4.5

Box 3.4 How has Bogota's TransMilenio affected the built environment?

The World Bank study team assessed the effect of TransMilenio on the built environment at the citywide, corridor, and neighborhood scales. It observed the impacts on a citywide and corridor scale mainly by measuring the change in building density, calculated using floor area ratio (FAR). It compared and contrasted the transformations of the built environment along the TransMilenio corridors ("affected areas" or "walkshed" in the study) and control areas outside the "affected areas" at the citywide scale. At the corridor scale, it used the different phases of construction to identify the influence of TransMilenio on land development. The study defined "affected areas" as areas that fell within a 1-kilometer radius of the main trunk lines and a 500-meter radius from the feeder lines.

At the neighborhood scale, the Bank team conducted matched-pair analysis by selecting station areas (target areas) and control areas (non–BRT stations) that were otherwise very similar (in terms of neighborhood incomes, land use, and subregional locations). Seven matched-pair analyses were conducted by selecting four pairs in the middle of TransMilenio corridors and three pairs at the end of corridors. Cadastral data from the City of Bogota for 2004 and 2010 were the main data source used for these analyses.

The study results suggest that a few key building density transformations have taken place across Bogota. At the city level, building densities increased overall, but they increased more away from TransMilenio stations than near them. The average increase in building density was 6 percent for areas affected by both the trunk and feeder lines; in the rest of the city, average density rose 10 percent (Figure B3.4.1).

Between 2004 and 2010, neighborhoods near peripheral feeder lines experienced more densification than areas along TransMilenio's trunk lines. The average increase in residential, commercial, and institutional densities was 6.3 percent for areas along peripheral feeder lines and 5.7 percent for neighborhoods along Bogota's main BRT corridors. (Building in Bogota is allocated as 85 percent residential, 6 percent commercial, and 5 percent institutional.)

Phase II has been a different story. For more recently built BRT corridors, building densities rose 7.1 percent along trunk lines and 9.0 percent along feeder lines. Substantial development took place in Phase II areas with vacant land. As expected, building densities along the major arterial roads—where most of the Phase II busway was constructed—were already comparatively high, thus relatively little new growth has occurred in these areas. Peripheral areas receiving new feeder services in Phase II, however, experienced more densification, in part because their prior densities were relatively low.

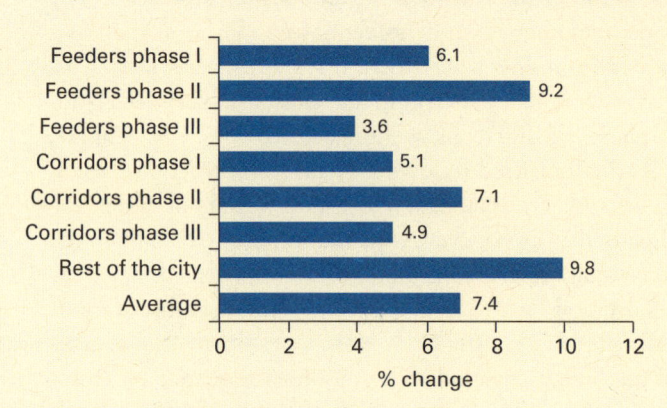

Figure B3.4.1 Changes in building density in areas of Bogota affected by the TransMilenio

Category	% change
Feeders phase I	6.1
Feeders phase II	9.2
Feeders phase III	3.6
Corridors phase I	5.1
Corridors phase II	7.1
Corridors phase III	4.9
Rest of the city	9.8
Average	7.4

Source: World Bank study team, based on cadastral data.
Note: Changes are between 2004 and 2010; building use includes residential and commercial.

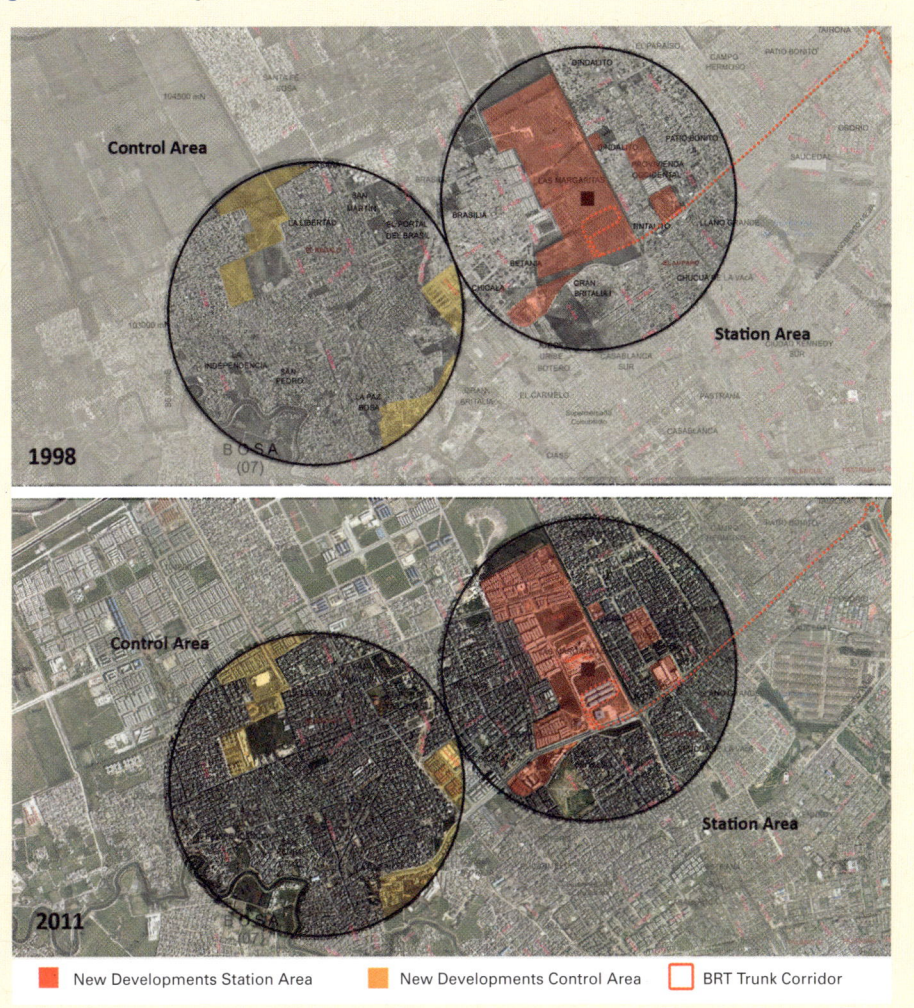

Figure 3.5 Development at end station of Bogota's TransMilenio, 1998 and 2011

■ New Developments Station Area   ■ New Developments Control Area   ☐ BRT Trunk Corridor

Source: World Bank study team, based on information from the Secretary of Planning, Bogota.
Note: By 2011, there was almost no vacant land available in the areas shaded in red, around the end station areas. Some land parcels were still available in the areas shaded in yellow.

percent, respectively, because high rises along Av. Suba, Av. NQS, and Av. Americas, all of which are located toward the city's periphery, were built. This pattern suggests that the market was more responsive in places where vacant parcels were readily available.

A micro-scale example also suggests that stronger market responses are evident in city's periphery. In 1998, there were almost no developments at the end station (Americas), located in the northeast of the city (figure 3.5). By 2011, the area boasted various commercial and residential buildings. Greater densification occurred on land closer to the stations than on land farther away. The closer-in locations attracted developers because the stations connect to the free feeder bus system and the trunk line was expected to attract more people to the area.

The corridors under Phase III, particularly along the Calle 26 corridor to the airport, are experiencing a boom in building construction, for several possible reasons. Many land parcels along the corridor are vacant; the El Dorado airport is expanding; and Phase III, connecting the airport with the city center, is under construction. Although identifying the true impact of the extension of TransMilenio on land-use development is difficult, densification along the BRT corridor can be interpreted as the result of substantial public infrastructure investments along this line, including the BRT extension.

Despite significant development, and to a lesser extent redevelopment, Bogota continues to suffer from a limited long-term vision, regulations that set uniform densities, and little formal TOD guidance. The city—including down to the district level, where detailed land-use planning is regulated and implemented—has yet to adopt and enforce even minimal changes in land use zoning, FAR policies, or other codes related to land development, even after the efforts of TransMilenio's mobility improvement (Bocarejo, Portilla, and Perez 2012). This lack of institutional support impedes efforts to shape effective use of land and decreases the ability to capitalize on the financial value created by new transit for additional betterment. As a result of overlooking the link between land use and TransMilenio investment, building volume in Bogota changed little between 2004 and 2010. As a result, low-rise buildings remain dominant, except in central business districts and suburban centers (figure 3.6). The FAR in Bogota remains low across the city (below 2, although it rose slightly in 2010) (figure 3.7). There is no difference in the rate of FAR changes in areas affected and not affected by the TransMilenio.

Factors Supporting Bogota's Progressive Development

Historically, TransMilenio triggered significant urban transformations through innovative development initiatives and strategies. Aligning these efforts with BRT system development helped upgrade the city to its current form and will continue to connect mobility and spatial use over the coming years. The real test for successful future integration depends on the way a city creates a synergestic environment into the community, which is sustainable and responsive to commuters' needs; Bogota's experiences are valuable to growing cities in the developing world.

Using transportation demand management. Many successful cities have alleviated traffic congestion by promoting TDM, which reduces demand for travel by private vehicles and encourages nonmotorized transport or transit use. Interventions include land-use regulation, pedestrian-oriented design, promotion and inclusion of bicycle-friendly environments, parking control and management, road-congestion pricing, and high occupancy vehicle (HOV) lanes, among others.

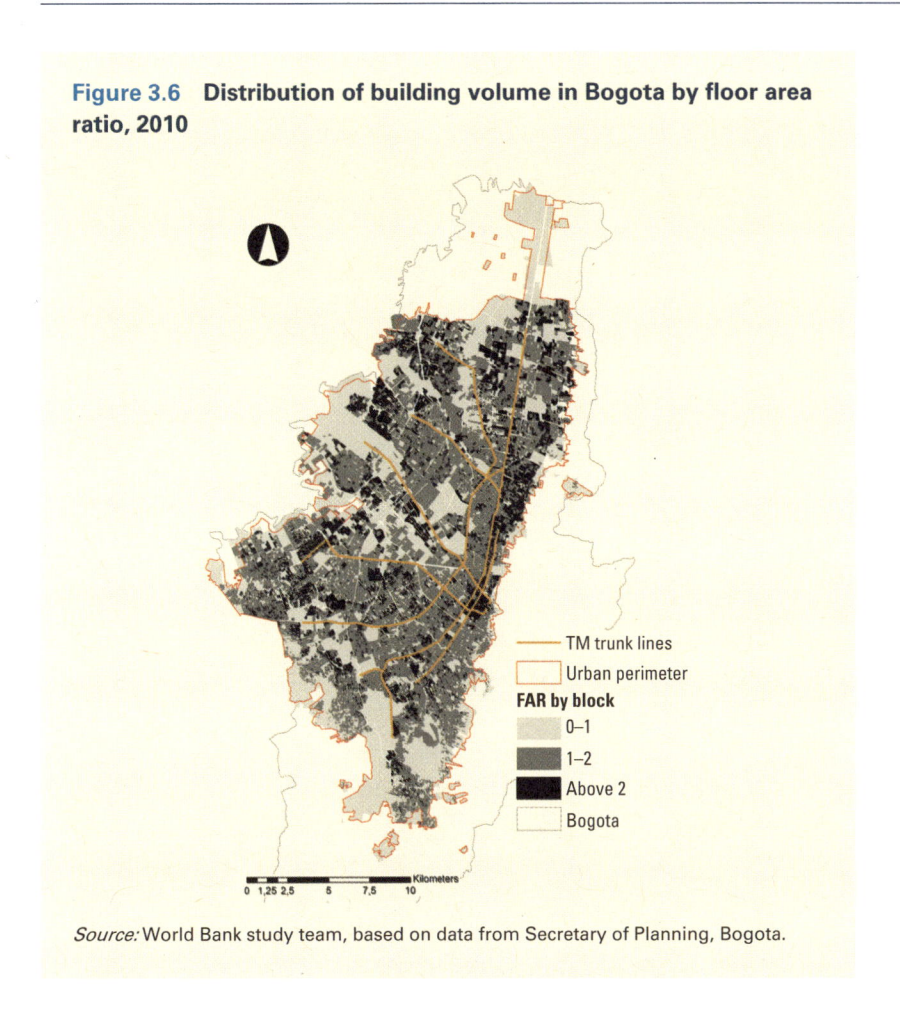

Figure 3.6 Distribution of building volume in Bogota by floor area ratio, 2010

Source: World Bank study team, based on data from Secretary of Planning, Bogota.

Bogota has adopted various progressive TDM initiatives, ranging from physical developments, such as bike and pedestrian paths, to policies and regulations that control automobile use. In 1995, for example, the city began construction of the 344-kilometer *cicloruta* (bike route), the largest network in Latin America. The city also closes road segments for selected hours on holidays and weekends, creating 121 kilometers of pedestrian and bike paths called *Ciclovia* (figure 3.8).[16]

On the policy side, in 1998, the city introduced the peak and licence plate program *(pico y placa)*, which regulates private automobile use during the morning and evening peak hours, based on the last digit of the license plate. Another initiative, car-free days *(sin mi carro)*, initated in 2000, aims to educate people on alternating transit modes. It is the world's largest car-free weekday event, temporarily removing about 1.5 million vehicles from the street.

Creating public and pedestrian spaces with good design elements has also promoted the use of nonmotorized transport in Bogota. Sidewalks and parks were first given back to citizens by removing parking and illegal settlements,

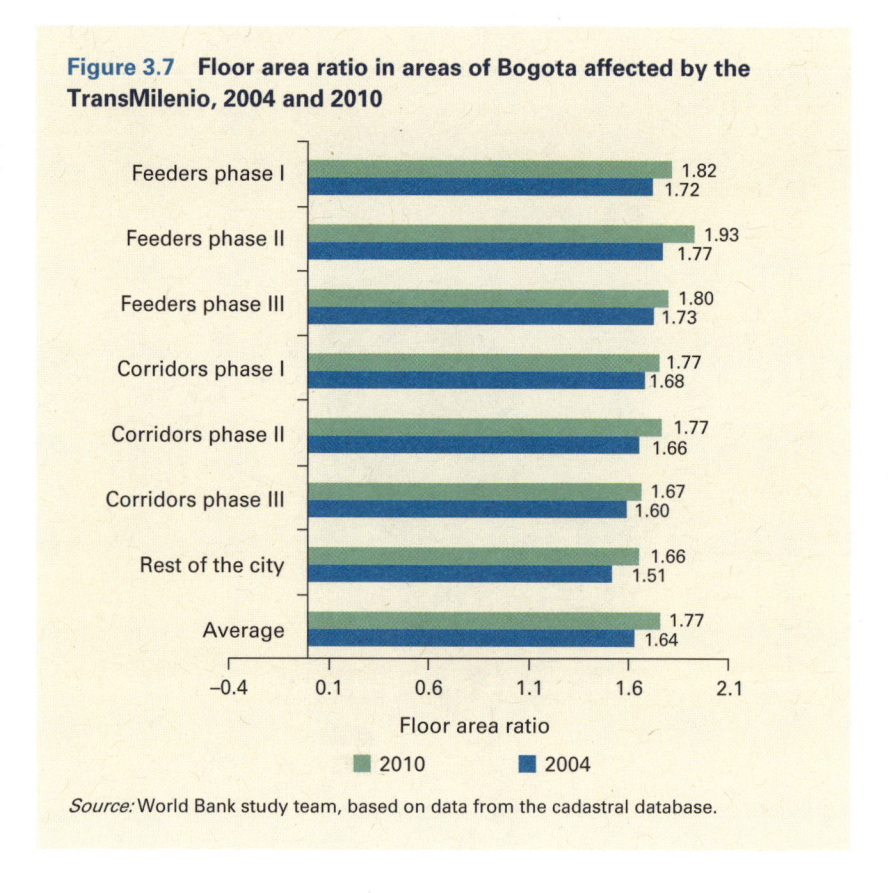

Figure 3.7 Floor area ratio in areas of Bogota affected by the TransMilenio, 2004 and 2010

Area	2010	2004
Feeders phase I	1.82	1.72
Feeders phase II	1.93	1.77
Feeders phase III	1.80	1.73
Corridors phase I	1.77	1.68
Corridors phase II	1.77	1.66
Corridors phase III	1.67	1.60
Rest of the city	1.66	1.51
Average	1.77	1.64

Source: World Bank study team, based on data from the cadastral database.

Figure 3.8 Joggers along Bogota's Ciclovia

Note: More than 1 million people use the Ciclovia every Sunday, according to the District Recreation and Sport Institute.
Photo by Kanako Iuchi.

Figure 3.9 Bike parking spaces at Portal de Suba, Bogota

Photo by Kanako Iuchi.

which previously occupied these public spaces. Pavement, street furniture, and greenery were added to create a more pedestrian-friendly space. Bike parking spaces are secured for easy transfer to TransMilenio (figure 3.9). Greenways, or *alamedas*, are currently expanding for the dedicated use of walking and cycling. One of them, the 17-kilometer Alameda Porvenir, is the world's longest pedestrian corridor. Located in a marginalized area of the city, it connects affordable housing, parks, the TransMilenio, and the city's library. Private developers have contributed to the effort by opening small cafes and shops to create an attractive open space.

Bogota has taken a holistic approach to promoting alternatives to private car travel. These initiatives have complemented transit services. Bicycle use has quintupled since the construction of the *ciclorutas*, the opening of the Ciclovia, and the introduction of other bicycle-use promotions.[17] Construction of public squares, improvements to sidewalks, and the development of pedestrian networks has also enhanced the public realm and pedestrian environments near some BRT stations. These improved enivornments have encouraged people to use the TransMilenio.

Connecting affordable housing for the needy: Metrovivienda. Like other cities in developing countries, Bogota faces major housing problems with respect to the underprivileged. The National Department of Statistics (DANE)'s population census indicated a shortage of about 370,000 units in 2005 (a decline from 550,000 units in 1993).

The Metrovivienda, which provides affordable housing near the TransMilenio system, is an innovative way of addressing housing needs by integrating transport and land use. The program was founded in 1999 to provide serviced land on which private developers could legally construct affordable housing for people who could not otherwise afford formal shelter. Lower-income residents—defined as people earning less than four times the minimum salaries set by the government (see, for example, Gilbert 2009), including people illegally living in hillside subdivisions—are the main target groups. The intent of the program was to better serve the underprivileged by building housing sites near TransMilenio stations and providing good access to social facilities (schools, hospitals, parks, and libraries). Before moving into Metrovivienda housing, many of these households devoted a large portion of their earnings to transportation (often about 20 percent) for rides serviced by informal operators in remote areas lacking good transit access or connectivity. Their livelihoods are expected to improve as a result of both better accessibility and environment and reduced transportation costs.

Metrovivienda operated as a PPP development scheme until 2007. It currently operates in partnership with local landowners, who receive the difference between the sales price and the cost needed to develop and service the area (Gilbert 2009). However, in case of opposition or refusal to participate, the city government has the ability to expropriate their lands.

Metrovivienda is responsible for developing and installing basic public infrastructure, including water and sewerage piping, parks, and roads. After construction, it is responsible for selling the rest of the land to developers for social housing. The system operates with the understanding that rural land prices freeze at the time of project approval, so that the agency as well as the eventual homeowners will not suffer from land price speculation. People who purchase the serviced sites are responsible for constructing houses; the city supports low-income residents by providing housing subsidies.

Most program sites are located in the southern and western peripheries of the city (figure 3.10). The planned sites are large, ranging from 0.35 square kilometers (La Palestina, Bosa) to 9.3 square kilometers (Operation Nuevo Usme, Usme), with about 2,000–36,000 housing units planned for each site. As the Metrovivienda needed to acquire lands quickly and at low prices before the construction of the BRT in order to keep housing affordable, most land is located in the city's outlying areas. Because Metrovivienda officials sit on the board of the TransMilenio, they can be strategic about connecting Metrovivienda sites and the BRT system.

Between 2001 and 2007, about 45,000 units were sold, mostly to low-income groups (Gilbert 2009). Needy populations who moved from the hillsides to the Metrovivienda currently enjoy better housing as well as shorter commutes and lower commuting costs. Before relocation, residents spent $1.40 a day on average for commuting. After moving, their daily commuting costs fell to $0.80, thanks to proximity to the TransMilenio stations (Cervero 2005).

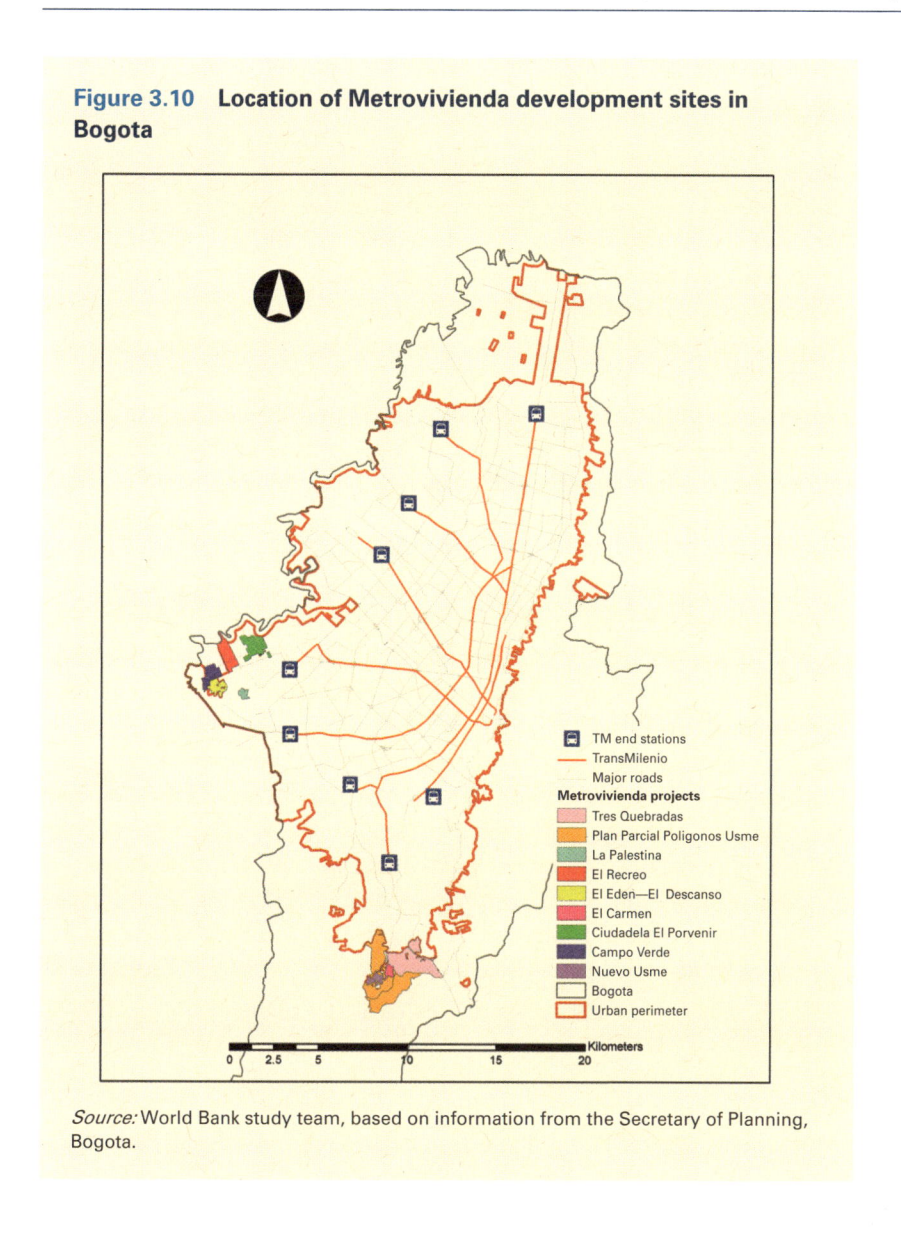

Figure 3.10 Location of Metrovivienda development sites in Bogota

Source: World Bank study team, based on information from the Secretary of Planning, Bogota.

Using innovative financing schemes. Bogota has an innovative land value capture scheme under which the city receives about 30–50 percent of the increase in land value that results from public investments (for example, parks, cycle ways, and pedestrian ways), which it uses for Metrovivienda projects and other social development purposes.

PPPs are also used in public infrastructure development and operation. TransMilenio is operated and managed by TransMilenio S.A., which was created by several public agencies under a PPP scheme. National and city governments financed the construction costs of the BRT infrastructure.[18] TransMilenio S.A. is responsible for designing, planning, and monitoring the system and monitoring the private operators in charge of system operations and maintenance, who are selected through a competitive bidding process.

Overcoming Obstacles to Sustainability

Bogota has adopted many progressive policies and innovative measures in making spaces more mobile and vibrant. But challenges remain, including the need to coordinate TransMilenio with land use. Institutional inefficiencies, weak regional coordination, ineffectual density policies, and a lack of physical design considerations and sensitivity exacerbate this disjoint.

Institutional difficulties with executing spatial plans. Bogota's planning system is considered to be one of the most sophisticated in Latin America. It follows the same hierarchically structured urban planning system found in some cities in developed countries, such as Barcelona, Spain. The system uses a Territorial Ordinance Plan (POT) to guide its spatial development.[19] Adopted in 2000, the current POT envisions Bogota evolving over the mid- to long-term into a dense, compact, and integrated city with a mobility system that gives priority to public over private transportation, and pedestrian over vehicular. As a spatial development strategy, it also envisages higher density in BRT corridors.

Three planning instruments fall under the POT: sectoral master plans (prepared every 12 years), a development plan (prepared every 4 years), and project budget plans (prepared annually). Under the POT are 112 smaller planning units—Zonal Planning Units (UPZ), which focus on district-level planning (Zonal Plans [PZ]). By statutory decree, the UPZs aim to define and regulate urban land use in detail—specifying maximum FARs, land use, and activities, for example—to realize the POT (Bocarejo, Portilla, and Perez 2012).

Of the 12 administrative offices in the City of Bogota, the 4 offices most relevant for transportation and urban development are the offices of mobility, planning, habitat, and culture. These offices are responsible for planning and implementing sectoral master plans from the POT in close collaboration as part of the development of an integrated development plan. Cross-sectoral coordination is often difficult, however, because many offices are decentralized and divided into diversified public offices, commerce and industry companies, and public utility companies with different functions. For example, the mobility sector, led by the Office of Mobility, consists of TransMilenio S.A. and the Urban Development Institute (IDU) acting as its special agency. The habitat sector, led by the Habitat Office, consists of Metrovivienda, the Urban Renovation Company (ERU), and the public utilities companies (figure 3.11).

Elected mayors are legally mandated to develop a four-year development plan for their term. Conceptually, the development plan needs to be aligned with the mid- and long-term POT. However, mayors often capitalize on this valuable opportunity to tie their campaign commitments to the city's

Figure 3.11 City offices in Bogota responsible for transportation and urban development

```
                        Mayor's office
        ┌───────────────┬───────────────┬───────────────┐
   Mobility Sector  Planning Sector  Habitat Sector  Culture Sector
```

Central level:
- Mobility Office
- Planning Office
- Habitat Office
- Culture and Sport Office

Decentralized level:
- Urban Development Institute (IDU)
- Transmilenio S.A.
- MetroVivienda
- Urban Renovation Company (ERU)
- Public Utilities Companies (EAAB-ETB-EEB)
- Recreation and Sport Institute (IDRD)

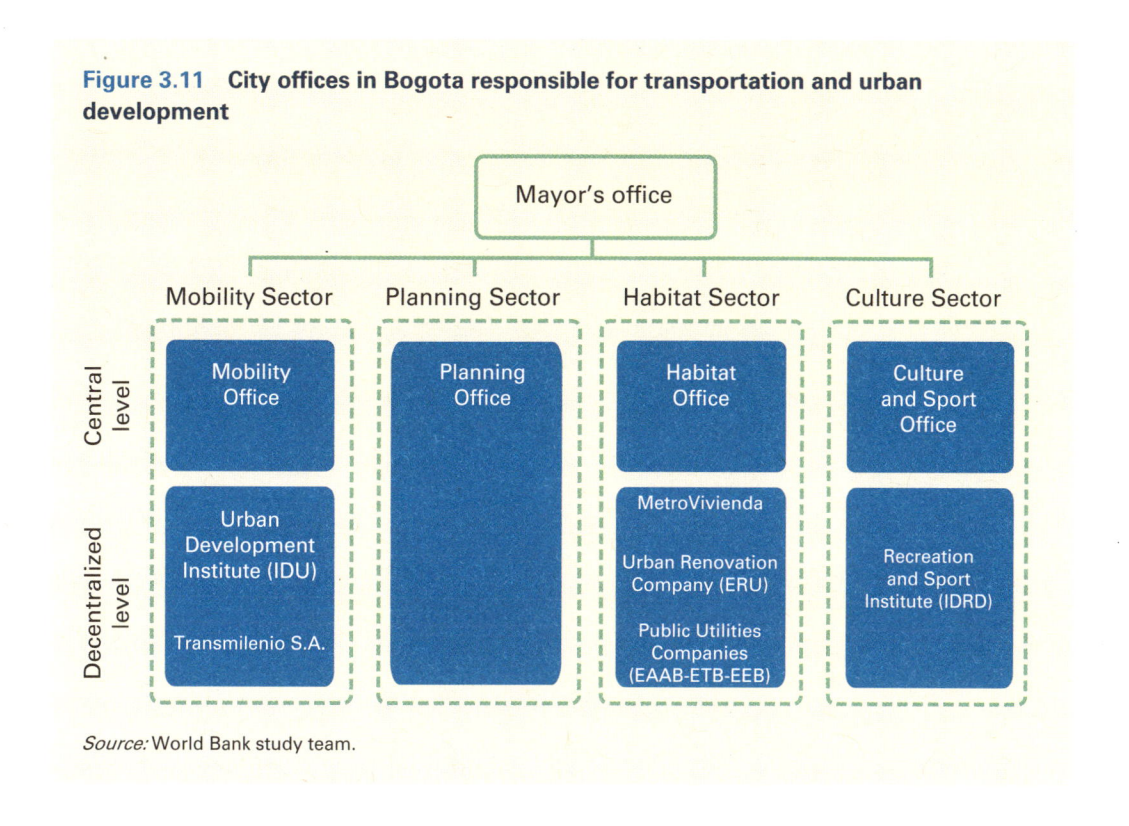

Source: World Bank study team.

spatial development, which they work hard to realize within their term. As a result, development plans are seldom consistent with the mid- and long-term POT and vary from term to term.

Executing spatial plans is often problematic under the current planning system and administrative structure. Although the decentralized administrative system is vertically aligned, allowing sectoral planning and development to be carried out seamlessly, horizontal connection across sectors is weak, making integration of planning visions and implementation difficult. The result is misaligned sectoral master plans, aims, and targeted time to completion. This administrative structure further complicates efforts to gain approval for annual budgets of planned projects.

There are also inconsistencies between master plans created under the POT, PZs, and UPZs. Despite the need for revising PZs and details of development in the UPZ in alignment with the revised POT and master plans, the contents of PZs are often infrastructure based and inherently less coordinated for integration. For instance, the strategy to increase building density along the BRT corridors as stated in the Bogota POT has not yet materialized, because of the unchanged FAR policies at the UPZ level. In addition, the three zonal plans—Zonal Plan North, Zonal Plan Centro, and Zonal Plan New Usme—do not necessarily align with the city-level master plans. As a result, POT implementation has not been as successful as envisioned.

Bogota's system of spatial planning and its decentralized administrative systems, with varied ownership, hinder sectoral collaboration and create plan inconsistencies. The system also makes implementation of development projects complicated and time consuming. Implementing a single plan in an integrated way requires working through several different administrative offices and entities at various hierarchical levels. Implementation becomes even more complicated if land parcels need to be consolidated. These institutional challenges are partially responsible for preventing developers from undertaking major urban development projects, particularly large-scale urban regeneration projects that would reflect new economic opportunities created by transit investments.

Weak regional coordination. The City of Bogota and the municipalities in the Cundinamarca Department (whose capital is Bogota) strongly recognize the need to coordinate spatially and systematically in order to accommodate growing population and economic activities. Several key efforts have been made. In 2008, the City of Bogota and surrounding municipalities created a metropolitan administrative unit (the "Regions Capital") to ensure implementation of well-integrated plans and programs, integral development, and timely and efficient service delivery. They are currently working on unifying various activities under the Regional Territorial Occupation Model, following the Territorial Ordinance Organic Law (LOOT) (figure 3.12).[20] Activities include interregional projects, such as the metro line, the regional train, and the revitalization of the River Bogota, to name a few.

As yet, weak horizontal connection between the City of Bogota and Cundinamarca's administrations make regional coordination complicated and inefficient. Like the City of Bogota's planning system, the regional system continues to be difficult to navigate. None of the plans and projects envisioned in the Regional Territorial Occupation Model for a more integrated metropolis has been implemented, and the planned regional transportation system has not yet achieved success.

Issues on policy regarding density. As seen in Ahmedabad, one of the key challenges for transit and land-use integration lies with the policy on land density. As the 2010 cadastral data of Bogota illustrate, the distribution of building density in Bogota is low, with an average FAR of less than 2 in most areas outside the central and subcentral business districts. The FAR ceiling in areas closest to the BRT stations and corridors remains unchanged, though their land values have increased as a result of the TransMilenio investment (Bocarejo, Portilla, and Perez 2012).

Some of the reasons why building densification along the TransMilenio station is not higher are technical and administrative complications associated with redevelopment. Tearing down old buildings and redeveloping the areas involved in land consolidation take much more time and money than developing greenfields. A low FAR reduces landowners' or private developers' interest in redeveloping stations areas that are already built

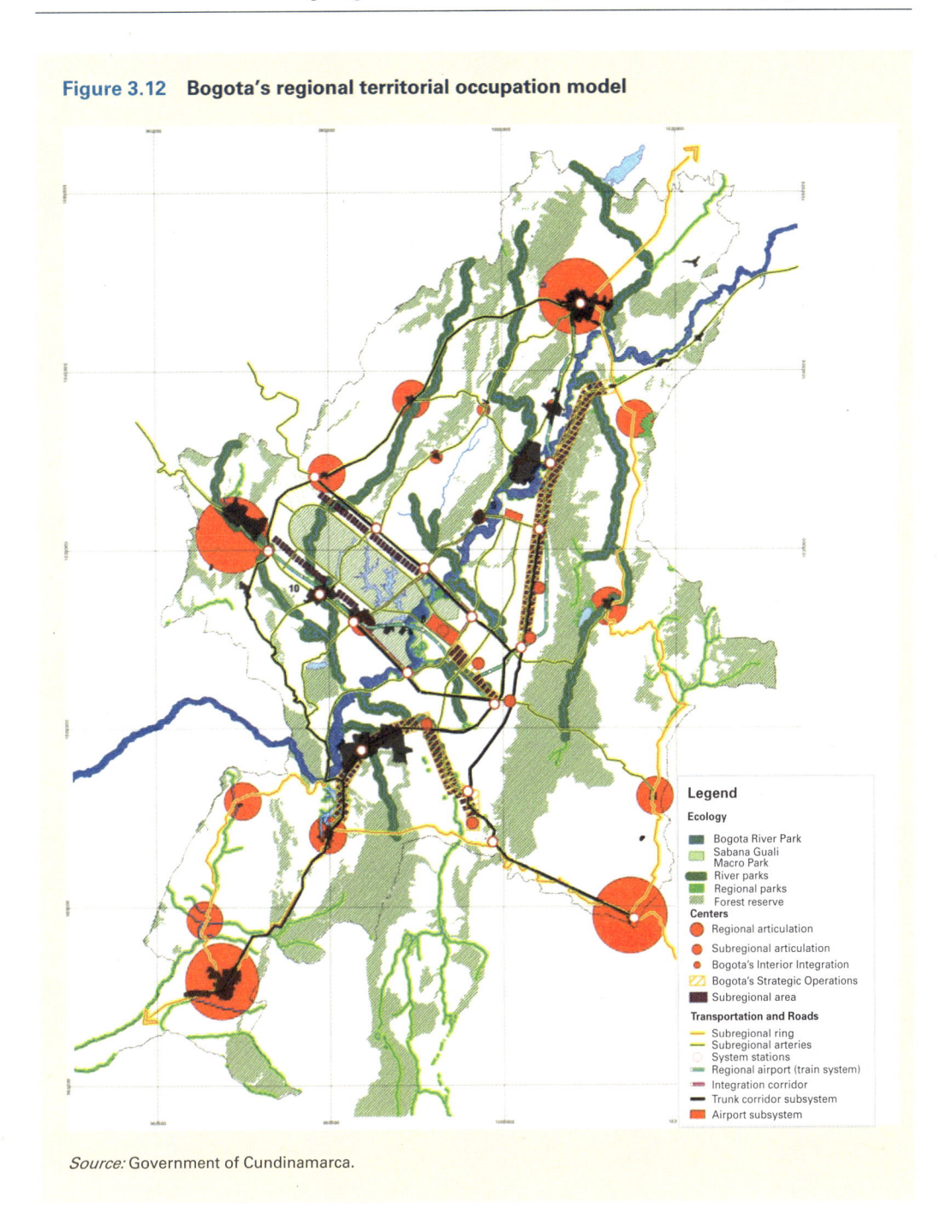

Figure 3.12 Bogota's regional territorial occupation model

Source: Government of Cundinamarca.

up. Greenfield development around peripheral stations is not eligible to take advantage of increasing building volume, which would have allowed accommodation of a growing population with good accessibility to cities.

Many North American cities aiming for transit-friendly spaces are developing TOD guidelines to establish close connections between transit and land use. These guidelines often focus on redevelopment and upgrading of areas around key transit nodes in order to minimize expansion of built-up areas while revitalizing underutilized or non-preferred portions of land. Local officials, private developers, landowners, and community members are included in this process; knowledge is shared and discussed with key stakeholders for optimal results. These TOD guidelines typically explain how TOD shapes the region and benefits people, and outline activities needed for success.

Guidelines detailing ways to develop a nexus of transit, urban development, and thriving communities have yet to be developed in Bogota. New legislation related to this nexus needs to be introduced to leverage TOD development and redevelopment.

Shortcomings in microdesign of the transit system. Physical design considerations are important for promoting transit usage. Many of the bicycle and pedestrian ways expanded over the past few years upgraded the city's mobility system by feeding into the TransMilenio. As an integrated system, the network has been providing opportunities to accommodate nonmotorized transport (for example, biking and using public transit) as an alternative to private automobiles.

Designs for the surrounding micro-spaces are still treated as afterthoughts, however. The skywalks that connect sidewalks to the entrances of TransMilenio are visually unattractive, resonate loud noises, and create inefficient, circuitous routes. They can be a challenge to use for older people and people with impaired mobility. Because only a few stations provide safe, secure parking for bikes, they are still not fully supported as a mode of access to TransMilenio, despite the connectivity with *cicloruta* and other greenways. Such design flaws inhibit maximum utility for transit riders.

The physical linkage of TransMilenio stations to immediately surrounding neighborhoods could be vastly improved. Open spaces where overpasses are located are often underutilized; they could be made more vibrant by adding design components and street furniture as well as designing them to reflect the flow of people. Stations at the end of the lines are often sterile, with no amenities other than large parking lots. Areas along the TransMilenio lanes were built without considering the urban facade. For example, while the BRT system was under development, TransMilenio S.A. acquired land along the Av. NQS lane to promote TOD along the corridor. These spaces between the transit system and other urban activities were left segregated, however, because ERU, which was in charge of developing them, had no incentives to create integrated space (figure 3.13). Lanes along Las Americas and Calle 26 suffer from the same problem.

Embracing Opportunities for Sustainable Growth

Bogota has significant opportunities to transform itself into a great transit-oriented metropolis. The city is filled with progressive development initiatives and few restrictive land-use regulations. It addresses urban poverty

Figure 3.13 Unattractive, disconnected space in the TransMilenio corridors

a. Urban facade in the NQS corridor

b. Urban facade in the Las Americas corridor

Photos by Alejandro Rodriguez.

inclusively, by connecting social housing sites with public transport. Despite various impediments to immediate TOD implementation, Bogota's continuing efforts with innovative TDM measures set the stage for advanced development toward integration.

Short-term congestion-relief objectives drove early phases of the TransMilenio. Many city stakeholders and government officials in particular are now reconceptualizing how transit and urban space should interact. National, regional, and city governments currently place greater emphasis on integration of the transit system, strategic spatial development with densification and mixed land use, spatial design for place-making objectives, and value capture for infrastructure investments. Redevelopment of the central station is an example of TOD in TransMilenio nodes. Opportunities to both develop and redevelop a better built environment by strategically integrating transit, such as a metro and green transit corridor on Carrera 7, are emerging.

To enhance mass transit, Bogota is developing a high-capacity metro system, which will be integrated with other public transit modes, including regional trains and extended BRT lines. This integrated transit system is being developed based on the concept of a Public Transportation Integrated System (SITP), created under the Mobility Master Plan, which aims to strengthen a unified and comprehensive transit system that facilitates modal exchange by integrating mass transit.[21] The metro system will eventually run throughout the city, beginning with the city's eastern edge (figure

Figure 3.14 Proposed metro network in Bogota

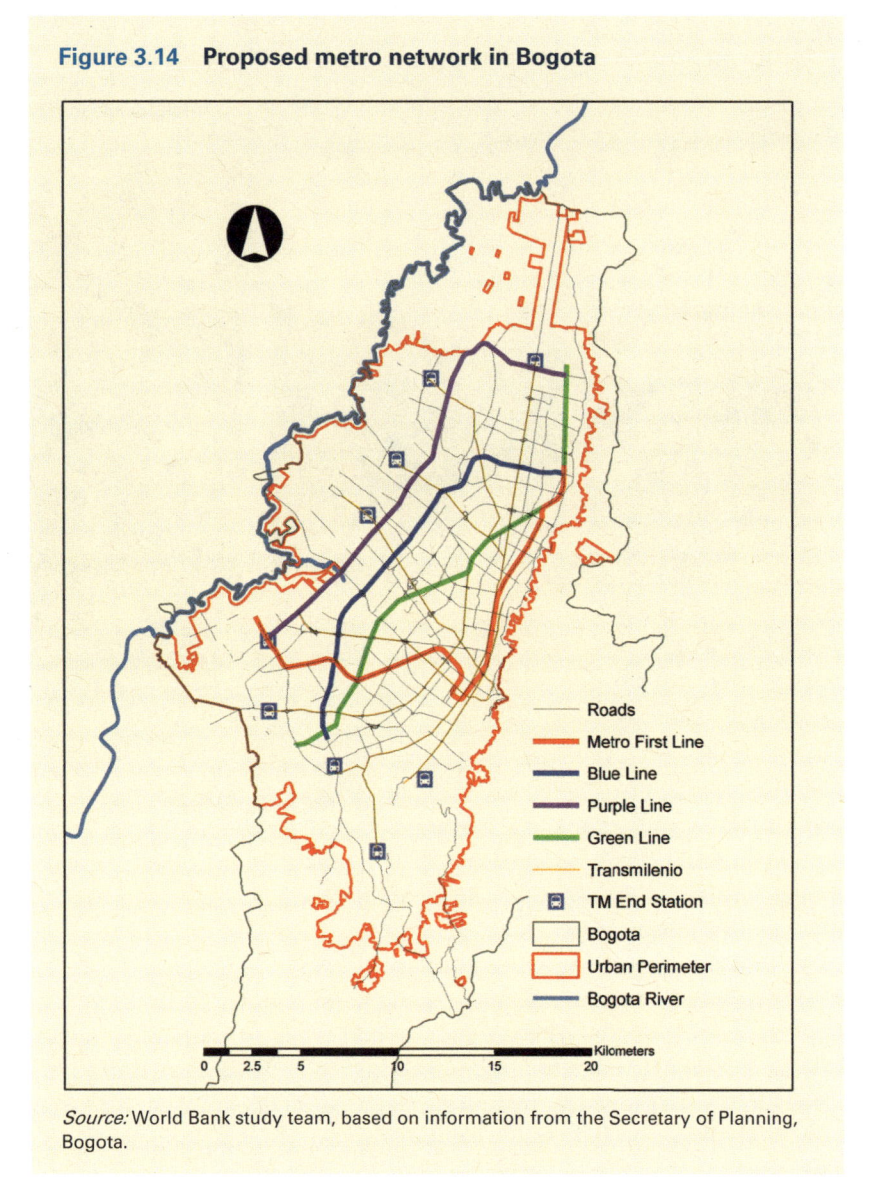

Source: World Bank study team, based on information from the Secretary of Planning, Bogota.

3.14). The plan has strategic implications for the sustainability of the urban districts as well as the increasing competitiveness of the expanded central business districts and regional nodes. As such, it has enormous potential to leverage TOD with legislative support on guidelines and effective utilization of the value capture system.

The Green Corridor project also has potential to radically change urban design and create a transit-supportive built environment in one of the busiest, most congested parts of the city. This project aims to solve the problems of mobility and pollution along Carrera 7 by integrating transit with the built environment. Plans include light rail and the promotion of New Urbanism, supported by an innovative financial system and a revised land-use policy for strategic densification.[22] Through these projects, Bogota's downtown could be transformed into one of the more economically active, environmentally friendly, and vibrant city districts. The gradual shift to a larger metropolitan transit system would also support longer-term development and redevelopment possibilities.

These new, integrated transit development projects would also provide excellent opportunities for the city to proactively pursue value capture financing schemes, by selling or leasing air or underground use rights in close collaboration with private developers. The revenue generated could finance a part of transit infrastructure costs, social housing costs, and investments needed for better place making in TOD areas.

Bogota could experience another stage of transformation by addressing the strategic development of space with transit improvement. For areas that are less developed, nodes of planned public transit—metro lines, regional rails, or the TransMilenio extension—should focus on shaping space to accommodate increased density with varied building heights and mixed-use zoning, as well as creating pedestrian-oriented areas with sidewalks, carefully articulated streetscapes, and parks. The redevelopment of areas along the TransMilenio system should be promoted through modified land-use and building regulations to obtain increased building volume and strategic land use.

Many factors favor sustainable development in Bogota, and the culture supporting integration has expanded among various urban actors. By addressing major impediments in the process of development and redevelopment—an ineffective planning system that hinders coordinated planning and implementation, micro-design shortcomings in transit–urban development linkages, outdated building density policies, and weak regional coordination—the city should be more livable, enjoyable, and sustainable (Bogota and its BRT system at a glance are shown in box 3.5).

Guangzhou: Adaptive Bus Rapid Transit

The city of Guangzhou is located in southwestern China, a 15-minute flight from Hong Kong SAR, China. It is the third-largest city in the country, with a population of almost 15 million. The city is the center of the northern Pearl River Delta urban cluster, with a population of 25 million—one of the world's largest urban agglomerations.

The Guangzhou Bus Rapid Transit System

Guangzhou opened its 22.5-kilometer BRT corridor in 2010, with the aim of cutting congestion on one of the city's busiest roads, Zhongshan Avenue, and improving the efficiency of the city's bus system. Today the Guangzhou BRT boasts 850,000 average weekday boardings, making it the busiest bus corridor in Asia (and the second-busiest bus corridor in the world, after Bogota), with more than three times the peak passenger flows of any other BRT system in Asia. Guangzhou's BRT is already carrying

Box 3.5 Bogota and its bus rapid transit system at a glance

Table B3.5.1 Population statistics for Bogota, Colombia

Item	Figure
Population 2010 (million)	
City	7.4
Metropolitan region	9.0
Area (square kilometers)	
City	1,587
(Urban area)	384
Metropolitan area	3,811
(Urban area)	488
Population density (people/square kilometer, urban)	
City	19,177
Metropolitan area	18,420
Annual population growth rate 2001–11 (percent)	
City	1.13

Source: World Bank study team.

Figure B3.5.1 Map of Bogota, Colombia

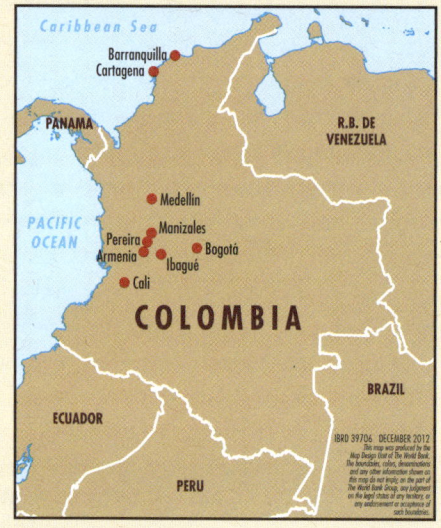

Source: World Bank.

Table B3.5.2 Capacity and infrastructure of the TransMilenio bus rapid transit (BRT) system

Feature	Figure
Daily carrying capacity	More than 1.5 million
Covered population	66% within 1 kilometer of the trunk and feeder lane buffer zone
Phase I	42 kilometers
Phase II	42 kilometers
Phase III	28 kilometers
Feeder system	200 kilometers

Source: World Bank study team.

Figure B3.5.2 TransMilenio bus in Bogota, Colombia

Photo by Hiroaki Suzuki.

more daily passengers than all five of the city's metro lines. According to the Institute for Transportation and Development Policy (ITDP), it has reduced travel times by 29 percent for bus passengers and 20 percent for drivers, for an aggregate annual time saving of 52 million hours, including 32 million hours for bus passengers, a value of RMB 158 million ($23 million). The system has also made the city's bus operations more efficient. After an initial capital investment of RMB 950 million (about $139 million) for BRT stations and lanes, the system reduced annual operating costs by more than RMB 90 million (about $13 million).

In addition to the BRT, Guangzhou created a new, high-quality greenway along the corridor. It also provides bike parking and a bike-sharing system at most BRT stations, as well as adjacent neighborhoods. The bike-sharing system consists of 5,000 bikes at 109 stations along the BRT corridor. The same smart card used for BRT station access is used to access the bike-sharing system, with free rides provided the first hour. Bike sharing allows the BRT to attract passengers from a wider radius. It also provides an option for passengers who would ordinarily travel just one or two stops, helping alleviate BRT crowding.[23]

The system has had a significant effect on the environment and public health. Together with the Guangzhou Municipal Engineering Design and Research Institute, the Institute for Transportation and Development Policy led the Guangzhou BRT planning and design from early conceptual planning in 2005 through to the planning, design, construction, and operation of the system. It estimates that Guangzhou's BRT will help reduce an average of 86,000 tons of CO_2 per year over its first 10 years (for a yearly certified emission reduction value of RMB 19 million [about $2.8 million]). The BRT will also reduce the emission of particulate matter, which causes respiratory illness, by an estimated four tons.

The Guangzhou BRT has several unique features:

- It is the first high-capacity BRT system in the world to use an open-system operational mode rather than a trunk-feeder model. Open-system operations mean BRT buses operate both inside and outside the BRT corridor, allowing passengers to make far fewer transfers and obviating the need for terminals and interchange stations.
- It is the first demonstration of the viability of metro-scale BRT in Asia.
- It features the world's first direct BRT–metro station connection (at Shipaiqiao Station), which also connects to a large adjacent new commercial development built by a developer from Hong Kong SAR, China.
- It is a model of highly cost-effective urban transport.
- It is the first BRT system in China to contract multiple bus operating companies for service provision. Bus operators are paid a percentage of the total passenger revenue based on the number of bus-kilometers they drive, with adjustments for service quality and performance criteria calculated monthly.

The Guangzhou BRT corridor along Zhongshan Avenue links some of Guangzhou's most developed areas to places where future growth is expected, such as the eastern portion of central Guangzhou (figure 3.15). The corridor begins at its western end in the Tianhe District, which has seen intense development over the past 20 years, including metro and railway stations, many high-rise residential developments, large shopping complexes, the huge Gangding computer and electronics center, and office towers in a new central business district area. The corridor continues 22.5 kilometers

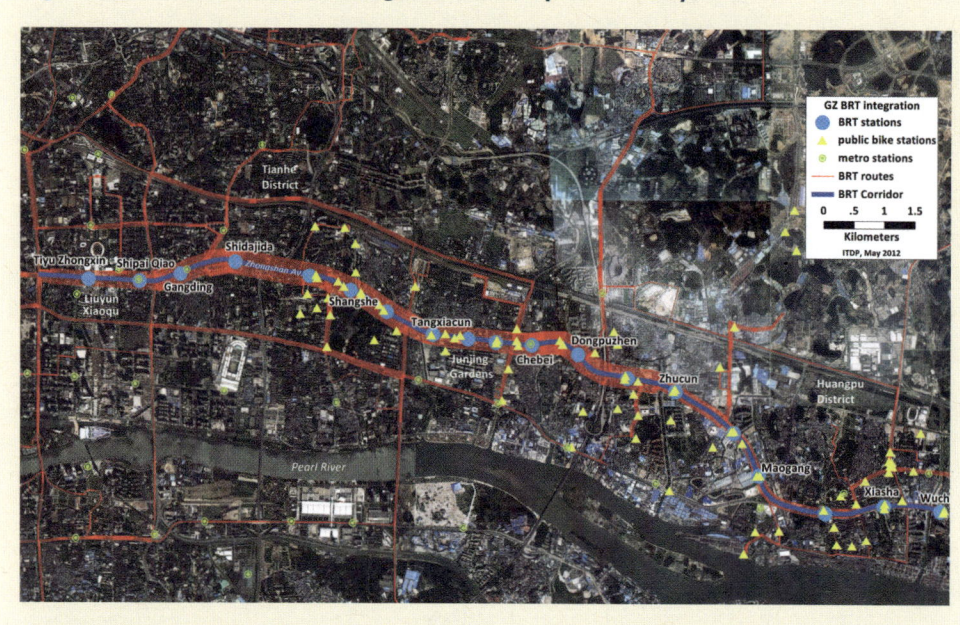

Figure 3.15 Aerial view of Guangzhou's bus rapid transit system

Source: Courtesy of ITDP.
Note: The 22.5-kilometer system has 26 stations.

through eastern Tianhe into the Huangpu District, which is dense, diverse in land uses, and growing quickly. Eastern Tianhe and Huangpu have old, ultra-dense, unplanned, low-rise "urban villages" like Tangxia; large new gated communities filled with dozens of high-rise residential towers such as Junjing Huayuan; large public parks; universities; large industrial sites; and even some agricultural sites on the as yet underdeveloped far eastern end of the corridor.

The BRT corridor along Zhongshan Avenue features 22.5 kilometers of fully segregated bus lanes, 26 BRT stations, and 31 bus routes (not including a dozen or so short routes, operating mainly during peak hours, and express route variations). All stations have overtaking lanes, allowing multiple substops, and express routes and are designed and dimensioned based on projected passenger demand and bus flows. Access to the center median stations of the BRT is through a combination of pedestrian bridges, at-grade crossings, and pedestrian tunnels. Intersections along the corridor have restricted left turns. Many BRT routes extend well beyond the BRT corridor itself, covering another 250 kilometers of roads with BRT service.

Before the BRT was built, about 80 bus routes serviced curbside stops in the Zhongshan corridor, although many serviced only short sections of the corridor. As curbside bus stops did not have sufficient length or capacity, buses were often prevented from stopping at the curb or close to the specified route stops, making access difficult and unsafe. Without segregated lanes for buses and mixed traffic, the frequently stopping buses slowed mixed traffic in the corridor.

Figure 3.16 Area around the Gangding station in Guangzhou before and after construction of the bus rapid transit system

a. Before construction of the BRT system   b. The BRT system in place

Source: ITDP 2011.

In 2010, the BRT bus fleet consisted of 980, mostly 12-meter long, low-floor buses powered by liquefied petroleum gas (LPG). In 2011, the fleet was expanded to include higher-capacity 18-meter long buses with three doors for boarding. Stations and buses are equipped with intelligent transportation systems that support real-time station arrival signage and enable centralized monitoring and control.

In the BRT corridor, passengers pay fares at station-entry turnstiles rather than on the buses. All stations have at-grade boarding. Low-floor buses provide easier entry and exit on and off the BRT corridor. Stations consist of multiple substops. BRT routes have been allocated to substops to maximize passenger convenience (for passengers who are going to an area served by several routes) and to ensure that queuing at one substop does not interfere with other substops.

Real-time digital displays at each substop within the station alert passengers to which buses will be arriving at which gates. For safety, each bus-boarding gate has sliding glass panels that open only when a bus has arrived at the gate. Each station has separate east- and westbound waiting platforms located on corresponding sides of the bus lanes. Stations have a sleek, modern look, are clean, and are well lit at night. Their sizes were calibrated to meet modeled demand and the needs of bus operations. Some stations are as short as 55 meters. Gangding, the busiest station in the world, at 55,000 daily boardings, is 250 meters long (one of the world's largest) and has multiple pedestrian bridges for access (figure 3.16).

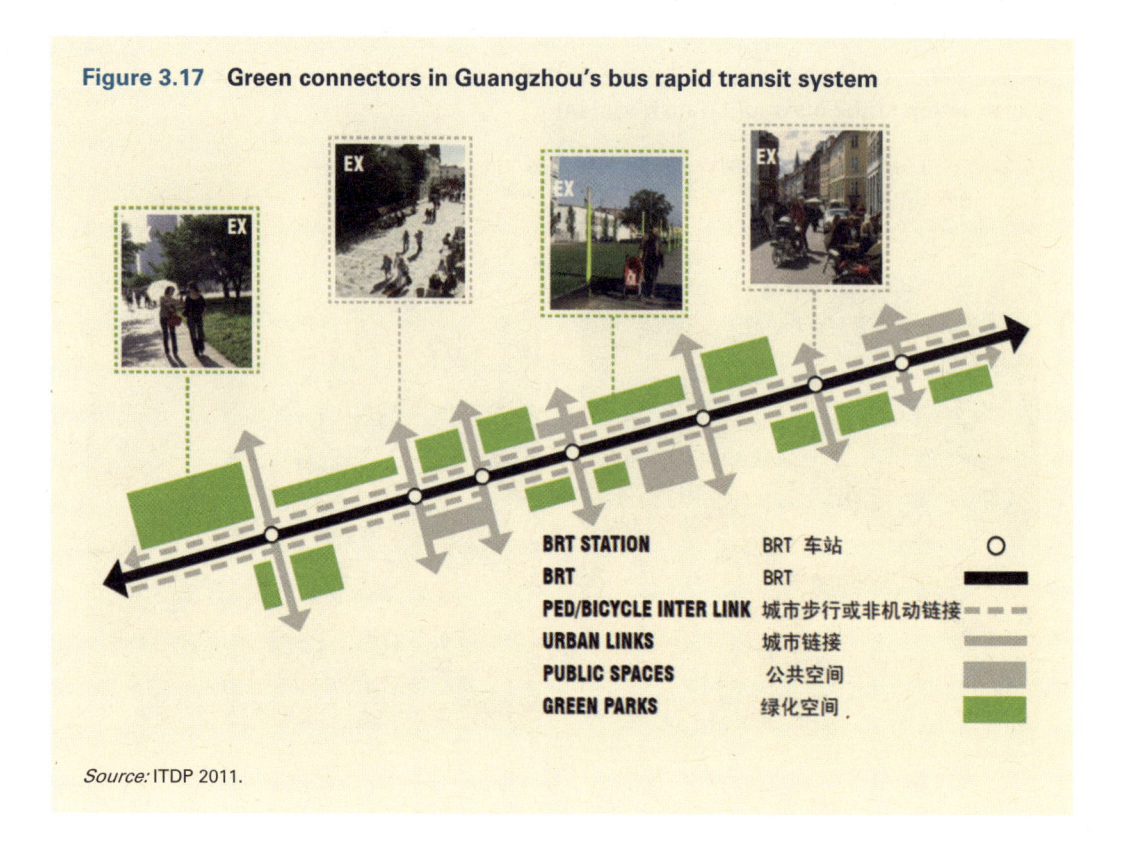

Figure 3.17 Green connectors in Guangzhou's bus rapid transit system

BRT STATION	BRT 车站	○
BRT	BRT	▬
PED/BICYCLE INTER LINK	城市步行或非机动链接	-----
URBAN LINKS	城市链接	▬
PUBLIC SPACES	公共空间	▬
GREEN PARKS	绿化空间	▬

Source: ITDP 2011.

Integrating Transit Modes and Improving Public Areas

Together with BRT development, Guangzhou is investing in facilities that promote modal integration between BRT and nonmotorized transport (figure 3.17). It has improved footpaths; installed escalators at key stations; added about 20 safe crossings along the corridor, effectively solving walkway crowding problems at bus stops; created bike lanes; and integrated free bicycle parking lots and bike-sharing systems at most BRT stations (figure 3.18).

These investments have significantly improved perceptions of pedestrian safety and the quality of the walking environment. Surveys by the Institute for Transportation and Development Policy record an increase in the percentage of respondents that agree with the statement, "I feel safe walking along Zhongshan Avenue" from 28 percent before the BRT investments to 68 percent afterward. The city is also making efforts to improve the quality of public space near the BRT, by developing linear parks and installing other civic amenities.

Greening the Bus Rapid Transit Corridor

Guangzhou began implementing a greenway improvement project in 2010, creating hundreds of kilometers of green corridors across the city. This scheme saw the restoration of the Donghaochong Canal, an ancient canal that dates back to the Song Dynasty, which several BRT routes serve. The

Figure 3.18 Bike-sharing station in Guangzhou

Source: ITDP 2011.
Note: The Huajing Xincheng BRT station is in the background.

Figure 3.19 Restoration of the Donghaochong Canal in Guangzhou

a. Before

b. After

Source: ITDP 2011.

effort is part of a major project to clean up waterways around the city, including several canals connecting with the BRT corridor.

Until recently, the Donghaochong Canal was a polluted ditch running mostly under an elevated expressway (figure 3.19). Uncontrolled urban development had encroached on the banks of the canal, and buildings were periodically flooded when waters overflowed the banks, sometimes spilling sewage into adjacent residential and commercial properties. Starting in 2009, a 3-kilometer stretch of land along the Donghaochong Canal was cleared and turned into a greenway, featuring world-class walking and cycling facilities and popular new green public spaces.

In the surrounding area, more than 329,000 square meters of new commercial real estate is being developed. The Donghaochong Canal Museum, housed in two historic villas, recently opened, providing information on the canal and its history. The greenway project attracts people to live, work, and play and has become a popular free swimming area in the summer.

Although the Donghaochong Canal restoration project was not directly coordinated with the BRT project, improvements in this area and in public spaces and pedestrian facilities along the BRT corridor will help retain high levels of transit passengers, by ensuring that corridors for accessing BRT by walking and cycling are attractive and vibrant. A similar transformation of a drab streetscape into a spectacular public space was achieved through the restoration of the Lizhiwan Canal, which also opened in 2010.[24]

Market Response

There was no corridor-wide institutional effort to coordinate transit and land use in the design of Guangzhou's BRT project, although, as discussed above, municipal agencies took many steps to link nonmotorized transport to station areas along the corridor. However, by serving the city's highest-density and most congested corridor, the Guangzhou BRT significantly improved public transit service in the city core, attracting new development.

With its very high capacity and ability to accommodate future growth along the corridor, the BRT system makes very high urban densities along the corridor a possibility, especially in the relatively less-developed eastern part of the city. Without BRT, residents of high-density developments would face daily gridlock. Before BRT, bus speeds were often as slow as 10 kilometers per hour—and poised to slow even more. Frequent, reliable, and comfortable transit services are necessary to attract private real estate investors. When complemented by supportive land-use zoning, attractive urban designs around stations, and other measures, such service can lead to compact, mixed-use development around BRT stations.

Although it is too early to evaluate the impact of the BRT on land-use patterns, the real estate market appears to be positively responding to the enhanced mobility provided by BRT. Densification and diversification of land use is taking place in the western part of the corridor. Many new high-rise buildings are being constructed in the less-developed eastern part of the corridor, previously occupied by degraded building stock and low-value land uses.

According to preliminary findings by ITDP, average residential and commercial real estate prices of properties along the BRT corridor increased more than 30 percent over the Tianhe district average during the first two years of BRT operation. The land-use pattern is also becoming more

Figure 3.20 Enhanced mixed land use of existing multistory apartment in Liuyun Xiaoqu community of Guangzhou

Source: ITDP 2011.

diversified and modernized. Service-oriented commercial, other facilities, and high-rise housing are replacing factory, logistical, and agricultural uses. Although no policy specifically promotes development along the BRT corridor, in practice, the city's planning authorities are more inclined to allow higher-density developments there, in recognition of the need for improved traffic conditions. The authorities are also open to relaxing minimum parking standards in light of the BRT's presence.

The most striking example of such densification is Junjing Gardens, an apartment complex housing more than 30,000 people. An expansion to the complex currently being built will increase the number of residents to more than 50,000. Because it is next to the central portion of the BRT corridor, most residents will be able to rely on BRT for longer-distance travel.

A related land-use development just south of the first BRT station is the revitalization of socialist-era *danwei* (work unit housing) at Liuyun Xiaoqu Community, where a major upgrade was completed in 2010. The community was fully pedestrianized, with beautiful landscaping; gates were torn down to allow public access; fancy boutiques and restaurants were installed on the ground floor; and a central pedestrian plaza replaced a road (figure 3.20).

Benefits for All

Both lower- and higher-income households along the BRT corridors are enjoying benefits from the project. During construction, many car owners opposed the BRT, fearing traffic conditions would worsen because of the reduced road space for cars. In fact, the BRT has improved not only bus speed and travel time but also private car speeds and travel time.

For people without cars, the BRT system has significantly enhanced regional accessibility by reducing the amount of time needed to travel around the city. It has also reduced travel costs, as users can transfer for free from BRT buses to other buses serving different routes. Preliminary analyses show that the BRT has also increased land values in the urban villages along the BRT corridor, although a longer time frame is needed before firm conclusions can be reached.[25] BRT has also improved environmental conditions, helping reduce tailpipe emissions by removing cars from the highway, conserving energy, and reducing greenhouse gas emissions.

Ho Chi Minh City: Building a Green Transit Corridor

Ho Chi Minh City, formerly called Saigon, is located on the banks of the Saigon River, 60 kilometers from the coast of the South China Sea and 1,140 kilometers south of Hanoi by road. It is the most populous city in Vietnam, with more than 7.3 million inhabitants in the city proper and more than 9.0 million inhabitants in the metropolitan area. The city's population is projected to reach 12 million inhabitants by 2020. Ho Chi Minh City is also the largest economic development center in Vietnam, generating roughly 20 percent of the national GDP and 71 percent of seaport throughput.

Much of the city's recent population and job growth has taken place on the city's periphery, particularly northwest of the city center. The central business district has also seen significant growth in the past few years, with the development of new office towers and apartment buildings.

Rapid economic and population growth has shaped Ho Chi Minh City's urban form into an increasingly sprawling city that is expanding outward but not upward. The mobility afforded by motorbikes has led to "leap-frog development," which has increased congestion.[26] More than 60 percent of passenger trips in the city are by motorbike—and less than 4 percent by bus.

Rapid growth in automobile use will quickly fill the limited road space. Although Ho Chi Minh City has the densities to support mass transit, infrastructure and commuter habits are not yet in place. Major metro investments are planned, but could take 15 years to yield a measurable impact. Meanwhile, worsening congestion is adversely affecting the city's competitiveness.

To address the problems caused by congestion, city officials asked the World Bank to help them develop and finance a new 25-kilometer BRT system (figure 3.21). The proposed system runs from the west along the

Figure 3.21 Proposed bus rapid transit system in Ho Chi Minh City

a. Proposed route of BRT system

b. Strategic green transit corridor study area

Source: World Bank 2012; maps and drawings prepared by Lyon Town Planning Agency/Deso.
Note: The red line in panels a and b shows the proposed BRT route. The green shaded area in panel b shows the strategic green transit corridor area.

Ben Nghe Tan Hu Canal, through the city center, and then east toward the new development area (District 2) (figure 3.22). City officials wanted to optimize the use of the proposed BRT investment as a catalyst project to redevelop a blighted canal area into a green transit corridor in order to enhance mobility, better utilize and capture the value of the surrounding land, improve the quality of life of the residents, and make the corridor a signature destination by creating an attractive environment with an infusion of new public spaces.

Figure 3.22 Current state of green transit corridor in Ho Chi Minh City

Source: Work Bank 2012.

Figure 3.23 Typical working sessions held to plan the Ho Chi Minh City bus rapid transit system

a. Large meeting with stakeholders

b. Smaller breakout session

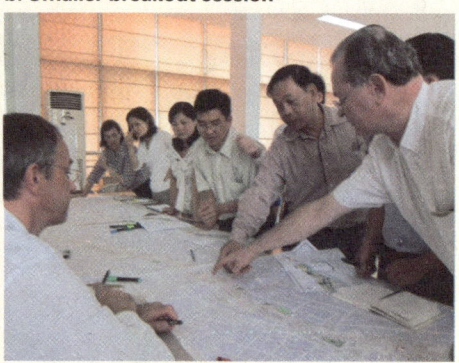

Source: World Bank 2012.
Note: Typical working sessions included large meetings with all key stakeholders and smaller breakout discussions. Facilitators ensured that all participants were actively engaged.

With the support of the World Bank and PADDI (a French planning organization dispatched to Ho Chi Minh City), in July 2011, Ho Chi Minh City's Department of Transport and Department of Planning and Architecture held a *charrette* to develop a key design concept for the green transit corridor. A *charrette* is a collaborative design and planning workshop that occurs during four to seven consecutive days, is held on-site, and involves stakeholders at critical decision-making points (NCI 2006).

Over the course of five days, event participants identified key concepts, design considerations, sitings of BRT stations, and strategies to optimize the built space to support transit use (figure 3.23). The end result of the *charrette* was a concept design, created through a consensus-based process that had strong ownership from all stakeholders. Collectively, stakeholders

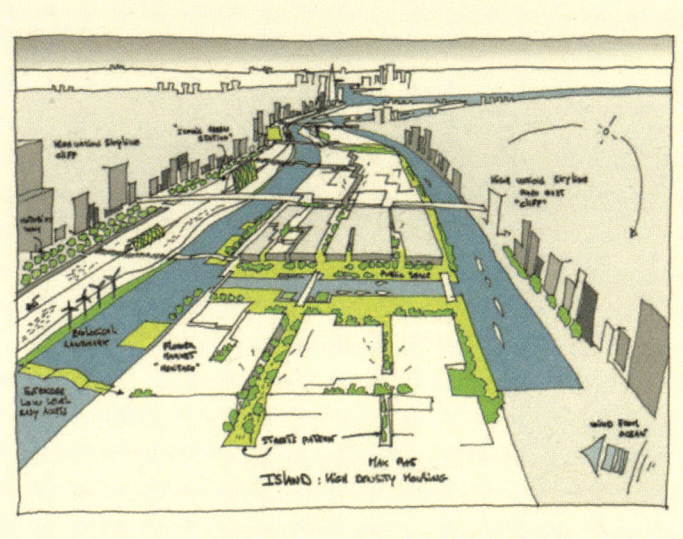

Figure 3.24 Preliminary sketches of the "island-valley" concept adopted for the Ho Chi Minh City bus rapid transit system

Source: World Bank 2012.
Note: The island-valley concept focuses on riverfront development, expansion of public green space, and high-density development on the edge of the BRT line.

developed feasible new ideas that went beyond the usual level of detail and scope.

The key design concept was a high-density BRT transit corridor surrounding a lower-density "island valley" (figure 3.24). The island valley provides areas for residential and recreational spaces and focuses on mixed-use riverfront development. Key elements of the concept include an enhanced focus on transit- and pedestrian-oriented design, greater emphasis on green space and public areas, identification of opportunities for private sector development and contribution to the transit greenway, improved connectivity to transit hubs/modes and key destinations, and the use of good design to create iconic and vibrant station areas (figure 3.25).

Before the *charrette*, various departments went on a study tour (sponsored by the South-South Experience and Exchange Trust Fund) of BRT systems in Brazil; Colombia; Hong Kong SAR, China; and Indonesia. This tour helped establish a community of practice, which was strengthened through the *charrette* process. The tour helped planners think like transport engineers, and transport engineers think like planners.

City officials were impressed with the rapid results and effectiveness of the *charrette*. The ideas and suggestions proposed have already been incorporated into the preparation of the feasibility study for Ho Chi Minh City by the World Bank, and the city has prepared a draft area development plan for the corridor.

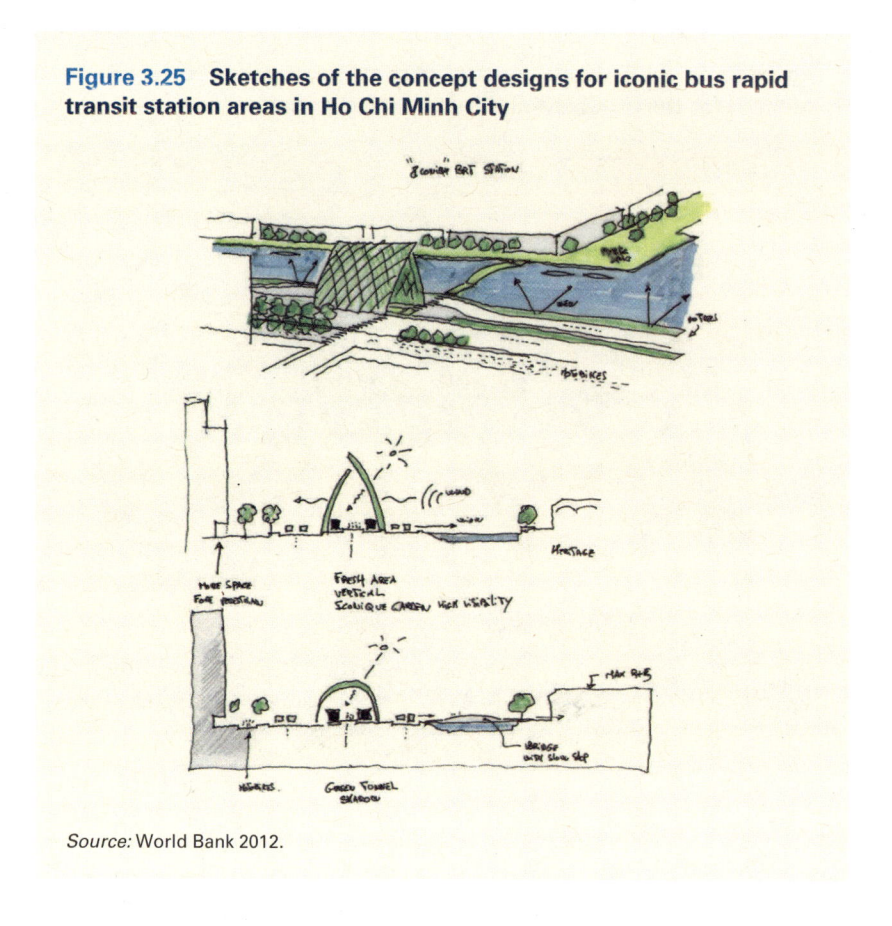

Figure 3.25 Sketches of the concept designs for iconic bus rapid transit station areas in Ho Chi Minh City

Source: World Bank 2012.

Notes

1. Delhi and Pune built busways before Ahmedabad completed its BRT system. Their busways are similar to the low-performing busways built in the 1970s and 1980s in some Latin American countries, however.
2. In 2010, the International Transport Forum and International Association of Public Transport recognized Janmarg for "outstanding innovation in public transport," and the Institute for Transportation and Development Policy (ITDP) awarded it the Sustainable Transport Award. Other organizations—including the Transportation Research Board Committee on Developing Countries, EMBARQ, the German Agency for International Cooperation (Deutsche Gesellschaft für Internationale Zusammenarbeit [GIZ]), the International Association of Public Transport (UITP), the United Nations Centre for Regional Development (UNCRD), the Clean Air Initiative for Asian Cities (CAI Asia), and Latin American Cities (CAI LAC)—have also recognized Janmarg (http://www.itdp.org/news/ahmedabad-wins-2010-sustainable-transport-award/).
3. Other investments include suburban rail transit systems, a metro system, and upgraded regular bus systems. Recognizing the importance of an integrated transport system, the AMC's vision aims to redesign

the city structure and transport systems to provide greater accessibility, more efficient mobility, and a lower carbon future.
4. Janmarg Phase I cost Rs 5,400 million ($100 million), of which JnNURM financed Rs 2,700 ($50 million), the Gujarat state government financed Rs 810 ($15 million), and the AMC financed RS 1,890 million ($35 million).
5. The surveys are conducted by the Centre of Excellence in Urban Transport at the Center for Environmental Planning and Technology (CEPT) University.
6. The Ahmedabad Urban Development Authority (AUDA) was originally established as an agency responsible for areas that fall outside the AMC but within the Ahmedabad Metropolitan Area. It currently manages an area of 1,295 square kilometers, 449 square kilometers of which belong to the AMC. Its responsibilities include preparing development plans, ensuring the availability of land for development, preparing the Town Planning Scheme, controlling development activities in accordance with the development plan, improving environmental conditions, and providing physical and social infrastructure.
7. The study team investigated Janmarg's impact on the built environment at three different scales: across the city, within its corridor, and in neighborhoods. The first two scales were observed by assessing the transformation of building footprints that fall within a 500-meter buffer of the trunk lines. A matched-pair analysis was conducted at the neighborhood level by selecting station areas (target areas) and control areas (non–BRT station areas) that were similar in social status and land use. The target areas were selected at the 500-meter buffer of the Janmarg stations, the control areas at 1,250 meters from the target area stations. Three pairs were selected for this analysis. The key data used for the three analyses were statistics on new construction and changes in building height between 2006 and 2011.
8. The ULCA was a national state regulation that set a ceiling on urban property ownership of 1,000 square meters per person in an effort to prevent the concentration of property in the hands of a small number of owners. The regulation was repealed in 1999.
9. The AMC is allocated 20 percent and private developers 80 percent.
10. The Lee Kuan Yew World City Prize recognized Ahmedabad's "early success in implementing a comprehensive city development plan, which aims to transform India's seventh-largest city into a more livable, equitable and sustainable metropolis with a dynamic multisector economy and an emerging auto-hub" (Lee Kuan Yew World City Prize 2012).
11. Developers who intend to redevelop textile mill sites usually purchase additional floor area ratio (discussed in the next section) to take full advantage of the property.
12. Possible financing schemes include cross-subsidization of affordable housing segments by high-income households and provision by the

local government of a bonus FAR, allowing the developer to construct more units.
13. In recognition of its success in reducing urban poverty, Ahmedabad received a national award for "Best City in the Implementation of Basic Services to Urban Poor (BSUP)" under the Jawaharlal Nehru National Renewal Mission program.
14. The Janmarg BRT (serviced by Ahmedabad Janmarg Ltd.) and the regular bus system (serviced by AMTS) are the two main public transit modes in the city. With 212 routes covering 550 kilometers of road network, AMTS covers about 97 percent of the AMC's developed area and carries 0.9 million passengers per day. It accounts for about 11 percent of all trips in Ahmedabad.
15. Phase I includes the Calle 80, Av. Caracus, Autonorte, and Av. Jimenez corridors. Phase II includes the Av. Americas –Calle 14, Av. NQS, and Av. Suba corridors.
16. nitiated in 1974, Ciclovia promotes nonmotorized transport and citizen's health. The initiative is implemented in most of localities in Bogota.
17. An estimated 300,000–400,000 bicycle trips are made daily in Bogota. The share of bicycle trips was 2.0 percent in 2008, up from less than 0.4 percent before the infrastructure was built (CCB 2009).
18. The estimated cost of Phase I and II projects is $1,970 million ($5 million per kilometer), of which the national government subsidized $1,296 million (66 percent), with the city financing the remaining $674 million.
19. The Territorial Ordinance Plan was created under Law 388 (1997) for territorial development, as an amendment to Law 9a (1989). It aims to ensure all citizens the right to the city, overcome urban informality, seek a more equitable land redistribution, and implement the constitutional principle of the social function of the property. The law requires all municipalities and counties in Bogota with a population of more than 100,000 to develop a POT.
20. The National Congress approved LOOT on June 28, 2011, making it the guide for the Territorial Ordinance in Colombia. LOOT aims to create directions for the organization of Colombia's territory, establish the guiding principles for ordinance, define the institutional framework and tools for territorial development, distribute the powers between the federal and regional authorities, and establish general rules for the territorial organization.
21. This integrated transit system is developed under the Mobility Master Plan by the Office of Mobility. SITP–targeted transit includes both publicly and privately owned public transportation. Detailed plans include networks of modal exchange, parking, and proposed tolls. Enhancement of institutional and organizational structures is also envisioned.

22. Initiated in the United States in the 1980s, the New Urbanism movement promotes space that is designed to be walkable and friendly and to serve mixed urban functions.
23. The Guangzhou BRT and integrated bike-sharing system won the 2011 Sustainable Transport Award. The BRT system has also been awarded city and provincial design prizes. It has been covered in magazines, major reports and publications, and other media. It accommodates hundreds of visiting delegations from China and around the world, inspiring many other cities to develop BRT systems, greenways, and bike sharing.
24. See http://www.chinabestpractices.net/lizhiwan.htm for more information.
25. "Urban villages" can be found in both city centers and at the periphery of megacities in China. These dense, overbuilt, medium-rise housing areas developed in an organic way without a formal road network in areas surrounding traditional villages, where land uses have changed from rural to urban and farmland has been built over. Temporary or unregistered migrants (called the "floating population") from rural areas tend to live in urban villages. In general, they are middle- to lower-income areas, with villages in the city center often also serving significant white-collar populations priced out of the more formal housing market in the city center. Although the housing stock in urban villages is poor and the areas lack direct light and open spaces, they are commercially and culturally vibrant places with a completely non-motorized core. The Guangzhou BRT corridor is lined with about 20 urban villages.
26. Leap-frog development is the development of new buildings in areas far from an existing urbanized area. It creates underutilized parcels of land between developed sites

References

AUDA (Ahmedabad Urban Development Authority). http://www.auda.org.in/about_us.html.

Bhatt, M. R. 2003. "The Case of Ahmedabad, India." In *Global Report on Human Settlements 2003: The Challenge of Slums*, ed. UN Habitat, 195–228. London: Earthscan.

Bocarejo, J. P., I. Portilla, and M. A. Perez. 2012. "Impact of TransMilenio on Density, Land Use, and Land Value in Bogota." *Research in Transportation Economics*.

CCB (Camara de Comercio de Bogota). 2009. "Movilidad en bicicleta en Bogota." Observatorio de movilidad, Bogota.

Cervero, R. 2005. "Accessible Cities and Regions: A Framework for Sustainable Transport and Urbanism in the 21st Century." Center for Future Urban Transport, University of California, Berkeley, CA.

CoE UT CEPT (Centre of Excellence in Urban Transport at the Centre for Environmental Planning and Technology University). 2009. Ahmedabad. http://www.cept.ac.in/index.php?option=com_content&view=article&id=86&Itemid=155.

———. 2011. *Integrated Mobility Plan for Ahmedabad.* Ahmedabad: CE UT CEPT.

Forbes. 2010. *In Pictures*: *The Next Decade's Fastest-Growing Cities.* http://www.forbes.com/2010/10/07/cities-china-chicago-opinions-columnists-joel-kotkin_slide_4.html. Accessed December 9, 2011.

Gilbert, A. 2009. "The Rise (and Fall?) of a State Land Bank." *Habitat International* 33 (4): 425–35.

Hidalgo, D., and EMBARQ. 2010. *Descripcion del sistema de transporte masivo transmilenio de Bogota.* Bogota: Estudio Elaborado para TransMilenio SA.

ITDP (Institute for Transportation and Development Policy), 2011. "Case Study of Guangzhou BRT as a Mass Transit Option." Presentation in Guangzhou, China, December 8.

Lee Kuan Yew World City Prize. 2012. *Special Mentions 2012.* http://www.leekuanyewworldcityprize.com.sg/special_mentions_2012.htm. Accessed May 15, 2012.

NCI (National Charrette Institute). 2006. *The Charrette Handbook.* American Planning Association, Chicago.

Sabarmati Riverfront Development Corporation, Ltd. 2010. Slide from presentation on the Sabarmati Riverfront Development Project, Ahmedabad, April 7.

SDP (Secretaría Distrital de Planeación). 2010. *Diagnostico POT Bogota.* Bogota.

World Bank. 2007. *World Development Indicators.* Washington, DC: World Bank.

———. 2012. *Vietnam Urban Review.* May 1, East Asia and Pacific Region, Washington, DC.

CHAPTER 4
Toward Sustainable Urban Futures

Faced with ever-worsening traffic congestion and deteriorating environmental conditions, many cities in developing countries have turned to public transit systems in an effort to reverse course. Transit investments, proponents hope, will also help reverse automobile-dependent patterns of urban growth.

The cases of Ahmedabad and Bogota (chapter 3) illustrate just how difficult it is to integrate transit and land use. Although both cities had forward-looking, long-term plans, visionary leaders, and world-class bus rapid transit (BRT) systems, neither has fully explored the potential of high-quality transit investments to catalyze an urban transformation. In both cities, the overarching objective in investing in BRT was to improve mobility, not explicitly to reshape and transform urban growth.

Based on an analysis of the case studies in chapters 2 and 3, this chapter identifies key constraints to integrating transit and land use in order to achieve more sustainable urban futures. It compares the approaches taken by Ahmedabad, Bogota, and other growing cities and highlights key barriers, challenges, and opportunities. It then draws lessons and makes recommendations for policy makers, government officials, urban and transport planners of rapidly growing cities in developing countries, and staff of development financial institutions.

Barriers to Integrating Transit and Urban Development

In adopting transit and land-use integration as critical strategy for sustainable urban development, cities in developing countries need to overcome multiple challenges. They include the urgency of short-term demands for improving mobility, which often override long-term visions for sustainable urban development; fragmented institutional frameworks, which make regional collaboration and city-level, cross-sector coordination extremely difficult; and regulatory constraints that hinder the capacity of real estate markets to respond to the economic value created by investments in transit.

The management of urban densities is also problematic. In many cities in developing countries, densities are not organized in relationship to high-capacity transit services. These cities often adopt uniformly regulated floor area ratios (FARs), which prevent land prices from reflecting location premiums. FARs near transit stations are too low in many cities in developing countries.

Inadequate policies and regulations, as well as redevelopment of built-up areas and neglected urban districts are also major challenges. The financial challenges of funding large, lumpy transit investments requires innovative solutions, especially given the many competing demands for fiscal resources and limits on government spending.

The Urgency of Short-Term Demands Overriding Long-Term Visions

Master plans in many cities in developing countries commonly identify viability and livability as long-term visions and goals. Cities often struggle to translate these objectives into concrete policies and land-use plans, however. Most developing cities are overwhelmed by the pressing demands of meeting day-to-day urban service requirements, which are exacerbated by aging infrastructure and rapid population increases. As a result, the responses of public authorities tend to be ad hoc and on a project-by-project basis rather than comprehensive and coordinated.

Compared with many other developing cities, both Ahmedabad and Bogota have the capacity to achieve long-term development goals. In fact, both the Janmarg (Ahmedabad) and TransMilenio (Bogota) are widely recognized as BRT success stories. In each case, transportation conditions improved following the initiation of BRT services. However, neither city has fully explored opportunities to enhance economic efficiency, improve environmental conditions, or enhance social equity by integrating their transit investments with urban development. Meanwhile, private developers have started to respond to new development opportunities and to capture the value created by these public transit investments, despite government inaction. More proactive public interventions would likely leverage even more private investments along BRT corridors.

Translating cities' visions into urban form and specific land uses is a lengthy process, requiring at least 10–20 years. The cumulative impacts of negative externalities caused by poorly integrated transit and land use—longer commutes, air pollution, increased greenhouse gas emissions, loss of preserved natural land—are difficult for most citizens to envision in the near term. Such outcomes unfold gradually and become noticeable only after many years. In contrast, political terms of mayoral office often span only three to five years—and in cities like Bogota, consecutive reelection of mayors is prohibited. Not surprisingly, politicians often focus on issues that can be addressed within their term in office.

For these reasons, city administrations and their transit agencies frequently focus primarily on the rapid construction of transit infrastructure (BRT/metro lines and stations) rather than working to integrate these systems with urban development. Integration requires time-consuming cross-sector coordination, which involves drawing on different sets of skills and disciplines, further hindering implementation. Transit agencies can control construction once rights-of-way are secured. In contrast, the city administration must go through a lengthy and complex deliberation process with commercial and residential property owners to develop or redevelop land near transit stations or corridors.

As a result, the integration of transit and land use becomes a low priority, despite its long-lasting positive impacts on the viability and livability of cities. The problem is the fundamental mismatch between the short-term parochial focus of many elected officials and the longer-term nature of the benefits conferred by integrating transit and urban development.

Ahmedabad has managed to partly overcome this political mismatch problem in several ways. Its mayor and elected council members make policy decisions, but implementation is left to a professional city manager (called the municipal commissioner). The municipal commissioner's three-year term can be extended up to six years, while the mayor terms out after three years. Ahmedabad also receives professional support from the Centre for Environmental Planning and Technology University (CEPT). Knowledge institutions like CEPT can not only provide technical support; they can also ensure political neutrality and institutional continuity.[1] These institutional and supporting mechanisms help Ahmedabad mitigate the negative impacts of short political terms on city development processes.

Bogota holds the Urban Development Institute (UDI) under the Mobility Secretariat, but its support is limited mainly to providing technical designs for infrastructure rather than overall urban planning. Bogota has a few well-respected universities with urban planning programs, but the city and universities have not collaborated closely. Bogota's Territorial Ordinance Plan (POT) articulates the city's long-term vision and integrated cross-sector needs. It outlines geographically specific urbanization aims toward the construction of a dense, compact, and integrated city. Little of this vision has been implemented, however, because of inconsistency between the city-level master plan, POT, and plans developed at the Zonal Planning Unit level.

However, Bogota has started to recognize the benefits of integrating BRT or future metros with urban development. For example, Phase III of the TransMilenio includes a large-scale land redevelopment project near a key node, connecting the new Av. 26 BRT line with the Av. Caracas line. Continuing market demand for good accessible locations will likely intensify land development near some TransMilenio stations in years to come.

Fragmented Institutional Frameworks

Fragmented institutional structures and governing arrangements are one of the biggest obstacles to transit and land-use integration. Although national and state governments set broad strategies and policies regarding urban development, metropolitan and municipal governments play the all-essential roles of translating regional or citywide strategies, policies, and plans into implementation. These regional and local governmental frameworks vary from country to country. India adopted the federal system, under which urban management is the responsibility of state governments, which delegate some of their functional and expenditure responsibilities to local governments. Colombia adopted the unitary system, under which all municipalities have equal legal status. Governance structures influence the way development is planned and managed at both the regional and local government levels.

At the city level, the "sector silo" behavior of decentralized departments and agencies often inhibits strategic and coordinated planning and investments. This institutional inertia—formed by parochial, unisectoral entities that view the world in silo terms—is a common challenge for most large institutions involved in many sectors, including the World Bank.

Lack of regional integration at the metropolitan level. At the metropolitan scale, governments need to closely coordinate land-use plans, infrastructure investments, and urban services. The management of a metropolitan region is an exceedingly complex task, because of the involvement of multiple governmental entities at multiple governing levels. By decentralizing, the national government devolves some of its decision-making powers and fiscal functions to lower-level governments. Doing so can isolate municipalities, however, making regional collaboration more difficult unless proper regulatory and institutional coordination mechanisms are incorporated.

Political and economic competition among municipalities often impedes the coordination of planning, investment, and service provision across administrative boundaries, a challenge Bogota and its neighboring municipalities currently face. Many low-income people who commute to Bogota from neighboring municipalities, such as Soacha, Cota, and Chila, are adversely affected by the fact that the TransMilenio is not well connected to other regional bus services. This deficiency arises because TransMilenio's service jurisdiction does not align with the regional division under which Bogota-Cundinamarca (Bogota's regional department) planning and policy making occurs. Recognizing these institutional shortcomings, in 2011, the national government enacted the Territorial Ordinance Organic Law (LOOT) law, which is intended to promote regional coordination.

Coordination of planning, investment, and service provision is smoothly implemented in the Ahmedabad metropolitan region, thanks to effective collaboration between Ahmedabad Urban Development Authority (AUDA), a metropolitan-wide urban development authority, and the Ahmedabad Municipal Corporation (AMC), which manages the city. The Gujarat state government supervises and facilitates regional coordination and provides funding support.[2]

Sector silo behavior and practices at the city level. At the city level, departments and agencies have varying missions, objectives, budgets, management styles, governance structures, and staff profiles. These differences often hinder cross-sector and interagency coordination needed to integrate transit and land use.

Transport department staff often have little knowledge of urban planning and design, and urban planners often lack knowledge of transportation, making it difficult for the two to work together to ensure seamless integration and implementation. Transport department staff have limited responsibilities to integrate transit and urban development (and often limited interest in doing so). Staff members from both departments work under different management and budgetary constraints; they have little incentive to coordinate day-to-day or long-term activities.

In Bogota, the Mobility Secretariat and TransMilenio S.A. developed TransMilenio without much coordination with the city's other relevant secretariats, particularly the Urban Planning Secretariat. New urban development near the BRT stations or corridors is minimal, except for the airport corridor and some commercial complex development near BRT terminal stations.[3] This lack of development may be related to the fact that the FARs of these areas have not been adjusted, even though land values near BRT stations and its corridors have increased. In addition, BRT station designs are not well integrated with the urban fabric of nearby neighborhoods and streets.

Ahmedabad has been able to coordinate cross-sector activities more comprehensively and decisively, through its City Development Plan. Janmarg's policy-making structure also allows for multisectoral inputs. The chairman of the Janmarg board is the municipal commissioner, and board members include representatives from various departments. Soliciting inputs from people representing urban planning interests and other sectors allows Janmarg to address a wider array of municipal concerns than simply moving people along busways. Coordination by itself, however, is not enough: Ahmedabad has yet to witness the focusing of new urban development along its BRT corridors.

Regulatory Constraints

Certain government policies and regulations may adversely affect transit and land-use integration by causing an under- or oversupply of urban land or delaying urban redevelopment and regeneration opportunities. Inappropriate density control in the form of FARs has the most adverse impact on integration. Other land and housing regulations as well as local governments' fiscal regimes also have unintended impacts on the spatial development of cities.

Lack of articulated density. Most large cities in Asia, and in most developing countries, have higher average population densities than those in land-rich

Australia, Canada, and the United States (both Ahmedabad, with 12,249 people per square kilometer, and Bogota, with 19,177 people, are among the world's densest cities). Most European cities fall in between these two groups (figure 4.1).

For various reasons, many politicians, planners, and citizens of high-density cities in developing countries have a desire to "deconcentrate," by spreading development to new areas rather than increasing density around BRT stations located in built-up areas. Their major concern is that concentrating growth around BRT stations will further deteriorate already unsatisfactory urban service provision and poor environmental conditions.

Most developing cities have difficulty providing adequate urban services, such as potable water, waste management, transportation, and electricity. They could improve service provision by addressing institutional and regulatory deficiencies, such as low levels of autonomy, accountability, inadequate cost recovery, and lack of professional management.

Instead, city authorities tend to consider population growth and the limited "carrying capacity of the city" as prime cause for their chronic demand-supply gaps. It is widely believed that cities in developing countries cannot accommodate additional growth or densification in built-up areas. Furthermore, cities tend to prefer development of peripheral greenfields to urban redevelopment in the city core, because development of greenfields is faster and costs less upfront (Burchell and others 2000).

Expansion of the built-up area of rapidly growing cities in developing countries is unavoidable to some extent. But urban growth need not always take the form of outward expansion, which requires expanding the infrastructure network (for example, water pipelines and sewerage network); operating and maintaining the expanded system; and converting agricultural land and open space, which are in short supply. Cities in developing countries often react to peripheral growth by allowing informal squatters to provide "self-help" infrastructure and services themselves (such as hauling water, using standpipes, creating dirt pathways). They do not try to serve the subsequent sprawling peripheries, resulting in few public services for the poor.

Although it logically follows that higher densities require an increased level of infrastructure investments, density does not necessarily lead to the deterioration of urban service provision. Large cities with high densities such as Seoul (16,589 people per square kilometer [UN 2009]) and Singapore (7,025 people per square kilometer [UN 2009]) are efficiently providing high-quality urban services while maintaining good environmental conditions. The Asia Green City Index of 2011, developed by the Economic Intelligence Unit (EIU), ranks Singapore in the well above average category and Seoul as one of the seven best cities in Asia (EIU 2011).

However, because higher densities are perceived to cause overcrowding, traffic congestion, and increased exposure to pollutants, policy makers and city planners in developing countries are often reluctant to ramp up urban density by raising the FAR. They also tend to apply a uniform or narrow

Toward Sustainable Urban Futures 153

Figure 4.1 Average population densities in built-up areas in 60 global metropolitan areas

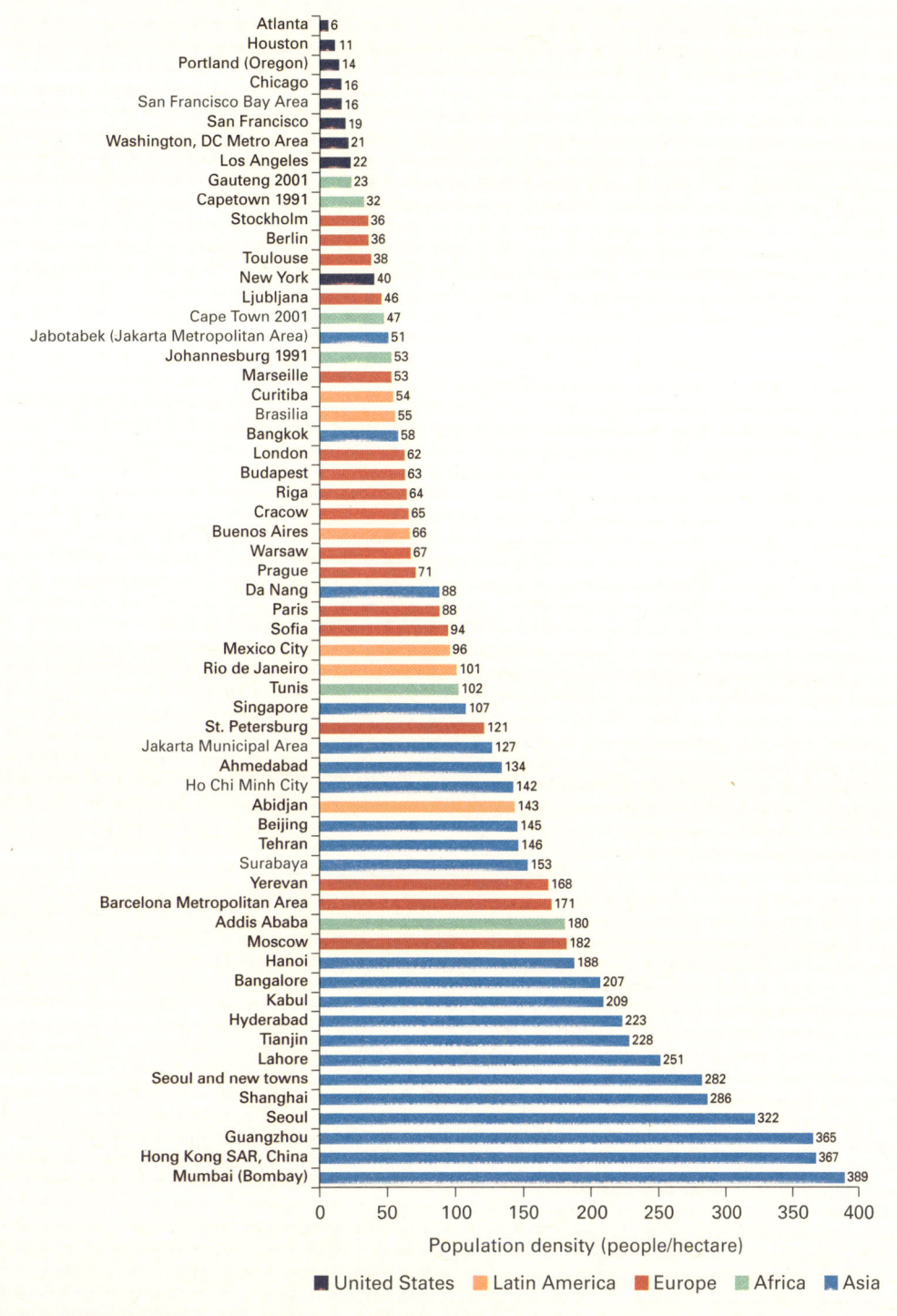

Metropolitan Area	Population density (people/hectare)
Atlanta	6
Houston	11
Portland (Oregon)	14
Chicago	16
San Francisco Bay Area	16
San Francisco	19
Washington, DC Metro Area	21
Los Angeles	22
Gauteng 2001	23
Capetown 1991	32
Stockholm	36
Berlin	36
Toulouse	38
New York	40
Ljubljana	46
Cape Town 2001	47
Jabotabek (Jakarta Metropolitan Area)	51
Johannesburg 1991	53
Marseille	53
Curitiba	54
Brasilia	55
Bangkok	58
London	62
Budapest	63
Riga	64
Cracow	65
Buenos Aires	66
Warsaw	67
Prague	71
Da Nang	88
Paris	88
Sofia	94
Mexico City	96
Rio de Janeiro	101
Tunis	102
Singapore	107
St. Petersburg	121
Jakarta Municipal Area	127
Ahmedabad	134
Ho Chi Minh City	142
Abidjan	143
Beijing	145
Tehran	146
Surabaya	153
Yerevan	168
Barcelona Metropolitan Area	171
Addis Ababa	180
Moscow	182
Hanoi	188
Bangalore	207
Kabul	209
Hyderabad	223
Tianjin	228
Lahore	251
Seoul and new towns	282
Shanghai	286
Seoul	322
Guangzhou	365
Hong Kong SAR, China	367
Mumbai (Bombay)	389

Legend: United States, Latin America, Europe, Africa, Asia

Source: Bertaud 2004.

band of FARs across a city, without capitalizing on location premiums, such as proximity to transit stations or corridors. Density control without consideration of a location's economic value prevents cities from effectively managing their use of land.

In Ahmedabad, the FAR is kept at a very low ratio of 1.80 throughout the city, although developers can purchase an additional 25 percent (that is, they can increase the FAR from 1.80 to 2.25) if a property is located on a street that is more than 18 meters wide, including BRT corridors. According to Ahmedabad's planners, allocating moderate FARs citywide is intended to disperse travel demand and thus decongest the city. Their approach is based on the fact that the majority of citizens in Ahmedabad travel less than 5.4 kilometers per day by walking, bicycling, or using a two-wheeler and that this dispersed population density contributes to relatively smooth traffic movement compared with other Indian cities of similar size.

Although in the near term this uniform density (spread out over a large geographic territory) may result in less traffic congestion, over the long term, it will result in an automobile-centric built form that is less conducive to patronizing high-capacity transit services. Cross-town, lateral trips induced by the need for suburb-to-suburb travel are the most difficult to serve by public transit and promote private automobile use. Given the rapid increase in car ownership, this urban form will eventually result in more traffic congestion and air pollution. The suppression of densities near BRT stations ignores the inherent location efficiency of transit-served properties.

Cultural sensitivities and political considerations partly account for the practice of uniformly distributing FARs in Ahmedabad. Landowners who are allowed to increase FARs stand to reap huge financial windfalls. The desire to avoid any appearance of favoritism by granting higher FAR concessions has prompted local government officials to assign the same FARs to everyone, regardless of whether or not a parcel is near a BRT station.

A similar approach prevails in Bogota. Except in the central business district, where no FAR restrictions exist, and in several other low-income areas with high density, Bogota's FARs are kept low (0–1.0 or 1.1–2.0), including in areas near BRT stations and corridors (box 4.1). Together with the difficulty of consolidating small properties, low FARs are one of the reasons why areas near TransMilenio stations and corridors are underdeveloped (the only exceptions are the large-scale commercial complexes at the terminal stations). Along the BRT corridors are two- to three-story buildings that were built decades ago. Neither their owners nor other investors have any incentive to construct new buildings. The low FAR prevents full economic use of the increased value created by the construction of the BRT system. Moreover, evenly spread density promotes an urban form that is suitable for private car use rather than public transit.

Altaf and Shah (2008) find similar FAR–related constraints in large cities in China, including Shanghai, Tianjin, and Zengzhou: "Gross FAR in major Chinese cities does not vary sufficiently across the urban space because of

Box 4.1 Articulated versus average density

What matters most for transit and land-use integration is not average population densities but "articulated densities"—densities that are strategically distributed across parts of a metropolitan area. The layout depicted in panel c of figure B4.1.1 is better suited for mass transit than the one in panel a, even though the two forms have the same average population density.

Figure B4.1.1 Importance of articulated density for mass transit

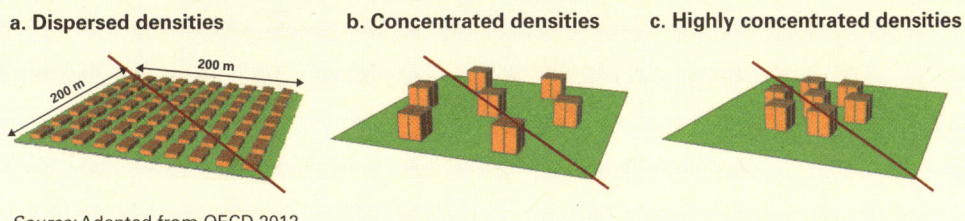

a. Dispersed densities   b. Concentrated densities   c. Highly concentrated densities

Source: Adapted from OECD 2012.
Note: Red line represents a mass transit line.

Curitiba, Brazil has created articulated densities along its BRT corridors (panel a in figure B4.1.2). Bogota, Colombia has not done so along its TransMilenio corridors (panel b). It maintains a low FAR (0–2), except within the central business district and a few other selected spots.

Figure B4.1.2 Densities along the bus rapid transit corridors in Curitiba and Bogota

a. Articulated densities in Curitiba

b. Unarticulated densities in Bogota

Source: IPPUC 2009.
Note: Buildings in Curitiba, represented in bright yellow and orange, are strategically built along the BRT corridors with good urban planning. The current urban form was developed under a long-term vision; a transit-oriented development (TOD) concept was first outlined in its 1965 Master Plan. Today, the city has lower greenhouse gas emission levels, less traffic congestion, and more livable urban spaces compared with other similar Brazilian cities. The red, green, and orange lines indicate the city boundaries.

Source: World Bank.

uniformly regulated FAR values that suppress location premiums from being reflected in the price of land. This leads to the dearth of strategically located high density nodes" (p. 3). Paradoxically, large Chinese cities with high average population densities keep lower FARs than large cities elsewhere, such as Manhattan, Seoul, and Tokyo. In contrast, city planning authorities in Guangzhou flexibly allow higher density development along the BRT corridor when requested by developers.

In the global transit-oriented cities analyzed in chapter 2, FARs vary more widely, even within the central business district area. For example, FARs range from 12 to 25 in Singapore; 1 to 20 Tokyo; 1 to 12 in Hong Kong SAR, China; and 8 to 10 in Seoul. All of these cities have developed varying levels of density in different areas, taking each area's social and economic features and infrastructure capacities into consideration. In general, all allow for high density around transit lines and stations to integrate transit and land use.

Other regulative and administrative constraints. In addition to FAR uniformity, certain national or local government regulations and administrative deficiencies adversely affect the smooth functioning of land markets. The result is an under- or oversupply of land, noncontiguous spatial development, and land-use patterns that respond only slowly to the provision of transit infrastructure. These regulations represent major barriers to transit-oriented spatial development.

Although Ahmedabad's capacity for planning is impressive, many national-level regulations restrict market forces, significantly limiting the ability of the city's planning instruments to direct real estate development toward a long-term spatial vision. For example, the Urban Land Ceiling Act of 1976 (ULCA) distorted land markets by preventing developers and individuals from owning large parcels, thereby hindering the redevelopment of vacant land, until the law's abolishment in 1999 (see chapter 3). The high stamp duty on land sales, rules setting minimum plot sizes, and the Rent Control Act are other examples of regulations that impede market-based property transaction and development.

Apart from the FAR restriction, Bogota has fewer national or local restrictive regulations constraining the smooth functioning of the real estate market than does India. Its problems stem from deficiencies in planning and implementation rather than regulatory constraints. Because of the inconsistency between the POT and Zonal Plans in Bogota, the long-term spatial vision of increasing densities along the BRT corridor cannot be implemented. In addition, it usually takes four to five years to obtain approval of land consolidation plans or a construction permit (Samad, Lozano-Gracia, and Panman 2012). This lag makes it difficult for developers to undertake urban redevelopment projects, particularly large-scale, mixed-land urban regeneration projects that require the consolidation of several pieces of land. Although TransMilenio has increased the economic value of land near

Figure 4.2 Fragmented land use in Chengdu, China

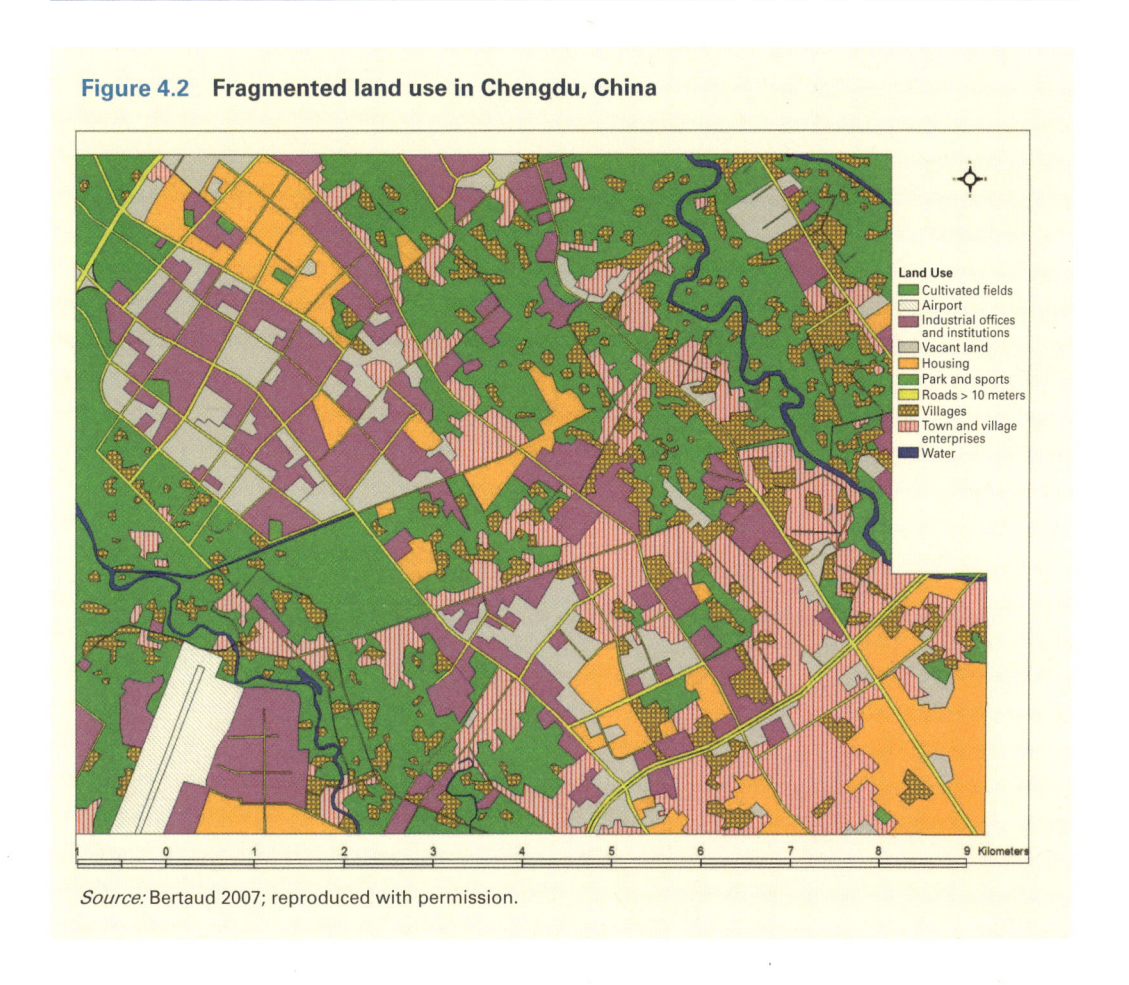

Source: Bertaud 2007; reproduced with permission.

BRT stations and corridors, these planning process deficiencies make it difficult for the private sector to respond.

The fiscal regime of local government revenue sources also adversely affects urban spatial development patterns. In China and Vietnam, land sales are major revenue sources for municipalities, which lack other significant sources, such as property taxes. To meet ever-increasing expenditure demands associated with rapid urbanization, local governments often convert rural land into urban land, which they then sell or lease to private developers. In this way, local governments effectively promote urban sprawl by creating vast low-density areas unsuitable for TOD.

In China, national regulations limiting land consumption by protecting farmland have the unintended consequence of fragmenting the urban periphery, leading to noncontiguous development of relatively high-density clusters, as exemplified in the periphery of Chengdu (figure 4.2). Regulations that do not discriminate sufficiently between agricultural lands within and outside the city boundaries exacerbate this fragmentation (Altaf and Shah 2008).

These unintended negative impacts of national regulations on urban spatial development are often overlooked.

Financial Constraints

As a result of unprecedented rapid urban growth, local governments in developing countries are facing enormous challenges to meeting competing funding demands for infrastructure investments and urban services. The large upfront capital investment required to develop a transit system is one of the largest obstacles to integrating transit and land use. In addition, at the operation stage, cities often need to provide subsidies to cover operational deficits or provide vouchers for low-income riders.[4] Scarce financial resources sometimes oblige transit companies to choose routes based on the cost of right-of-way acquisition rather than on the long-term development potential of the areas served. System design is driven primarily by the desire to minimize construction costs—for example, siting stations in the median of thoroughfares, reducing the need for costly land takings and disruptions—often ignoring opportunities to maximize development.

In 2011, both Ahmedabad and Bogota plan to construct new metro lines, at a cost of $1.8 billion in Ahmedabad (18 times the cost of the Phase I Janmarg system) and $1.5 billion in Bogota. Bogota needs to finance at least 30 percent of the total estimated construction cost of its metro ($450 million). Both cities need to find ways to finance these huge investment needs, including nonconventional approaches.

As most of both cities' transit investment funds are earmarked for the construction of major trunk lines and stations, few resources are available to facilitate modal integration between transit and nonmotorized transit or to improve the quality of public places near transit stations and corridors. These "green connector" investments—which include the creation or enhancement of footpaths, bicycle lanes, streetlights, parks, and street furniture—are important for both creating spaces that are effectively integrated into the surrounding community and cultivating an enjoyable transit experience.

The main issue local governments face is finding ways to finance these investments and leverage the associated long-term economic and environmental benefits when they are struggling to meet current demands for public services and investments. Yet both Ahmedabad and Bogota have strong financial management capacities, including innovative infrastructure financing tools, such as municipal bonds, public-private partnerships, Town Planning Schemes, and land value capture. They have also secured strong financial support from higher-level governments for their BRT investments. In order to upgrade their transit systems as their populations continue to grow, they will need to mobilize more resources. Partnering with the private sector to share the rewards and risks of TOD through various value capture approaches is one possibility, as discussed later in this chapter.

Neglected Urban Design at the Neighborhood and Street Level

Transit shapes urban development, and land-use patterns affect travel demand. Land-use variables reflect attributes not only of the trip (travel time, costs between trip origins and destinations) but also of the origins and destinations (density, degree of land-use mixture). This complementary relationship is the impetus for the discussions of the importance of density and its strategic control through FARs. However, density is not the only important element of land use and built environments. Other factors, such as carefully articulated land-use mixtures; safe and smooth access to transit stations (footpaths, bike paths, street lights); and amenities (benches, parks, landscaping, libraries) contribute to the development of a good built environment. Design measures (such as sound walls, pedestrian flyovers, context-sensitive design, and traffic-calming interventions) that help mitigate negative externalities also affect where people live and how they travel. Improving the quality of places and streets near transit stations and corridors can help cities attract people to these areas and encourage them to actively choose transit over cars.

Most users of public transit spend more than half their travel time walking (from home to the station and from the station to office) and waiting. Traditional public transit improvements focus only on the journey itself. The new "whole journey" approach focuses on the entire trip, from origin to destination. It involves issues such as walkability, safety, and accessibility, which are not only transit but also land-use planning issues.

Ahmedabad's BRT features some attractive design elements, such as the construction of bicycle lanes. But these were not well thought out. Stations are tucked in the center of roads, requiring pedestrians to cross streets at grade, creating conflict points with car traffic and reducing the likelihood of good public place making. Most passengers have to walk in the carriageway to reach the BRT stations, as most streets in Ahmedabad—and elsewhere in India—lack a separate space for pedestrians (figure 4.3) Bicycle lanes are parallel systems, largely duplicating and perhaps even competing with BRT. In place of these disparate systems, Ahmedabad planners should concentrate on creating a complementary feeder system that provides well-designed bike and pedestrian connections to BRT corridors.

Ahmedabad has a long way to go to develop high-quality public places with well-integrated urban design at the neighborhood and street level. City planners have started to address these challenges, beginning with accessibility to BRT stations. In one notable example, they created a vibrant cultural and recreation area (Kankaria Lake Park) by rehabilitating a neglected and polluted lake located next to a BRT station. Both the Indian government and nongovernmental organizations (NGOs) have started to produce guidelines for street design and land-use planning. A department of the Delhi Development Authority—the Unified Traffic and Transportation (Planning & Engineering) Centre (UTTIPEC)—has recently released guidelines for street design, setback removal, and land-use planning around

Figure 4.3 Street without footpath in Ahmedabad, India

Source: ITDP 2011.

metro stations. The Institute for Transportation and Development Policy (ITDP), India, has also published a guideline for street design (ITDP 2011).

Bogota's TransMilenio has improved mobility, particularly for the poor. But its design does little to promote station integration with surrounding communities. For example, some BRT stations are located in the medians of six- to eight-lane highways, requiring passengers to walk across long steel flyovers (figure 4.4). At peak hours, these flyovers resonate like giant drums, creating significant noise pollution. This partly explains the decline in some nearby property values. Under Phase III, the city is constructing concrete pedestrian bridges that should moderate noise problems; it has not improved the quality of public places along most BRT corridors, because redevelopment plans are still incomplete. A long line of unadorned walls occupies the space between BRT corridors, creating a visual and psychological barrier between the transit system and surrounding neighborhoods. Their presence does not promote the reconfiguration of the city layout along the BRT lines in a way that fosters vibrant urban life and economic activity.

Guangzhou's BRT system is notable not only for its large boarding capacity but also for its good corridor and street design, which promotes modal integration and improves the quality of public space. Its key design features include escalators at stations, 20 safe crossings, and bicycle lanes connected with BRT stations. The city is also making efforts to improve the quality of public space near BRT lines and stations by developing linear parks (strips of long park located next to railways, bus lines, roads, canals, or rivers) and creating hundreds of kilometers of green corridors.

Ho Chi Minh City is developing a BRT greenway corridor in collaboration with the World Bank. The draft concept integrates a BRT system along an existing highway corridor (figure 4.5). Such integrated design will

Toward Sustainable Urban Futures 161

Figure 4.4 Flyover in Bogota's TransMilenio bus rapid transit system

Photo by Allaeddin Twebti.

Figure 4.5 Integrated solutions proposed for greenway corridor in Ho Chi Minh City

Source: World Bank 2012.
Note: A well-integrated bus rapid transit (BRT) lane, business and residential areas, and green amenities (a canal and park) create a vibrant and livable urban space.

not only improve mobility but also transform this corridor into a pleasant and vibrant space. The proposal includes plans to provide better access to pedestrians, create green and public spaces, and allow mixed-use developments highlighting the identity of the city along the Saigon River (Moffat, Suzuki, and Iizuka 2012).

The Retrofitting Problem

Most transit investments in cities in developing countries will first take place in already urbanized areas, because the priority is to meet current traffic demand and stave off congestion. Retrofitting these areas in response to new development opportunities created by transit is more complex and difficult than TOD in greenfield development.

Retrofitting built-up areas is complicated for two reasons. First, private businesses or households own most of the property in TOD areas, leaving the government with little control. In comparison, the government can control the construction of transit once it secures the right of the way and construction funds. Second, as its name indicates, the redevelopment of built-up areas requires the demolition of physical assets, such as infrastructure and housing stock, and their reconstruction. Such decisions have both economic and social implications, including the need to resettle displaced residents.

Guangzhou's BRT line serves high-density areas in which commercial and residential developments co-exist. Supported by the city's liberal FAR policy, BRT accelerated the densification of its corridor, transforming it into vibrant TOD areas.

Mixed-use TODs have not yet materialized in Ahmedabad or Bogota. Except for the vacant land from closed textile mills in Ahmedabad, most areas near BRT stations and corridors had already been developed with low-rise buildings. In Bogota, except for the central business district, most of the structures along BRT lines and corridors are two- to three-stories high. The slow pace of transforming these areas partly reflects restrictive FAR controls and the lengthy approval processes for urban regeneration projects. The huge development potential of these areas remains unexploited.

Significant increases in land values created by new transit investments provide good development opportunities in BRT-served districts. Particularly when large vacant lands become available in the central city, local governments could undertake large-scale strategic urban regeneration projects that integrate transit. In Ahmedabad, for example, redevelopment of the closed textile mill sites near BRT stations is taking place mainly under the initiative of private real estate developers. Given the scarcity of large vacant land parcels in central cities, the local government could be more aggressive in converting former mill parcels into vibrant new activity centers, such as multipurpose cultural and sport complexes that are well integrated with BRT.

Large-scale urban regeneration can have a transformative impact on economic efficiency, environmental improvement, and social conditions. Such projects require close collaboration by the city administration, private developers, and citizens.

Local governments can also proactively develop new urban land by redeveloping the river or ocean front, as shown in the Sabarmati Riverfront Development Project in Ahmedabad. Alternatively, land-scarce cities in developing countries could rehabilitate and convert brownfields into models of livable eco-districts or vibrant economic areas, as Stockholm has done in Hammarby Sjöstad (see chapter 2).

The Power of Vested Interests

The vested interests of users and operators of transit modes, developers, and specific industries make it difficult for cities to formulate a shared spatial vision that promotes transit and land-use integration. A real estate developer holding a large land site close to a future BRT station, for example, would be unlikely to release it, preferring to hold onto it in expectation of an increase in value. The result is leap-frog urban development (box 4.2). For their part, operators of taxis and para-transit vehicles would oppose the construction of the transit system for fear of losing customers. Unless rule-based and transparent processes are in place, corruption can drive policy and transit line or station location selection, dashing hopes for successful integration of transit and land use.

Box 4.2 How land speculation contributes to sprawl

Transit infrastructure created to facilitate development often perversely fosters sprawl, which in turn requires more land (and more investment in infrastructure) to serve a given number of households and businesses. At fault is not the infrastructure itself, but the way landowners are allowed to appropriate value created by public investment.

Hoping that the land will appreciate after a metro or BRT is built, owners of sites near public transit often hold on to the sites, preventing integration with land use. The worst consequence of this speculative landholding is the incentive created to develop cheaper sites farther away from transit networks, which often leads to urban sprawl. Once this cheaper land is partially developed and inhabited, the new occupants often create political pressure to extend the infrastructure to their area. Once the infrastructure is extended, land prices at these formerly remote and inexpensive areas begin to rise, choking off development there (even though additional capacity exists) and continuing the cycle by driving developers and users even farther away. This type of sprawling urbanization—discontinuous development often characterized by noncontiguous land uses and low average densities—inhibits walking, cycling, and the use of transit. It increases the need for automobiles, creating externalities such as air pollution.

Source: Rybeck 2004.

Figure 4.6 Automobile-dependent urban development in Kuala Lumpur, Malaysia

Source: http://eyeonmalaysia.wordpress.com/2007/03/18/sri-hartamas.
Note: Kuala Lumpur has expanded outward along highways.
Photo by Chua Soo Kok.

In the United States, the automotive, highway construction, and oil industries have influenced governments' urban development and infrastructure policies, which have fostered automobile-dependent urban sprawl. The availability of cheap oil through the early 1970s combined with the availability of land helped fuel this trend. Rising levels of automobile ownership and usage prompted governments to build more roads through the post–World War II era, which spurred sprawl and encouraged longer and longer automotive trips. This vicious cycle of rising car ownership and suburban sprawl is difficult to reverse once set into motion.

Kuala Lumpur, Malaysia has followed an urban development path that is somewhat similar to the United States' (figure 4.6). In 2010, for example, it had 3,838 people per square kilometer, one of the lowest densities among East Asian capital cities. Its low density partly reflects the fact that Malaysia has adopted automobile-dependent urban development policy—influenced, at least in part, by a national strategy promoting the domestic automobile manufacturing industry.

In 2009, car ownership in Malaysia (313 cars per 1,000 people) exceeded car ownership in the Republic of Korea (267 cars per 1,000 people) (World Bank website), even though its per capita income was much lower. Malaysia's greenhouse gas emissions are also high for a country with its per capita income and level of development.[5] According to the United Nations Development Programme (UNDP 2007), in 2004, per capita carbon dioxide emissions were 114 percent higher than the average for countries in East Asia and Pacific and 88 percent higher than the global average for all middle-income countries.

The automobile industries are not the only influences on the government's urban and transit policies. Private sector firms engaged in highway construction and toll road operators share the same interest in maintaining automobile-dependent urban development.

The Challenge of Inclusive Transit-Oriented Development

One of the major social ramifications of ill-conceived spatial development is the burden placed on residents who cannot afford to purchase a private vehicle or are unable to live close to work and schools. Many of the poor must consequently endure long-distance commutes to make ends meet.

Transit investments help increase mobility and accessibility. But investment in public transit also increases property values near transit corridors and stations, raising housing costs and rental prices. Higher property values and gentrification continually force low-income residents farther and farther out toward the periphery.

Local governments must consider mitigation measures for the resultant shortage of affordable housing while promoting TOD investment. In response to the decline in affordable housing, the city of Vancouver increased the supply of rental houses by promoting "secondary suites" in existing homes and the construction of "laneway (driveway) houses" on existing properties (box 4.3).

In developing countries, informal settlements often become de facto affordable housing. In promoting TOD, it is important that local governments include residents of these informal communities in the development process. The ideal approach would be to coordinate low-income housing programs and transit development such as BRT so that the beneficiaries of social housing programs also benefit from improved mobility. In the long term, a socially inclusive and diversified community will enhance social capital, improve political stability, and increase economic viability.

Both Ahmedabad and Bogota are making considerable efforts to enhance social equity by combining social housing programs with public transit. Ahmedabad has allocated 10 percent of the land pool in its Town Planning Scheme and 10 percent of the government-owned textile mill site for economically weak segments in an effort to provide affordable social housing across all city areas, especially newly gentrified areas. It remains to be seen whether the Ahmedabad Municipal Corporation can secure enough land to provide social housing for everyone who needs it.

Bogota is more economically and socially segregated: the affluent live in the northern areas, and the low-income population lives in the peripheral

Box 4.3 Reducing housing costs and improving livability in Vancouver

On June 10, 2008, the Vancouver City Council unanimously adopted the EcoDensity Charter and a set of initial actions. The charter commits the city to make environmental sustainability a primary goal in all planning decisions, in ways that also support housing affordability and livability. The initial actions provide the roadmap to begin implementation of the EcoDensity Charter.

The EcoDensity Charter promotes a gentle, hidden, invisible form of density. Initial actions provide the framework for future work and implementation of the EcoDensity commitments, including secondary suites (invisible density) and laneway (driveway) housing (hidden density) as solutions to the shortage of affordable housing (figure B4.3.1). These optional modifications increase the supply of rental housing, improve the affordability of home ownership (financial institutions take income into consideration for mortgage calculations), and provide more housing while retaining neighborhood character.

Figure B4.3.1 Laneway housing

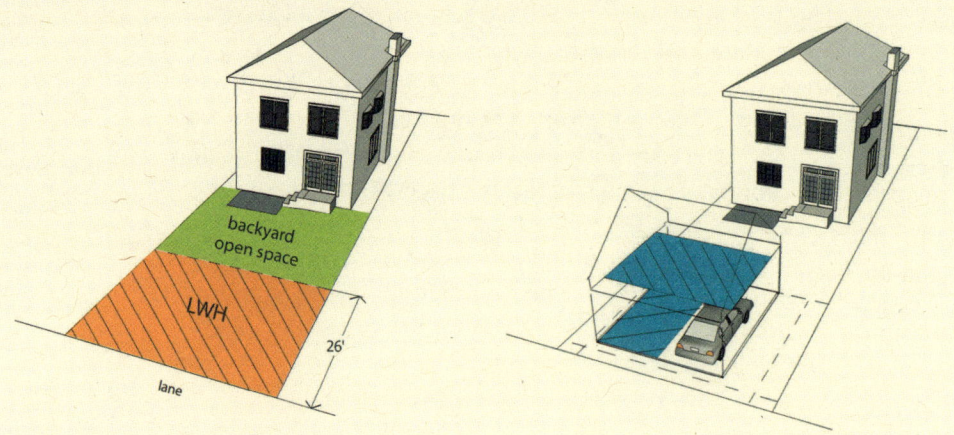

Source: OECD 2012.
Note: Part of the backyard (left) will be used to construct a laneway house (right) as a secondary suite that will be rented.

Vancouver first adopted regulations allowing secondary suites in single-family homes in 2004 (City of Vancouver 2011). Homeowners may add laneway housing while retaining the existing main house, build a laneway house alongside a new main house, or add a laneway house to the main house as a secondary suite. Laneway housing is intended to respond to the need for diverse types of rental housing in Vancouver. Although it cannot be sold, it provides ideal accommodations for family members, caregivers, or renters.

areas of the south and southwest. This spatial pattern is reflected in Bogota's social housing policy and measures. Although Bogota's administration cannot provide social housing in the city center, it has increased accessibility to BRT feeder lines by locating social housing, good infrastructure, and public amenities such as schools and health care facilities in key locations. The city's Metrovivienda program provides a good example of how low-income housing programs can be linked to a transit system, although it faces the challenges of finding land near transit stations and financing the program given a limited government budget.

Toward Successful Integration: Recommendations

The case experiences reviewed in this study underscore the challenges of placing rapidly growing cities on sustainable pathways. These challenges are magnified in developing countries. Integrated spatial development—particularly the coordination of transit and land-use plans and programs—must be a central component of any strategic effort to create more sustainable cities and regions. In the words of the Director of the European Commission's Directorate General for Regional Policy, European Commission, "Sustainable cities will never appear if the transit system is not sustainable. Increasing energy consumption, extensive travel and poor natural resource management must be redirected. Urban sprawl and the need to commute great distances for work and shopping must be curbed" (Kazlauskiene 2009).

Policy makers worldwide, particularly in developing countries, are in dire need of best-case examples of cities that have turned the tide, creating more sustainable mobility options and harmonizing urban transit systems and land-use patterns in sustainable ways. Chapter 2 highlighted several best-case examples; more success stories are needed, particularly in cities in the developing countries. Chapter 3 examined the constraints and opportunities associated with transit and land-use integration in several rapidly growing cities in developing countries. The cases of cities that have aggressively invested in mass transit systems highlight the contexts and challenges of integrating major transit investments with urban development.

The insights gleaned from these case experiences point to specific policy recommendations and measures for implementing them that deserve consideration at different levels of strategic decision making and planning. Based on these insights, this section examines four critical issues: creating a vision and an enabling institutional and regulatory framework, adopting a city-level planning approach, promoting and implementing TOD, and capturing the value from transit infrastructure and neighborhood improvements.

Creating a Vision and an Enabling Institutional and Regulatory Framework

Any initiative on sustainable spatial integration begins with a city's well-articulated vision of a desirable future. This vision is then translated into plans and actions that promote integration with statutory master plans, which are sensitive to the market and are realistic regarding financing. Transit and land-use integration are considered convincing approaches for sustainable urban forms; they need to be guided by the master plans.

Developing strategic plans. Strategic planning is an indispensable component of successfully integrating transportation and urban development. Cities must have a thoughtful, collaborative, and inclusive process for planning; the process must yield a well-articulated and defensible long-range master plan for guiding regional growth; and the institutional capacity and wherewithal for carrying out the plan at multiple geographic scales must be in place.

As global best-case practices reveal, effective planning starts with a long-range vision of a desirable built form and settlement pattern. Many cities have a clear vision of the future transit network but a fuzzier sense of the communities and places that will be served. Visioning "place" ahead of "mobility" recognizes that transit is a means to an end—figuratively and literally—a vehicle for connecting people to places and creating the kinds of cities and neighborhoods where people want to live, work, play, learn, and interact. Only through visioning and planning for a desirable city form and pattern of land uses can investments in expensive transit systems become not only mobility projects but city-shaping and community-serving ones as well. Framing urban futures means the planning emphasis shifts from accommodating movement to promoting accessibility as well as other goals, such as livability, economic prosperity, and social inclusiveness. Visioning and planning for a desirable city form and its land-use pattern require a shift in focus from vehicles and channel ways to people and places. Visions and plans must be market sensitive and rooted in fiscal realities lest they become pipe dreams.

Visions matter, as all of the experiences reviewed in this study show. Whether it was a future vision of compact, walkable, low-carbon cityscapes (as in Singapore) or BRT services that cater to a range of urban forms (as in Ottawa), all success stories shared a long-range land-use vision that guided transit investments and service deployments. In all of these cities, the "land-use horse" led the "transit cart."

Visions need visionaries, people like Curitiba's Mayor Jaime Lerner and Seoul's Mayor Myong-Bak Lee. Such luminaries not only provided compelling visions of the future and decisive political leadership, they also nurtured a local culture that enthusiastically embraced the idea of sustainability to ensure that a succession of like-minded progressive mayors advanced the original plans and visions.

Advancing long-range visions and plans requires broad-based public support, without which a plan is likely to become an administrative document used and recognized by public officials but few others. Plans that have drawn broad public attention have adopted metaphors, such as Copenhagen's Finger Plan and Singapore's Constellation Plan. Such expressions are effective marketing tools for the plan and the planning process. They enable the average citizen to comprehend and relate to the plan and provide the kind of broad-based, popular support often needed for political traction.

Plans that make a difference extend beyond a single sector. They are multisectoral, holistic, and cross cutting. Such characteristics are important partly because of the co-dependence of urban systems: urban growth induced by a world-class public transit investment increases demand for expanded sewerage and water capacity, new housing, and business centers. Multisectoral planning also exploits opportunities for economizing on the costs of urban services and infrastructure—for example, using the rights-of-way for a new fixed-guideway transit line to lay broadband cable, storm-runoff channels, and utility lines. Crafting long-range visions and plans is a major challenge in developing countries, where most city officials are preoccupied with day-to-day urban service demands and face huge backlogs of infrastructure investments. Some cities have plans, but the concept of merging mobility and land use is alien. In other cities, the problem is the failure to integrate planning and implementation, institutionally or financially.

To endow strategic planning with teeth, it is often necessary to make the creation and implementation of a master plan a statutory requirement. Doing so usually means that stewardship must start at higher (national or state) levels of government. Authorizing legislation is needed that empowers planning agencies to create and enforce the master plan and enables the plan to be translated into specific sectoral actions and district plans. The planning process must be dynamic and fluid, changing if necessary as market conditions and local priorities shift. This agility and flexibility are particularly critical for rapidly growing and changing cities in developing countries.

Creating a supportive institutional and government environment. Local authorities are best able to gauge the land-use preferences of local residents and businesses. For this reason, land-use controls are and should be a local prerogative. However, it is important that local authorities weigh the broader desirable and undesirable repercussions of their decisions. Desirable effects include the economic efficiency gains and environmental benefits realized by a well-integrated regional transit network. Undesirable effects include negative externalities, such as generating car trips that impinge on surrounding communities.

Localities must be accountable for nonlocal impacts of their land-use decisions, which can be measured through various mechanisms, such as regional impact assessments or the formation of regional governing bodies that have the capacity to override local decisions that are incompatible with regional plans and visions. Global experiences with regional planning and growth management—in Copenhagen and Ottawa, for example—underscore the critical importance of establishing an institutional framework that prompts municipal authorities to "think globally and regionally and act locally." Support for this kind of regional planning and institutional frameworks must come from the top, along with enabling legislation that allows this governing model to function.

Although regional and local governments are responsible for measures related to urban transit and land-use integration, national governments can play important roles in promoting this integration. To promote such integration, it is important that the national government articulate its policies

> **Box 4.4 Integrating land-use and transit policy planning in India**
>
> Cities in India vary considerably in population, area, urban form, topography, economic activities, income levels, growth constraints, and other features. The design of the transit system depends on all of these city-specific features. Transit planning is also intrinsically linked to land-use planning. The two need to be developed together, in a manner that serves the entire population and minimizes travel needs. An integrated master plan needs to internalize the features of sustainable transit systems.
>
> In developing such plans, attention should be paid to channeling the future growth of a city around a preplanned transit network rather than developing a transit system after uncontrolled sprawl has taken place. Transit plans should enable a city to take an urban form that best suits the geographical constraints of its location; these plans should support the key social and economic activities of the city's residents. In practice, transit planning has not received the attention it deserves in strategic development and land-use plans.
>
> The government of India would promote the development of integrated land-use and transit plans for all cities. Management of all state-level urban development and planning bodies would be required to include in-house transit planners and representation from transit authorities. The national government would extend support for the preparation of such integrated land use and transit plans to the extent of 50 percent of the cost of developing such plans, provided the city demonstrates its willingness to act in accordance with them.
>
> In order to create models for possible learning and replication, the government of India would fully support pilot studies in a few sample cities, of different characteristics and in different regions of the country. As part of this exercise, each city would be encouraged to identify potential corridors for future development and then establish a transit system that would encourage growth around it. For example, radial corridors emerging from the city and extending 20–30 kilometers could be reserved for future development. To protect such corridors from encroachment, physical barriers would have to be erected along them and roads would have to be built on short stretches even before settlements were developed. Stretches of the corridor would guide the location of the settlements, preventing sprawl.
>
> A scheme already exists under which the central government provides partial financial support for traffic and transit studies in cities. This scheme would be modified to enhance the extent of central government support and make these studies more broad based to integrate transit and land-use planning, keeping projected populations in mind.
>
> *Source:* Ministry of Urban Development, Government of India 2006.

as part of a national urban development or national urban transport development strategy. Few national governments in developing countries have such policies. One of the few that does is India. Its National Urban Transport Policy of 2006 includes integrated urban transit and land-use planning as its first objective (box 4.4). By providing funds through the Jawaharlal Nehru Urban Renewal Mission in exchange for certain urban reforms, India's national government supports local governments' efforts to develop infrastructure for public transit and nonmotorized transportation infrastructure, such as bicycle lanes. As most mass transit investments require national budgetary support, local governments may be required to adopt certain policy measures to promote transit and land integration as a condition of receiving funds.

At the city level, the administration must have the capacity and political backing to overcome the inertia formed by parochial, unisectoral entities that view the world in silo terms. Such behavior has been a major obstacle to integrating transit and land use in Bogota. This common institutional barrier is found in many governmental organizations worldwide.

Cross-sector coordination does not require the creation of a super organization that absorbs all relevant departments and agencies: such an organization would not easily resolve the problem of integration, as subsector units would simply be created under an umbrella organization, leaving the lack of coordination across units unchanged. Overcoming these problems requires articulating the process of cross-sector coordination, identifying coordination-related issues, and ensuring that the management and staff concerned understand how these processes work.

In *Human Transit*, Walker (2011) explains that the complex nature of the planning process requires conversation in three dimensions: between land-use and transit investments, between long-range and short-range planning, and between different levels of governments. He concludes that "in each case, consolidating bureaucracies is tempting, but iteration is often a better path" (p. 221). He suggests a process of coordination between land-use planning and transit planning agencies using dialogue boxes that works as follows:

> The land planners do a long-range sketch of urban structure and this goes up on the wall in the transit planner's office, so that it guides daily thinking as well as long-range planning. The transit planner does a similar sketch of a long-range transit network, and this goes up on the wall in the land-use planner's office. That way, when developments are being approved, the short-term land-use planner can check whether the location is a good or bad one for transit and can judge developments accordingly. Meanwhile, as the long-term land-use planners stare at the transit map, they have new ideas for how to build communities around the proposed line and stations (see figure 4.7).

Removing restrictive regulations and setting the right prices. As explained in the case study of Ahmedabad in chapter 3, some policies and regulations adopted by the national or local government have adversely affected the smooth functioning of the land market by distorting prices. These distortions lead to an under- or oversupply of land and noncontiguous spatial development; they also inhibit the ability of transit infrastructure to change land-use patterns. It is important that the national government review the impact of these regulations on the functions of the land market. If the impact is found to be negative, the government needs to either repeal the regulations or introduce necessary mitigation measures.

Regarding the choice of transit mode, the most important policies concern energy prices, including taxation and subsidy policies, and import duties and fees on automobile registration, and use. It is important that the national government help manage the balance between private automobile use and public transit by removing subsidies for automobile use—by, for example, modifying fuel prices, parking prices, and toll charges.

Figure 4.7   A healthy conversation between transit and land-use planning officials

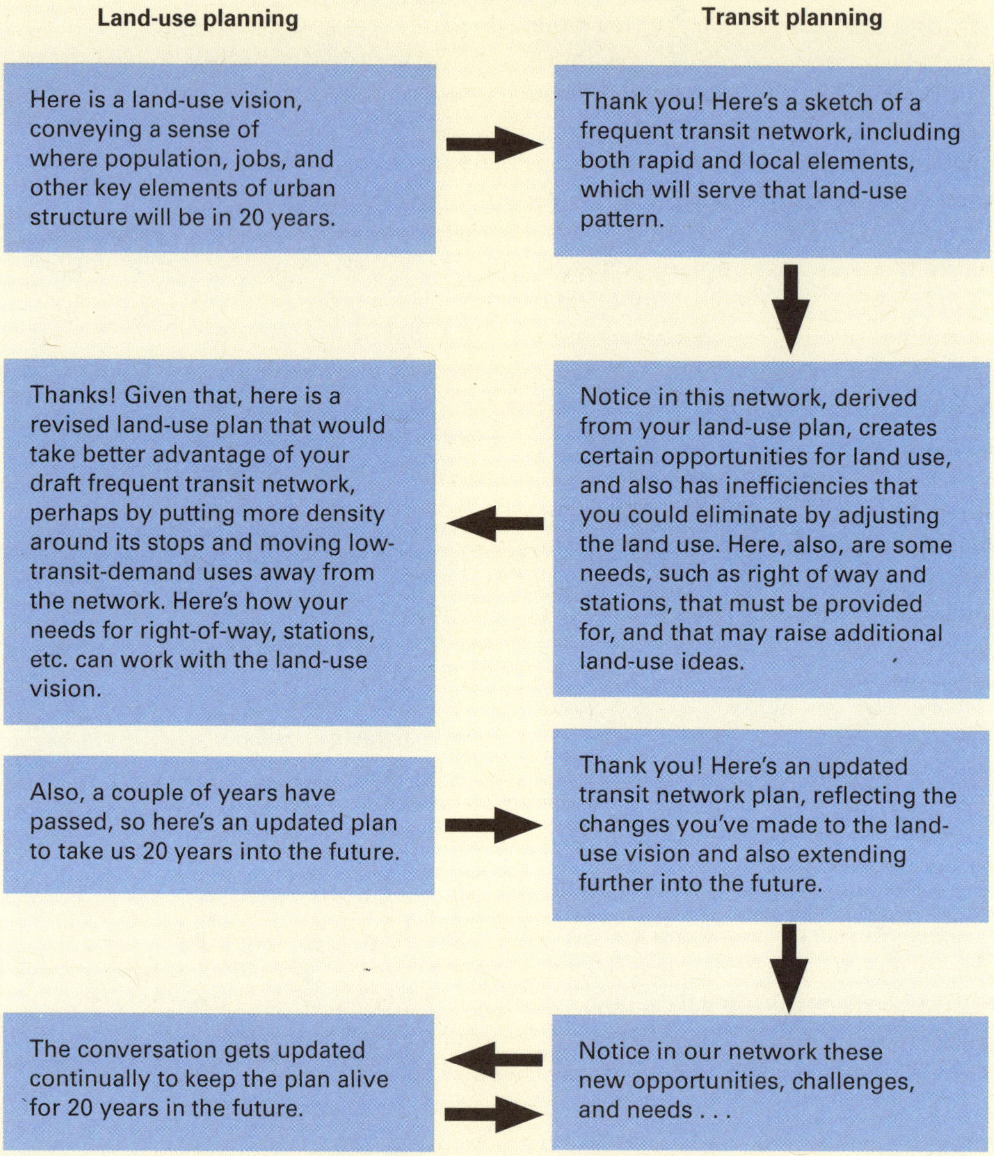

Land-use planning	Transit planning
Here is a land-use vision, conveying a sense of where population, jobs, and other key elements of urban structure will be in 20 years. →	Thank you! Here's a sketch of a frequent transit network, including both rapid and local elements, which will serve that land-use pattern.
Thanks! Given that, here is a revised land-use plan that would take better advantage of your draft frequent transit network, perhaps by putting more density around its stops and moving low-transit-demand uses away from the network. Here's how your needs for right-of-way, stations, etc. can work with the land-use vision.	← Notice in this network, derived from your land-use plan, creates certain opportunities for land use, and also has inefficiencies that you could eliminate by adjusting the land use. Here, also, are some needs, such as right of way and stations, that must be provided for, and that may raise additional land-use ideas.
Also, a couple of years have passed, so here's an updated plan to take us 20 years into the future. →	Thank you! Here's an updated transit network plan, reflecting the changes you've made to the land-use vision and also extending further into the future.
The conversation gets updated continually to keep the plan alive for 20 years in the future. ← →	Notice in our network these new opportunities, challenges, and needs . . .

Source: Walker 2012; adapted with permission from Island Press, Washington, DC.
Note: Similar conversations happen between land use and road planning, or between transit and road planning, etc., for other infrastructure or government objectives.

Achieving short-term mobility objectives and creating sustainable urban form goals in parallel. The natural instincts of local governments embarking on major new transit investments is to view such investments principally in mobility terms—as a solution to traffic congestion and air quality woes, and perhaps an opportunity to inject badly needed capital into the local economy. This near-term, congestion-relief focus is understandable, if undesirable, in light of political exigencies that mandate rapid improvements. The benefits of careful transit and land-use integration do not reveal themselves for decades, a time line that does not square well with the three- to five-year terms of office of many local politicians.

Most of the international best-case practices reviewed in chapter 2 framed transit investments well beyond the singular, near-term objective of enhancing mobility. Long-term indirect benefits, such as contributing to a less automobile-dependent and more sustainable urban form, were equally important.

In contrast, BRT investments in Ahmedabad, Bogota, and indeed most rapidly growing cities embarking on major new transit programs have been framed and envisioned as mobility rather than city-shaping investments. Experiences in cities like Copenhagen, Curitiba, Seoul, Stockholm, and metropolitan Washington, DC, reveal that transit investment is not an "either-or" proposition. Good integrated spatial development can provide both near-term congestion relief and longer-term urban-form benefits. Changes in urban form do not happen automatically, however, and they cannot be an afterthought once the system is already in place. Rather, the long-term urban-form objectives that are tied to infrastructure investments must be a strategic focus from the very beginning, marked by a firm and proactive commitment to incentivizing desired land-use outcomes through tools like permissive zoning and complementary neighborhood improvements.[6,7]

Adopting a City-Level Planning Approach

Once a vision is in place, a planning process must be established to execute the vision. Global experience suggests the kinds of forward-looking actions and steps—such as concentrating new urban growth around stations—that are of critical importance.

Establishing articulated densities. Among the physical features of the cityscape that are critical to the success of public transit, urban densities are the most important. Simply stated, mass transit needs "mass," or density. Higher densities along transit-served corridors ensure a critical mass of trip origins and destinations to fill up trains and buses, increasing cost-effectiveness. Very low-density cities with a predominantly polycentric form are automobile-centric (figure 4.8). In spread-out cities like Atlanta, for example, public transit has a difficult time competing with private vehicles. Only when urban densities are very high and a large share of jobs and retail activities are concentrated in the urban core, as in Shanghai, is public transit cost-effective. Many cities, such as Jakarta and Paris, lie somewhere between these extremes, where private and public transit can compete equally for trips.

Citywide average densities can be deceptive and even misleading: using citywide data to relate densities to transit success can lead to fallacious inferences, because cities are the wrong ecological unit.[8] What matters is

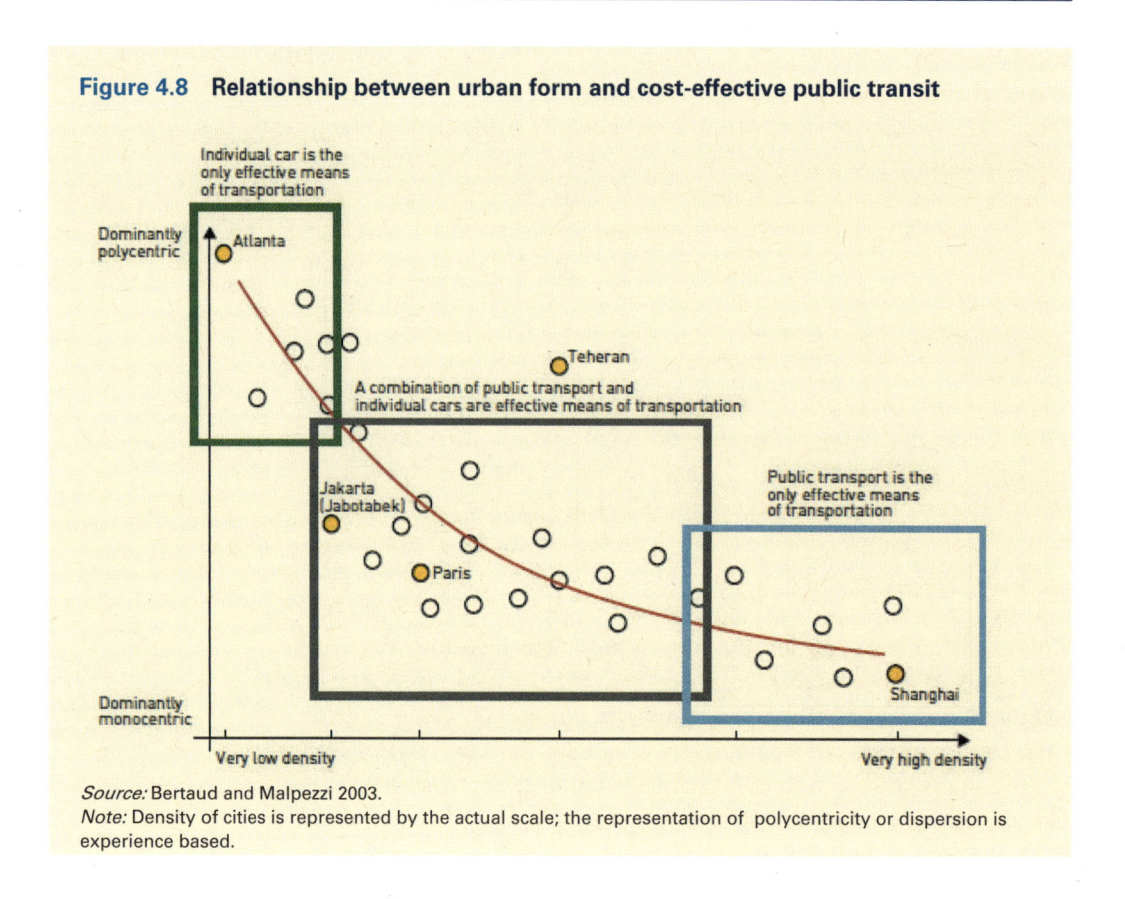

Figure 4.8 Relationship between urban form and cost-effective public transit

Source: Bertaud and Malpezzi 2003.
Note: Density of cities is represented by the actual scale; the representation of polycentricity or dispersion is experience based.

not average densities but how densities are organized in relationship to high-capacity transit services. Average densities in Curitiba are not high citywide, for example, but densities are high where they matter—along BRT corridors. Curitiba enjoys "articulated densities"—high densities in high-quality, transit-served corridors and the acquiescence to market-driven spread-out patterns of development in highway corridors.

In contrast, in cities without a legacy of forward-looking planning, densities tend to be unarticulated. Los Angeles, the most automobile-dependent city in the United States, averages the highest overall population density in the country. Its thicket of crisscrossing freeways and major arteries form a dense road network. The city also averages the highest level of vehicular travel per capita and typically the worst traffic congestion in the country, according to the Texas Transportation Institute (Cervero and Murakami 2010). This dysfunctional combination of high population and road densities has been called the worst of all possible worlds, because traffic congestion and the externalities associated with car travel increase exponentially with car density and city size. The suburbs of Los Angeles are dotted with three- to four-story garden-style walk-up apartments, horizontally stretched within superblocks, creating long walking distances. Densities in Los Angeles are too high for an automobile-dependent city, but they are not organized along linear corridors, as they are in transit-friendly cities like Curitiba and Stockholm, making it difficult to draw sufficient travelers to public transit.

Combining higher densities with diverse land uses and pedestrian-friendly design. By themselves, higher densities are insufficient for promoting sustainable travel. High-rise residential towers in isolated superblocks far removed from retail districts are unlikely to promote walking and cycling, and they are associated with high vehicle kilometers traveled (VKT) per capita.[9]

In addition to higher densities, diversity of land uses and pedestrian- and bicycle-friendly designs are needed (Cervero and Kockelman 1997; Ewing and Cervero 2010). Diversity refers to the mix of land uses (for example, jobs and housing), the degree to which these uses are balanced, and the variety of housing types and mobility options available. Mixing land uses can shorten trips, encouraging nonmotorized travel and internalization of travel (the replacement of trips by private car to external destinations with trips within a neighborhood in the form of foot travel). Other benefits of mixed land uses include opportunities for shared parking and a more even distribution of trips (and thus a flatter peak period) throughout the day and week. As shown in the cases of Arlington County, Virginia; Curitiba; and Stockholm, mixed-use transit corridors can also produce efficient bidirectional travel flows.

The design of pedestrian-friendly environments is also crucial to successful TOD. High-quality urban design softens peoples' perceptions of densities, allowing building heights to be increased beyond what residents would otherwise accept in order to sustain cost-effective transit services. Studies from Bogota; Hong Kong SAR, China; and Taiwan, China reveal that urban design features like block sizes and the levels of street connectivity can affect travel behavior more than urban densities (Cervero and others 2009). Perhaps because they are in such short supply in the developing world, pedestrian-friendly environments there strongly influence how people travel. Road networks with branching loops, cul de sacs, and dead ends provide poor connectivity to pedestrians, forcing them to follow circuitous, indirect pathways. Grid street patterns allow pedestrians to reach desired destinations more quickly. As connectivity increases, block sizes typically shrink. In one Ahmedabad neighborhood, for example, only 13 percent of trips with an average block size of 4 hectares were by foot, compared with 36 percent in an otherwise similar neighborhood in which the average block size was just 1.2 hectares (based on the World Bank's study in Ahmedabad). Combining higher densities with diverse land uses and pedestrian-friendly designs at and around transit stations, experience shows, is an effective way to induce sustainable travel and create a sustainable city form.

Creating a supportive environment to leverage transit-oriented development. High-capacity transit services ensure that large volumes of people can reach a site. Without the expansion of other urban infrastructure and services, however, or the appeasement of current residents in an area, highrise development will not take place.

Knight and Trygg (1977) reviewed experiences in San Francisco, Toronto, and other North American cities. They identified a number of prerequisites for significant land-use shifts around newly opened metrorail stations (figure 4.9). Their recommendations are as valid today as they were in 1977.

The decision to develop land is made by a private real estate developer, but it hinges on the "commitment to a specific improvement"—another way of saying that the public sector must have the will and capacity to follow through with transit investments that contribute to achieving land-use and urban form visions of the future. Implementation of this commitment enhances accessibility to particular parcels of land. The unleashing of this dynamic, coupled with other supportive factors, results in the decision to develop land and the consequent impact (for example, TOD, reduced traffic congestion, better air quality).

Among the key factors leading to successful linkage of urban transit and land use is the presence of nearby land developments, spurred by public sector urban renewal projects or private developers reacting to market opportunities. Another is the availability of developable land, which could be assembled by developers or the public sector (using eminent domain powers, for example). In Ahmedabad, the pattern of land parcelization—many small lots, as a result of the Urban Land Ceiling Act—has thwarted TOD.

A third factor is the physical environment, which needs to be reasonably attractive if a site is to be developed. Sites need to have good access (for example, good pedestrian connections at transit stations). They also need to be free of blight, crime, and incompatible land uses (such as factories if high-end residential housing is being developed). The presence of blight and stagnant surrounding districts has stymied urban regeneration and TOD around a number of Bogota's BRT stations.

A fourth factor is the existence of strong regional demand for growth. New transit investments have largely redistributive rather than generative effects on growth: rather than create new jobs and businesses in a region through productivity gains, they help determine the specific locale in which growth in a region takes place.[10] If a region is not growing, there are no new households or businesses to redirect from highway to transit corridors; railways and busways will have negligible impacts on land use in areas with weak regional economies. In the United States, cities like Buffalo and Pittsburgh invested in expensive fixed-guideway rail systems in the 1970s–90s. Little TOD occurred, in large part because their regional economies were stagnant (Cervero 1998).

A fifth factor for leveraging TOD is supportive government policies, such as tax policies and complementary infrastructure. In distressed urban districts, tax-exempt bonds or tax abatements within enterprise zones may be necessary to reduce investment risks and attract private capital. Expansion or upgrading of sewerage and water trunk-line capacities, stormwater

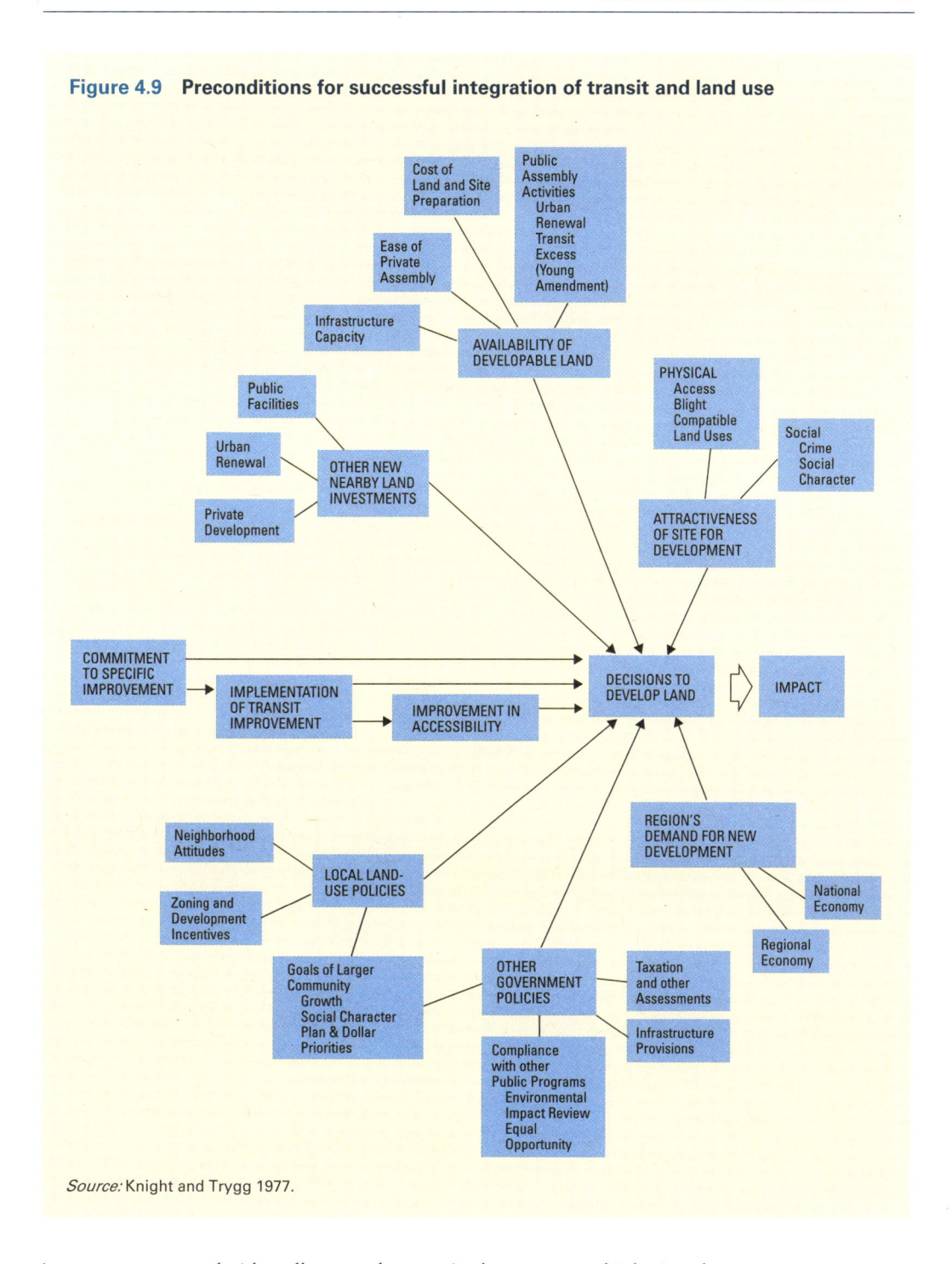

Figure 4.9 Preconditions for successful integration of transit and land use

Source: Knight and Trygg 1977.

improvements, and sidewalks may be required to support high-rise clustered development.

Figure 4.9 identifies other local government policies that may have to accompany transit investments, such as zoning that allows increases in density and the inclusion of neighborhood viewpoints in neighborhood designs, in order to head off not-in-my-backyard (NIMBY) resistance to clustered development. The *charrette* method, which Ho Chi Minh City used to bring together the relevant departments to jointly develop a green transit corridor project (see chapter 3), can be applied to include communities through participatory planning for TODs. *Charrettes* facilitate local government's solicitation of broad-based public input into the planning and design of its transit system.

Exploiting implementation tools. A host of regulatory and incentive-based tools is available for promoting transit and land-use integration. Several that are particularly well suited to the challenges facing cities in the developing countries deserve particular attention:

- Redevelopment authorities can be created and granted special powers and privileges to redevelop distressed and blighted urban districts. Normal redevelopment powers include the right to underwrite the costs of land development through such mechanisms as tax-increment financing and assistance acquiring/assembling land through eminent domain powers.[11] The creation of redevelopment zones has the potential to transform distressed or marginal urban areas near BRT stations in Ahmedabad and Bogota into economically viable transit-accessible districts.
- Land consolidation and readjustment schemes can be used to assemble land and finance local infrastructure improvements around major transit stations. Experiences from Japan, the Republic of Korea, and Taiwan, China show that land adjustment techniques work best when first introduced in agricultural settings, where land prices are low and landholdings can be easily assembled and reconfigured. In Japan, a land readjustment scheme has also been used in urban redevelopment projects. As Ahmedabad already has expertise and experience with town planning schemes, it could consider applying them, with necessary adjustment, to urban redevelopment projects, including TOD in already urbanized areas.
- Process-related tools, such as streamlining development reviews and fast-tracking project permitting, can be used to incentivize private development around stations. Private developments that are consistent with and reinforce station-area master plans should be exempted from prolonged environmental reviews and permitting requirements. Other pro-development actions that could be taken to leverage TOD in rapidly growing cities include as-of-right zoning (development that complies with all zoning regulation and does not require special permission from the city), the provision of density bonuses for mixed-use developments, and tax-exempt bond financing of urban renewal.

Guidelines for TOD and for site and street design can be introduced to ensure that investments feature an efficient arrangement of land uses; good circulation options, including nonmotorized forms of accessing stations;

and provision of parks and open spaces.[12] Examples and normative standards for street widths, intersection designs, site layouts, building densities, landscaping, and the like can ensure that station areas are both functional and attractive. Design shortcomings sometimes deter land development. In Bogota, for example, the siting of BRT stops in the medians of busy thoroughfares coupled with unattractive metal pedestrian bridges for accessing stations has created unattractive station environments. Passage of enabling legislation by higher levels of government is often needed to empower local authorities to introduce such tools. Pilot testing to overcome political and institutional inertia to any efforts to depart from business as usual may also be needed.

Rationalizing mainline transit investments and feeder systems. TOD hinges on the presence of high-quality transit services—services that are not only time competitive with private automobiles but are also free from extreme overcrowding, are reasonably on time, and have exceptionally high-quality feeder access. There needs to be some level of compatibility between a BRT system's design, operations, and the feeder networks that link to stations.

All transit users are pedestrians at some level. Experiences in cities like Copenhagen; Curitiba; and Hong Kong SAR, China point to the importance of providing well-integrated, seamless pedestrian connections between surrounding neighborhoods and transit stops. Particularly important are green connectors, which provide perpendicular bikeway and pedway linkages to transit stations and surrounding areas. Among the BRT cases reviewed in this study, Bogota has linked its bikeway (*cicloruta*) and pedway networks to TransMilenio stations, significantly improving feeder access. In contrast, Ahmedabad aligned its cycle tracks along Janmarg BRT corridors, effectively creating a parallel (and thus potentially substitutable) mobility option rather than a more complementary perpendicular one. Although there is no doubt a financial logic to co-building BRT and cycle-track systems on the same corridor, unless a circulation plan is in place for ensuring that secondary modes efficiently tie into and link with mainline BRT services, there is likely to be a disconnect between core transit services and the distribution-feeder systems that tie into them.

The design and operation of the BRT system itself partly defines the importance of integrated feeder connections. In Ahmedabad, the Janmarg BRT operates as a "closed system" (buses on the busway never leave the facility), effectively providing trunkline services that rely on other modes (foot, bicycle, car, two-wheeler, or another bus) for station access. Closed systems require exceptional feeder connections as well as intermodal transfer facilities for handling the logistical needs of connecting modes. The absence of integrated networks of green connectors as well as staging areas for efficient, seamless intermodal transfers suggests a lack of congruence between a closed-system BRT operation and the network of complementary feeder services. An alternate approach, practiced in Guangzhou and Ottawa, is an "open system," in which some buses function as both mainline carriers and feeder connectors. Having buses that operate at higher speeds along a busway morph into neighborhood feeders when they leave the busway can reduce or even eliminate what is often the scourge of transit riding for choice (that is, car-owning) users: the dreaded transfer. Such integrated bus services reduce the pressures of building complementary, secondary networks of bikeway/pedestrian bus feeders.

The open system is one of the factors contributing to the metro-like carrying capacity of the Guangzhou BRT system. It reduces the size of BRT stations, because it does not require additional space for connecting feeder lines. The smaller area needed for stations is a particular advantage when BRT systems must be built in narrow and crowded corridors. From a land development perspective, open systems also effectively extend the spatial reach of the busway, allowing for a form of extended TOD—that is, development that is less concentrated around transit stops but is reachable by high-quality feeder connections. Guangzhou's open system design combined with high-rise development along main-line corridors has meant that it has effectively taken on features of both an adaptive city and adaptive transit, as discussed in chapter 2. The simultaneous creation of a flexible bus-based transit network and leveraging of dense, mixed-use development along busy corridors is a unique feature of Guangzhou's highly successful BRT investment.

In Ottawa, an open-system BRT has meant that some development, mostly office and commercial buildings, has concentrated within a five-minute walk of BRT stops. Other development, notably single-family and even some multifamily residential housing, has occurred farther away but still within a reasonable distance by integrated-feeder bus or bike access.

Promoting and Implementing Transit-Oriented Development

In promoting and implementing TOD, each city needs to develop a diverse portfolio of TODs, taking account of local conditions. Based on these, cities can introduce prototype TOD projects as a way to test the waters, in both market and political terms. As a complementary measure, cities also need to introduce transportation demand management (TDM) and aggressively pursue affordable housing policies to address the needs of lower-income residents.

Creating transit-oriented development typologies. TOD is not suitable everywhere. Some stations function as logistical interchange points where buses, taxis, private cars, pedestrians, delivery trucks, and the like converge. Few people want to live near such areas. Other stations are in established residential neighborhoods, where residents are happy with what they have and do not want any land-use changes.

All cities seeking to achieve a more transit-oriented built form should aim to build a typology of transit station environments and TODs, backed by realistic market assessments and illustrative design templates. Even in places ripe and ready for change, a typology of TODs should be considered for market and practical reasons. For example, some station areas may be better off with fairly modest densities, predominantly residential development, and a scattering of retailers that serve mainly local markets. Other station settings may evolve into large mixed-use centers that are all-day/all-week trip generators servicing a regional customer base. Some TODs might be assigned a strong public place–making role—serving, for example, as focal points for reenergizing stagnant urban districts and reorganizing development by providing urban amenities like neighborhood libraries, retail plazas, and civic squares. Other TODs might be better suited as compact commercial districts with relatively little housing. A diverse portfolio of TOD types is more likely to reflect market realities and factors, such as the availability of sufficient and buildable supplies of land, than a one-size-fits-all approach to TOD planning and design.

Creating transit-oriented development prototypes. For cities with little history of TOD or even transit/land-use integration in general, it is important that prototypes be introduced as a way to test the waters, in both market and political terms. Each city presents a unique context for creating TOD prototypes. In Ahmedabad, closed textile mill sites offer tremendous opportunities for leveraging large-scale TOD. As large, preassembled plots of land, these brownfield sites allow project-level master plans to be drawn and large-scale, mixed-use redevelopment projects to be built. Adaptively reusing former textile mill land is all the more important given legislation that resulted in ownership of small parcels, which can thwart efforts to leverage TOD. Local agencies should focus on creating a few prototypes for each class of TOD, using a *charrette* process, perhaps even pursuing joint development (as in the Washington, DC metropolitan area) as a way to divide both risks and reward between the public and private sectors.

Combining transit-oriented development and transportation demand management. TOD can be viewed as a "hardware" solution—a physical design that promotes transit ridership and nonmotorized access. This hardware needs supportive "software," including TDM measures. Combining transit incentives with automobile disincentives, experiences show, can yield synergistic outcomes, including higher ridership gains.

Bogota has been particularly aggressive in pursuing TDM, in the form of car bans, a day-without-a-car initiative, parking reforms that have forced parked cars off sidewalks, bikeway (*cicloruta*) networks, and an assortment of improvements to pedestrian and civic spaces. The city has taken a holistic approach to promoting alternatives to private car travel by introducing a set of reinforcing and interlocking demand-management strategies. It has largely failed, however, to capitalize on these complementary TDM measures to promote a denser, mixed-use, pedestrian-friendly environment around key TransMilenio stations. To date, TOD has not been a part of Bogota's portfolio of progressive urban initiatives. Future phases of BRT expansion, as well as new investments in metrorail services and the green corridor light-rail system, could become part of the city's urban agenda.

Making cities inclusive. The ability of transit to enhance access to jobs, educational opportunities, retail outlets, and other valued destinations benefits households across the income spectrum. However, land markets typically respond by raising land prices around transit stations, which can displace low-income households. When possible, local authorities should aggressively pursue affordable housing policies, locating social housing near transit stops, providing density bonuses for the inclusion of mixed-income housing within projects, and requiring developers to set aside at least 15 percent of new units as below market-rate housing in return for tax credits and other financial incentives, for example. TOD should not be just about creating an efficient and sustainable urban form; it should also help redress the most serious problem facing many cities of the developing world: crippling urban poverty and deprivation.

For many households, transportation and housing are co-dependent, bundled goods. Some households end up trading off low housing costs on the metropolitan periphery for high transportation costs incurred in reaching jobs and amenities in the urban core. Programs like Bogota's Metrovivienda aim for "win-win" solutions by building affordable housing near transit terminals. Such programs are designed for low-wage households that can afford a titled, serviced property and public transit fares. Metrovivienda has struggled to achieve its program objectives partly because of poor enforcement of property rights laws and administrative shortcomings, such as the granting of overly generous concessions to private property developers. As is often the case in the developing world, the problems are less a product of flawed theory than outcomes of institutional inertia and shortcomings.

Capturing the Value from Transit Infrastructure and Neighborhood Improvements

Value capture is a promising source of income for building transit infrastructure and neighborhood improvements. As discussed in chapter 2, it has been successfully applied in Hong Kong SAR, China and Tokyo, through the sale of development rights by the transit agency to real estate firms in Hong Kong SAR, China and the granting of a development franchise to railway consortia that co-develop new towns and rail transit systems in Tokyo.

An important lesson from these cases is that the integration of transit and land use can be remunerative, yielding income needed to expedite and solidify the process. Value capture is particularly suited for financing transit infrastructure in dense, congested settings where a high premium is placed on accessibility and the institutional capacity exists to administer the program. Accessibility benefits get capitalized into land values, presenting tremendous opportunities to recapture some of the value created by the transit investment, as a supplement to fare-box income and other revenue sources. In addition to generating income to pay off the bonds and loans for transit infrastructure, value capture can produce income that goes to improving station-area environments. Value capture can also suppress land speculation by returning some of the value added to the public sector.

Even in ultradense, transit-friendly Hong Kong SAR, China, railway investment is not financially viable on its own. Value capture and joint development not only generate income to help retire rail capital investment bonds and finance operations, they also create market demand that ensures high-ridership services. Hong Kong SAR, China's version of public-private partnership is not about offloading the cost of building railways to the private sector. Rather, it is about co-development in which each sector brings its comparative advantage to the table (land acquisition powers in the case of the public sector, access to equity capital in the case of the private sector). The resulting "win-win" situation not only leads to financially viable investments, it also establishes an intimate connection between rail systems and nearby real estate development that attracts tenants, new investors, and transit riders. This model is currently being extended to Shenzhen, which over time could open the door to its application in other Chinese cities, including Guangzhou.

Greater Tokyo's private railways have historically practiced transit value capture on an even grander scale, building massive new towns along rail-served corridors and cashing in on the construction, retail, and household service opportunities created by these investments. In both Tokyo and Hong Kong SAR, China, rail and property development has created a virtuous cycle of viable railway operations and a highly transit-oriented built form.

Important to the success of transit value capture in both cities has been institutional adaptation and change. Over time, Mass Transit Railway (MTR) Corporation executives gained an appreciation of urban design, pedestrian circulation, and public amenities—all particularly important in a dense, crowded city like Hong Kong SAR, China—in creating financially successful Rail+Property (R+P) projects. The city's emergence as an international gateway, combined with its economic transformation from traditional manufacturing to a service-based economy, opened up new possibilities for R+P in both shaping growth and serving new market demands. MTR built high-quality, mixed-use R+P projects on greenfields en route to the new international airport as well as on brownfields served by central-city railway extensions. These projects have proven to be wise investments: recent R+P projects that functionally and architecturally blend well with surrounding communities have outperformed earlier projects in terms of both ridership gains and real estate market returns.

Experiences in Tokyo, and to a lesser degree Seoul and Stockholm, also underscore the importance of market adaptation. The downturn in the Tokyo region's real estate market, slowing economic growth, and changing demographic structure prompted private railway companies—both new and old—to seek new market opportunities, most notably infill housing and mixed-use developments around major central-city railway terminals. Such redevelopment complements the earlier-generation new towns built by private companies. To appeal to professional-class workers and a more youthful labor force, Tokyo has created high-quality urban spaces in and around joint development projects. Resiliency in the design and planning of new-towns/in-towns has also been a hallmark of recent urban regeneration successes in Seoul and Stockholm.

Value capture need not always occur directly, through land ownership and joint development. It can also occur indirectly, by extracting surplus from other property owners through betterment taxes, benefit assessment districts, and gains in regular property tax proceeds.[13] In Los Angeles, for example, nearly 10 percent of the $4 billion price tag for building the Red Line metrorail system came from benefits assessments exacted from nearby commercial property owners.

Successful value capture schemes depend on a supportive institutional environment. In the Washington, DC metropolitan area, a single transit authority was formed and given the resources needed to leverage TOD. Particularly important was the formation of a proactive real estate development department within the organization, staffed by seasoned professionals with private sector experience who brought a more entrepreneurial approach to land development. Management gave these professionals the resources and latitude needed to amass a portfolio of real estate holdings, carry out market pro formas, and seek out private sector partners with whom it forged successful public-private partnerships. Creating a town planning and urban design department to ensure that joint development projects are of high quality and architecturally integrated can be another key institutional reform, as demonstrated by the case of Hong Kong SAR, China.

Moving from the theory to the practice of value capture can be difficult in the developing world, where institutional support for progressive financing schemes is often lacking. Ahmedabad recaptures value by selling FAR bonuses to property owners along Janmarg corridors, but this program appears to generate relatively modest levels of funding.[14] Value capture in Bogota yields only a fraction of the municipal budget.

Another means of indirectly recapturing transit-induced gains in land value is the introduction of split-rate property taxes, as practiced in the state of Pennsylvania. This mechanism imposes higher taxes on land than on buildings, as a means of prodding owners to develop land more fully and intensely. The higher tax rates plus the intensification of development increases revenue while contributing to a more transit-supportive built form.

One possible way to stimulate transit value capture in developing countries is to involve the private sector, in the form of public-private partnership schemes. Private participants not only bring a more entrepreneurial mindset and business acumen to the table, they also provide access to private capital and spread the risks inherent in land development.

Sometimes a culture change within the transit organization is needed in which land development becomes a legitimate mission. In Hong Kong SAR, China, the mission of the MTR included not only serving market demand but also shaping the market to ensure financial viability. This redefined business model allowed it to take advantage of land value capture and commercial sales opportunities in and around stations. Strong real estate markets, significant institutional capacity, and clear policy guidelines are needed to successfully pursue joint development and public-private partnership schemes, especially in developing countries (Mathur and Smith 2012).

Experiences from Hong Kong SAR, China, Tokyo, and metropolitan Washington, DC, point to other prerequisites for value capture schemes and successful joint development projects:

- *high densities*, which although they give rise to severe traffic congestion, create market demand for property development in highly accessible locations like transit station areas
- *a supportive legislative environment* that empowers transit authorities to pursue joint development projects
- *organizational cultural change* that embraces property development as a legitimate mission of the transit organization, in recognition of the fact that successful transit operations are not just about running trains and buses on time, but also about shaping markets and ensuring high levels of future ridership by steering larger shares of future land development to transit station areas
- *creation of a real estate development division* within the organization whose charge is to seek out promising joint development opportunities and leverage "win-win" partnerships with private sector interests.

Probably the most challenging issues in applying value capture to cities in developing countries are the lack of transparent property right registration systems and the complex procedures associated with land acquisition and transaction. Without more straightforward and efficient regulations and procedures, the application of the value capture financing scheme will be difficult, if not impossible.

The presence of informal settlements makes the redevelopment of built-up areas difficult. However, as the land value of TOD-associated areas is high, local governments or transit companies could use the revenues mobilized from value capture to cover the resettlement costs of the affected people. Another approach is to require developers to set aside a percentage of new residential buildings for local residents affected by changes, reducing the social and economic impacts of relocation.

Another major risk is that value capture finance mechanisms can lead to corruption, if transactions are not conducted in a competitive and transparent manner. An additional technical difficulty is estimating the base value of the land as well as its future value after transit construction. It is also important to make a conservative estimate of the value capture amount, if land speculation trends are observed in the market.

Core Lessons on Transit Investments and Urban Growth

The steps and proactive measures discussed earlier and outlined in figure 4.9 are necessary, but they are hardly sufficient for promoting successful linkages between transit and land use in general and TOD more specifically. Several other lessons emerge from the global experiences.

- *Land-use impacts are greatest when transit investments occur just before an upswing in regional growth.* Experiences show that the timing of transit investments matters. Some 70 years ago, sociologist Homer Hoyt observed that urban form is largely a product of the dominant transportation technology in place during a city's prevailing period of growth (Cervero 1998). Toronto's subway investment during a period of rapid immigration in the late 1950s was fortuitous; many new housing projects were built within walking distance of rail stations. In contrast, in Los Angeles, which invested heavily in subway, light rail, and commuter rail lines in the 1990s, much of the region's urban growth had already taken place. These public transit improvements proved to be too little, too late. For many rapidly developing cities, investing in transit during growth spurts can translate into significant land-use impacts.
- *Building rail in advance of market demand can yield positive economic rewards if a visionary land-use master plan, a well-functioning planning regime, and institutional apparatus are in place.* Although rapidly growing cities in the developing countries are best poised to be fundamentally reshaped by high-quality transit investments, they need the institutional capacity and wherewithal to leverage land development opportunities.
- *Radial fixed-guideway transit systems can strengthen downtown cores.* Experiences from Hong Kong SAR, China; San Francisco; Tokyo; Toronto; and elsewhere show that radial rail systems lead to increased employment growth in urban centers, the places that enjoy the largest gains in regional accessibility (figure 4.10). Although the regional shares of jobs and retailing in center cities often fall in the wake of new rail and busway investments, they would have fallen even more were it not for central business district–focused railway services.
- *Transit systems generally reinforce and often accelerate decentralization trends.* By improving accessibility to different parts of a region, extensive railway and BRT networks, like their highway counterparts, generally encourage suburbanization, to some degree. Although growth may be funneled in a particular direction as a result of new transit services, more often than not this direction will be outward.
- *Proactive planning is necessary if decentralized growth is to take the form of subcenters.* Whether decentralized growth takes a multicentered form (that is, TOD) rests largely on the degree of public commitment to strategic station-area planning carried out on a regional scale. Experiences in cities like Stockholm, Tokyo, and Toronto show that an aggressive stand to leverage the benefits of mass transit services can lead to more concentrated forms of decentralized growth.

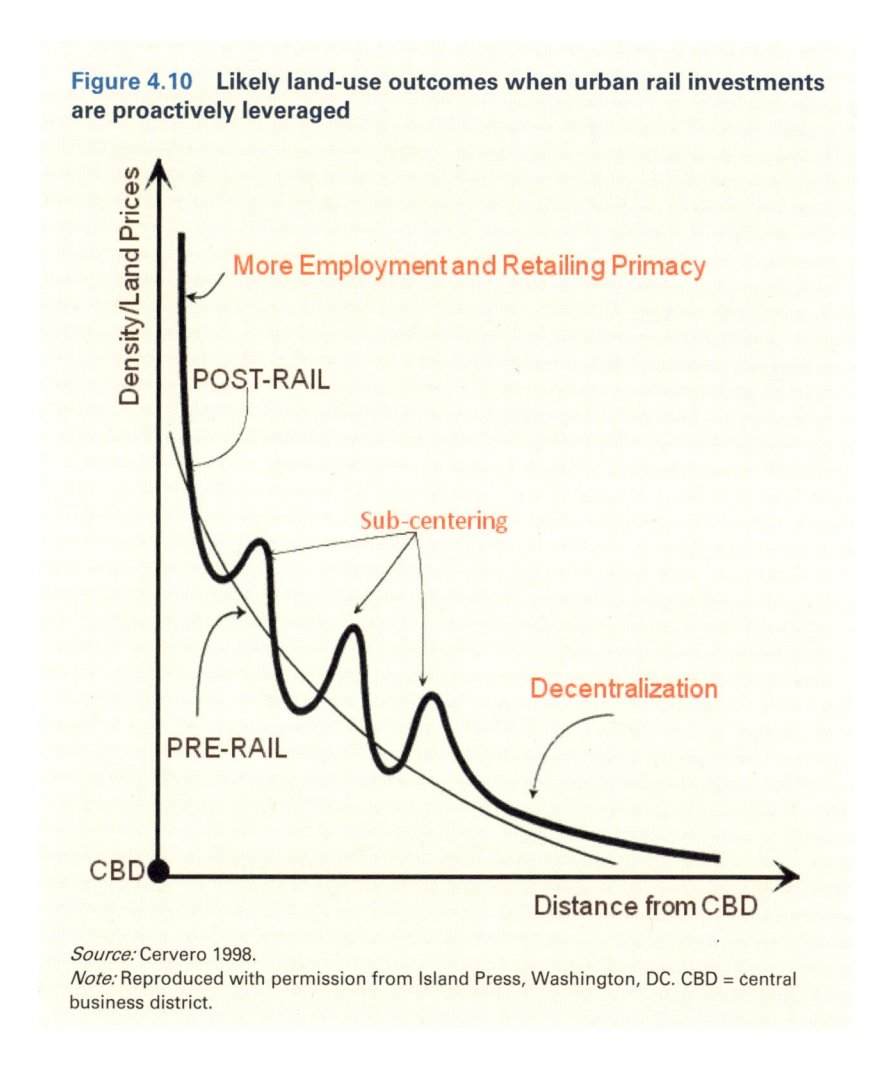

Figure 4.10 Likely land-use outcomes when urban rail investments are proactively leveraged

Source: Cervero 1998.
Note: Reproduced with permission from Island Press, Washington, DC. CBD = central business district.

Given public resource commitments, railways and busways can not only strengthen the core but induce selected subcentering. Although railways and busways contribute to outward growth, they can help to more efficiently organize whatever development occurs within traditional built-up areas.

- *Railways and busways can spur redevelopment* of *the central city under the right conditions.* When government agencies are willing to absorb some of the risks inherent in redeveloping depressed and economically neighborhoods, railways and busways can help attract private capital and breathe new life into struggling areas—as they have in the San Francisco Bay area, Tokyo, and metropolitan Washington, DC. There must be an unwavering public commitment to underwrite redevelopment costs and provide needed financial investments. The quid pro quo is the sharing of upstream risks, which allows the public sector to eventually share in the downstream reward of urban redevelopment. Experiences suggest that even with such investments, however, it is difficult to revitalize distressed urban districts where crime, intergenerational poverty, and private disinvestment remain serious problems.

- *Other pro-development measures must accompany railway and busway investments.* In addition to financial incentives, other "software" policies are needed to make transit "hardware" attractive to land developers. These measures include permissive and incentive zoning, such as density bonuses; the availability of nearby vacant or easy-to-assemble and develop parcels; support for land-use changes by local residents (that is, the absence of organized opposition and NIMBY forces); adequate water and sanitation trunk-line capacities and underground utilities; and complementary public improvements, such as the upgrading of sidewalks and the removal of physical constraints, including the preemption of land development by park-and-ride lots (see figure 4.9).
- *Network effects matter.* For fixed-guideway railway and busway systems to induce large-scale land-use changes, they must mimic the geographic coverage and regional accessibility of their chief competitors—limited-access freeways and highways. The strong city-shaping influences of metros in London, Paris, and Tokyo owe much to such network effects. The addition of a new exclusive-guideway line creates spillovers and synergies, benefiting not only the newly served corridors but also existing ones. Cities with growing BRT networks are poised to become more time competitive with private cars, increasing their shares of future trips.

Institutions and regulations. As stressed throughout this study, supportive institutional and regulatory environments are critically important to successful transit and land-use integration. Of particular importance is the presence of a regional governance structure that gives rise to inter-municipal cooperation, fosters accountability (in order to reduce negative spillovers across jurisdictions), and provides a territorial context for coordinating growth within a region's commuteshed and laborshed.

Ottawa's success in promoting bus-based TOD stems in part from the presence of a metropolitan government structure (the Ottawa-Carleton municipality), which prepared a visionary long-range master plan to guide growth, and introduced regulatory controls that enabled the body to override local zoning and land-use actions deemed inconsistent with this plan. The statutory authority to require that all regional trip generators and large-scale land developments, like shopping malls, were within walking distance of Ottawa's busway stations also ensured that a transit-supportive built form took shape.

Being effectively city-states with strong central government controls, Hong Kong SAR, China and Singapore have taken a largely unitary governmental approach to urban planning and growth management. This approach provides the kind of political continuity and firm oversight of private development often needed for a coherent and well-orchestrated form of transit-oriented growth to take shape.

Denmark's tradition of national government directives and a top-down, hierarchical approach to financing infrastructure played a role in prodding municipalities like Copenhagen to proactively plan for transit and land-use integration. The high fees and taxes on private cars set by the Danish government played a role in encouraging use of public transit and promoting efficient development patterns. Both integrating transit and land use and discouraging private car use are important in a land-constrained, low-lying country that is vulnerable to the negative consequences of global climate change, like rising sea levels.

Roles of Development Financial Institutions

Given the body of evidence showing that denser, transit-oriented built forms result in more cost-effective transit investments and integrated sustainable urban development, a sensible policy would be for development financial institutions to tie financial assistance to bona fide local efforts to improve the coordination and integration of transit and land development projects. Such an approach could also support and leverage national governments' own sustainable urban and transit programs, such as India's Jawaharlal Nehru Urban Renewal Mission (JnNURM).

Development financial institutions could help cities in developing countries nurture the institutional capacity needed to design and implement prototype TOD projects by facilitating technical and knowledge transfers of global best practices and the experiences of other developing cities. In particular, they could help cities committed to implementing TOD develop the institutional capacity and tools to implement value capture financing. Probably the most effective approach would be to integrate institutional capacity development with the implementation of a prototype TOD project financed by a loan.

Conclusion

This study builds on the World Bank's Ecological Cities as Economic Cities (Eco^2) concept, which promotes cross-sector integration, by focusing on integrated transit and land-use development as a promising strategy for advancing environmental sustainability, economic development, and inclusive development. If done well, integrated spatial development, particularly the physical linkage of transit investments and urban development, can create positive and meaningful Eco^2 outcomes.

A financial model to sustain TOD can occur at two levels and in two directions. The top-down, macro perspective of sustainable financing is critical. Pursuing a strategy of compact, mixed-use, high-quality development—whether TOD or smart growth in general—at a citywide or even metropolitan level can become an effective regional economic development tool, making city regions more economically competitive in the global marketplace. A high-quality, functional regional transit system that links high-quality urban centers creates the kind of built environment that is of increasing importance to amenity-conscious employers and employees. Blending good urban design with compact, mixed-use TOD becomes an effective tool for attracting outside investments and knowledge-based companies and professional businesses, which increasingly place a premium on livability and quality of place. Cities that manage to create attractive environments around transit stations can enjoy a competitive edge in recruiting and retaining highly sought businesses, which grow regional economies. Experiences with orienting growth in transit-served corridors matched by high-quality urban design—in Hong Kong SAR, China; Seoul; Singapore; and Stockholm, for example—reveal that good urbanism is wholly compatible with economic prosperity and competitiveness. Given that cities contribute 75 percent of global gross domestic product (GDP), this macro perspective should also be of prime interest to national governments.

At the micro, bottom-up level, financial sustainability can take the form of value capture as a tool for generating revenues—funds that pay not only for the investment (for example, stations, tracks, vehicles), but also for the upgrades and enhancements that are needed within a half-kilometer, five-minute walk of stations to create a high-quality, live-work-play-learn environment. This revenue can also finance social housing and associated facilities for low-income people. As experiences in Hong Kong SAR, China and Tokyo reveal, using some of the profit from selling land or development rights to the private sector to embellish public spaces and pedestrian environments around stations can improve a project, allowing it to generate higher profits as well as higher property tax revenue. The resulting TOD is not only environmentally but also financially sustainable. A virtuous cycle is set in motion in which denser, high-quality TOD generates higher profits and fiscal revenue, some of which can go into creating future high-quality TODs.

A point emphasized throughout this book is the importance of visioning urban futures. Experiences from Copenhagen and Stockholm reveal that a cogent regional vision helps ensure that high-capacity transit investments produce desired urban-form outcomes. Experiences from these and other cities suggest that station-area planning needs to be carried out selectively and judiciously. In many settings, planning efforts should be devoted to developing or redeveloping no more than a handful of rail and BRT stations, in order to concentrate resources and increase the odds of a "win-win" arrangement in which both public and private interests share the benefits conferred by new rail investments. Demonstrating that positive land-use changes are possible in conjunction with a rail investment is important to produce models the larger development community can emulate as well as to convince banks and lenders that investing in station-area projects can be financially remunerative.

As urban growth shifts to cities in the developing world, unprecedented opportunities will arise for linking land development and transit infrastructure. Although the rate of motorization is slowing in the developed world, it is growing exponentially elsewhere. The potential payoffs from successful transit and land-use integration in the Jakartas, Mexico Cities, and Nairobis of the world are therefore huge.

Given that the vast majority of urban growth is projected for cities with less than half a million people, a bus-based form of TOD interlaced with high-quality infrastructure for pedestrians and cyclists may be appropriate in many settings. Many cities in the developing world have the prerequisites needed if railway and BRT investments are to trigger meaningful land-use changes, including rapid growth, rising real incomes, and increased motorization and congestion levels. Supportive planning and zoning, public sector leveraging and risk sharing, and the capacity to manage the land-use shifts put into motion by transportation infrastructure investments are also needed.

Cities are well positioned to learn from international experiences with transit-induced land-use changes. Few, however, have adopted the practices of cities like Hong Kong SAR, China; Tokyo; and Washington, DC, in engaging private investors to co-finance capital investments through ancillary land development. Such value capture initiatives could go a long way toward putting cities in developing countries on more sustainable pathways, in terms of both facility financing and future patterns of urban development. Among all the tools available, value capture combined with TOD offers the most promise of putting the Eco^2 concept of sustainable growth and economic prosperity into practice.

Notes

1. In Curitiba, Brazil, the Institute for Research and Urban Planning (IPPUC) has provided essential technical input to support the city's sustainable urban development.
2. The same institutional framework has not always been successful in other Indian states.
3. As analyzed in chapter 3, the new development along the airport corridor is the result of the combined effects of the expansion project of the international airport and TransMilenio.
4. To prevent the operational inefficiency of transit companies, it is desirable that local governments provide operational subsidies to their transit companies to compensate mainly financial losses attributable to regulatory requirements, such as serving remote areas and ensuring late-night and early-morning services.
5. The official estimate of national greenhouse gas emissions is 292.9 Mt CO_2e in 2007 (10.8 t CO_2e per capita) (World Bank 2011).
6. In the absence of a variance or special exception, such an ordinance generally prohibits uses of land unless permitted as primary uses or

can be found to be accessory to a permitted use (New Hampshire Office of Energy and Planning).
7. Permissive zoning refers to land-use regulations that permit higher densities and different land uses than typically allowed in an urban area in recognition of factors such as a parcel's proximity to a transit station.
8. *Ecological fallacy* is a term used in research design that indicates that the wrong "ecological unit" was used to study a phenomenon. The proper unit of analysis is the one that best captures behavior. In the case of density, the correct unit of analysis is people or neighborhoods, not cities. Ecological fallacies typically refer to aggregation biases when using citywide data.
9. A new developing town in the western part of Ahmedabad is following this kind of automobile-dependent development pattern.
10. Redistribution itself can eventually yield economic productivity benefits by increasing agglomerations. Increasing densities near transit stops can increase economic outputs of knowledge-based and service industry firms that benefit from urban agglomeration through knowledge spillovers, quicker access to specialized labor, and new opportunities to collaborate.
11. Tax increment financing (TIF) is a method of mobilizing financial resources for the redevelopment of targeted areas by issuing bonds against future incremental tax revenues as a result of the improvement of the targeted areas. Cities need a well-functioning property tax system to adopt TIF.
12. Examples from Dallas and the San Francisco Bay Area, in the United States; Edmonton, Canada; and Queensland, Australia are available at http://www.dart.org/economicdevelopment/DARTTODGuide lines2008.pdf; http://www.bart.gov/docs/planning/TODGuidlines.pdf; http://www.edmonton.ca/city_government/documents/TODGuide-lines_February_2012.pdf; and http://www.dlgp.qld.gov.au/resources/guideline/tod/guide for-practitioners.pdf. See also http://www.itdp.org/library/publications/better-streets-better-cities.
13. One example is Ahmedabad's "guidance value"–based property tax.
14. FARs should not be driven by value capture opportunities, but by factors such as the carrying capacity of local infrastructure and environmental impacts on air quality and local traffic conditions, for example.

References

Altaf, A., and F. Shah. 2008. "The Spatial Growth of Metropolitan Cities in China: Issues and Options in Urban Land Use." World Bank, East Asia Region, Transport, Energy, Urban Sustainable Development Unit, Washington, DC.

Bertaud, A. 2004. "The Spatial Organization of Cities: Deliberate Outcome or Unforeseen Consequence?" http://alain-bertaud.com/images/AB_The_spatial_organization_of_cities_Version_3.pdf.

———. 2007. "Urbanization in China: Land Use Efficiency Issues." http://alain-bertaud.com/AB_Files/AB_China_land_use_report_6.pdf.

Bertaud, A., and S. Malpezzi. 2003. "The Spatial Distribution of Population in 48 World Cities: Implications for Economies in Transition." University of Wisconsin, Center for Urban Land Economics Research, Madison, WI.

Burchell, R. W., G. Lowenstein, W. Dolphin, and C. Galley. 2000. "Costs of Sprawl 2000." Report No. 74, Transportation Research Board, National Research Council, Washington, DC.

Cervero, R. 1998. *The Transit Metropolis: A Global Inquiry*. Washington, DC: Island Press.

Cervero, R., and K. Kockelman. 1997. "Travel Demand and the 3 Ds: Density, Diversity, and Design." *Transportation Research Part D* 2 (3): 199–219.

Cervero, R., and J. Murakami. 2010. "Effects of Built Environments on Vehicle Miles Traveled: Evidence from 370 U.S. Metropolitan Areas." *Environment and Planning A* 42: 400–18.

Cervero, R., O. Sarmiento, E. Jacoby, L. Gomez, and A. Neiman. 2009. "Influences of Built Environments on Walking and Cycling: Lessons from Bogotá." *International Journal of Sustainable Transport* 3: 203–26.

City of Vancouver. 2011. "Laneway Housing: How to Guide." http://vancouver.ca/commsvcs/lanewayhousing/pdf/LWHhowtoguide.pdf.

EIU (Economic Intelligence Unit). 2011. *Asian Green City Index*. Munich: EIU.

Ewing, R., and R. Cervero. 2010. "Travel and the Built Environment." *Journal of the American Planning Association* 76 (3): 265–94.

IPPUC (Instituto de Pesquisa e Planejamento Urbano de Curitiba). 2009. Slide from presentation, April 2, IPPUC, Curitiba, Brazil.

ITDP (Institute for Transportation and Development Policy), and EPC (Environmental Planning Collaborative). 2011. *Better Streets, Better Cities: A Guide to Street Design in Urban India*. Ahmedabad: ITDP and EPC.

Kazlauskiene, N. 2009. "The EU Can Help—But Cities Need to Act." In *Cities: Part of the Solution*. Stockholm: European Commission, Directorate General for Regional Policy, Swedish Presidency of the European Union.

Knight, R., and L. Trygg. 1977. *Land Use Impacts of Rapid Transit: Implications of Recent Experience*. Washington, DC: Office of the Secretary of Transportation.

Mathur, S., and A. Smith. 2012. *Decision Support Framework for Using Value Capture to Fund Public Transit: Lessons from Project-Specific Analysis*. San Jose, CA. Mineta Transportation Institute.

Ministry of Urban Development, Government of India. 2006. *India National Urban Transport Policy*. New Delhi: Government of India.

Moffat, S., H. Suzuki, and R. Iizuka. 2012. *ECO² Cities Guide: Ecological Cities as Economic Cities*. Washington, DC: World Bank.

OECD (Organisation for Economic Co-operation and Development). 2012. *Compact City Policies: A Comparative Assessment*. Paris: OECD.

Rybeck, R. 2004. "Using Value Capture to Finance Infrastructure and Encourage Compact Development." *Public Work Management & Policy* 8(4): 249–60. http://www.china-up.com:8080/international/case/case/1495.pdf.

Samad, T., N. Lozano-Gracia, and A. Panman, eds. 2012. *Colombia Urbanization Review: Amplifying the Gains from the Urban Transition*. Directions in Development. Washington, DC: World Bank

UNDP (United Nations Development Programme). 2007. *Human Development Report 2007/2008: Fighting Climate Change: Human Solidarity In a Divided World*. New York: Palgrave Macmillan.

Walker, J. 2011. *Human Transit*. Washington DC: Island Press.

World Bank. n.d. worldbank.org/indicator/IS.VEH.PCAR.P3.

———. 2011. *Malaysia Economic Monitor*. Bangkok: World Bank.

———. 2012. Materials for discussion at The Ho Chi Minh City Greenway Concept Workshop, July 4–8, 2011 in Ho Chi Minh City, Vietnam.

Index

Boxes, figures, notes, and tables are indicated by b, f, n, and t following the page numbers.

A

adaptive transit cities, 49–94
    Arlington County, Virginia, 78–82, 80f
    bus rapid transit in, 82–89, 83f, 85f, 87–88f
    Copenhagen, 4b, 53–56, 53f, 56f, 90t
    Curitiba, 82–84, 83f, 90t
    economic growth in, 50, 52, 52t
    Hong Kong SAR, China, 7f, 61–64, 63f, 90t
    Ottawa, 84–89, 85f, 87–88f, 90t
    population density in, 50, 51f
    Seoul, 64–70, 66–67f, 69t, 70f, 90t
    Singapore, 4–5b, 70–73, 71f, 90t
    Stockholm, 56–61, 59–60t, 90t
    Tokyo, 74–78, 75–78f, 90t
    transit and land-use integration in, 52–82
    transit ridership in, 50, 51f, 52t, 90t
    transportation modes in, 90t
    Washington, DC metro area, 78–82, 80f, 90t
administrative capacity, 8, 12, 156–58, 170–71
affordable housing, 101–3, 119–20, 121f. *See also* inclusive transit-oriented development
Africa, traffic accidents in, 32. *See also specific countries and cities*

Ahmedabad, India, 96–109
    challenges for, 8, 105–8
    collaboration in, 104–5
    density limitations in, 10, 105–7, 154
    design issues in, 107–8, 159–60, 160f, 175
    FAR limits in, 105–7
    financing schemes in, 14, 19, 103, 158
    future plans and recommendations for, 108–9, 142–43n3
    inclusive TOD in, 165
    institutional framework in, 103–4, 105b
    Janmarg BRT in, 97–99, 98–99f, 110b
    land regulations in, 107, 176
    long-term TOD goals in, 148
    new-town developments in, 108
    public housing linked to transit in, 101–3
    regional coordination in, 151
    regulatory framework in, 156
    retrofitting problems in, 162
    Sabarmati Riverfront Development Project, 101b
    transit corridor development in, 100–101, 101b, 102f
    value capture in, 184
Ahmedabad Janmarg Ltd. (AJL), 99

Ahmedabad Municipal Corporation
    (AMC), 97, 102–5, 107, 142–43n3,
    150, 165
Ahmedabad Municipal Transport
    Services (AMTS), 107
Ahmedabad Urban Development
    Authority (AUDA), 99, 103, 104–5,
    143n6, 150
Alameda Porvenir (Bogota), 109–10,
    119
AMC. *See* Ahmedabad Municipal
    Corporation
Arlington County, Virginia. *See also*
    Washington, DC metro area
        as adaptive transit city, 78–82,
            80f
        mixed-use development in, 175
articulated density
    average density vs., 11b, 155b
    lack of, 151–56, 153f
    recommendations for, 15, 173–75,
        174f
    regulatory framework for, 10–12
Asian Green City Index, 152
as-of-right zoning, 79, 178
Atlanta, Georgia
    environmental footprint of, 34, 34b
    transit vs. private automobile costs
        in, 173
AUDA. *See* Ahmedabad Urban
    Development Authority
automobile-dependent development.
    See also private automobile
    ownership
        consequences of, 3, 29–33, 30–32f
        interest groups and, 163–65, 164f
        new-town developments as, 108
        reversing culture of, 35–38, 35f,
            37–38b
average density vs. articulated density,
    11b, 155b

B

Bangladesh, traffic accidents in, 33
Barcelona, Spain, environmental
    footprint of, 34, 34b
Ben Nghe Tan Hu Canal (Ho Chi Minh
    City), 139
betterment taxes, 20
bicycle-friendly design
    in Ahmedabad, 107, 159–60, 179
    in Bogota, 116, 117, 119f, 126,
        144n17, 179
    in Copenhagen, 53–54
    density and, 175
    financing of, 158
    in Guangzhou, 131, 134, 135f

in Stockholm, 58
TOD and, 37b
transportation demand
    management and, 36
bike lease programs, 54
bike-sharing systems, 131, 134, 135f
Bogota, Colombia, 109–29
    affordable housing in, 119–20, 121f
    challenges for, 8, 122–29
    density regulations in, 10, 124–26,
        154
    design issues in, 126, 127f, 160,
        161f, 175
    financing schemes in, 14, 19,
        121–22, 158
    future plans and recommendations
        for, 126–29, 128f
    inclusive TOD in, 165–67, 182
    institutional framework in,
        122–24, 123f
    long-term TOD goals in, 148
    regional coordination in, 9, 124,
        125f, 151
    regulatory framework in, 156
    transit corridor development in,
        113–16, 114b, 115f, 117–18f
    TransMilenio BRT in, 111–12,
        112f, 114b, 130b
    transportation demand
        management in, 116–19,
        118–19f
    unarticulated density in, 11b, 155b
    value capture in, 184
brownfield development
    in Ahmedabad, 100
    regulatory framework for, 17
    in Stockholm, 58, 163
Buffalo, New York, rail infrastructure
    in, 176
"bull's eye" development, 79, 80f
bus rapid transit (BRT). *See also specific
    BRT systems*
        in adaptive transit cities, 82–89,
            83f, 85f, 87–88f
        closed system operations, 179
        defined, 26b
        in Guangzhou, China, 129–33,
            132–34f, 145n23
        Janmarg BRT (Ahmedabad),
            97–99, 98–99f
        open-system operations, 131,
            179–80
        in Seoul, 67–68, 67f
        transit-oriented development and,
            25
        TransMilenio BRT (Bogota),
            111–12, 112f, 114b, 130b

Index

C

CAI Asia (Clean Air Initiative for Asian Cities), 142*n*2
CAI LAC (Clean Air Initiative for Latin American Cities), 142*n*2
Calgary, Canada, light rail system in, 86
carbon dioxide emissions, 32, 32*f*, 57, 60. *See also* greenhouse gas emissions
car-free days, 117, 181
cars. *See* automobile-dependent development; private automobile ownership
car-sharing companies. *See* shared vehicle fleets
Center for Clean Air Policy, 52
Central Japan Railway Company (JR Central), 77, 78
Centre for Environmental Planning and Technology (CEPT) University, 99, 104, 143*n*5, 149
charettes, 140–41, 178
chawl houses, 102
Cheong Gye Cheon (CGC, Seoul), 66, 66*f*, 68
China. *See also specific cities*
    greenhouse gas emissions in, 32, 32*f*
    motorization rates in, 30, 30*f*
    regulatory framework in, 157
"Cities on the Move" (World Bank), 39
City Bikes (bike lease program), 54
city-level planning, 15–18, 173–80
Clean Air Initiative for Asian Cities (CAI Asia), 142*n*2
Clean Air Initiative for Latin American Cities (CAI LAC), 142*n*2
climate change, 32
closed-loop eco-cycle model, 58
closed system operations, 179
collaboration and coordination. *See* regional coordination
Colombia. *See also* Bogota
    institutional framework in, 150
    regulatory framework in, 12
congestion. *See* traffic congestion
congestion pricing
    in Bogota, 116
    in Singapore, 72, 73
    in Stockholm, 60
Constellation Plan development, 5*b*, 71, 71*f*, 168
Copenhagen, Denmark
    as adaptive transit city, 3, 4*b*, 49, 53–56, 53*f*, 56*f*
    demographics of, 50
    "finger plan" development in, 4*b*, 53, 53*f*, 56*f*, 168

    institutional framework in, 189
    regional planning and coordination in, 169
    transportation modes in, 90*t*
corruption, 163
cross-sector coordination, 148, 171
Cundinamarca Department (Colombia), 124
Curitiba, Brazil
    as adaptive transit city, 49, 82–84, 83*f*
    articulated density in, 11*b*, 41, 42*f*, 155*b*, 174
    environmental footprint of, 50, 83
    mixed-use development in, 175
    transportation modes in, 90*t*
cycling. *See* bicycle-friendly design

D

DANE (National Department of Statistics, Colombia), 119
decentralization
    as barrier to collaboration, 9, 124
    sector silo behavior and, 150
    transit system's impact on, 20, 186
Delhi Development Authority, 159
Delhi-Mumbai Industrial Corridor, 96
demographics of urbanization, 26–28
density
    in adaptive transit cities, 50, 51*f*
    in Ahmedabad, 105–7, 154
    articulated density vs. average density, 11*b*, 155*b*
    as barrier to integration of transit and urban development, 151–58, 153*f*, 155*b*
    in Bogota, 114*b*, 115–16, 123, 124–26, 129, 154
    economic productivity and, 192*n*10
    in Guangzhou, 156
    recommendations for, 15–17, 173–75, 174*f*
    regulatory framework for, 10–12, 124–26
    in Seoul, 64, 152
    in Singapore, 152
    social equity and, 35
    transit ridership associated with, 50, 51*f*
    urbanization and, 28*b*
    value capture and, 185
design issues
    in Ahmedabad, 107–8, 159–60, 160*f*

design issues *(continued)*
 as barrier to integration of transit and urban development, 8, 13, 159–62, 160–61f
 in Bogota, 126, 127f, 160, 161f
 density and, 13, 175
 in Guangzhou, 160
 in Ho Chi Minh City, Vietnam, 160–62, 161f, 162
 radial design, 21, 56, 71, 71f, 186
 trinary road system design, 82–83, 83f
Deudeshwar–Delhi Darwaza corridor (Ahmedabad), 100
developing world integration of transit and urban development, 95–146
 Ahmedabad, 96–109, 98–99f, 101b, 102f, 105b, 110b
 Bogota, 109–29, 112f, 114b, 115f, 117–19f, 121f, 123f, 125f, 127–28f, 130b
 Guangzhou, China, 129–38, 132–35f, 137f
 Ho Chi Minh City, Vietnam, 138–41, 139–42f
 lessons from case studies, 7–14
development financial institutions, 21, 189
distance-based pricing, 68
Donghaochong Canal (Guangzhou), 134–36, 135f
Downtown Tunnel (Ottawa), 89
driveway houses, 165, 166b

E

EcoDensity Charter (Vancouver), 166b
ecological fallacy, 192n8
Eco-Metropolis for 2015 (Copenhagen), 54
economic growth
 in adaptive transit cities, 50, 52, 52t
 automobile-dependent development and, 31, 31f
Economic Intelligence Unit (EIU), 152
"Eco² Cities: Ecological Cities as Economic Cities" (World Bank), 14, 25, 38–39, 40b, 189
Edmonton, Canada, light rail system in, 86
electronic road pricing (ERP), 60, 72, 73
enterprise zones, 176
environmental conditions
 automobile-dependent development and, 31–32, 31f
 density and, 10
 in developing countries, 7–8
 private automobile ownership and, 25
 in Seoul, 69, 70
 urbanization and, 27
ERP. *See* electronic road pricing
European Commission, 167

F

FAR. *See* floor area ratio
feeder systems, 17–18, 36, 179–80
financing
 in Ahmedabad, 103
 as barrier to integration of transit and urban development, 2, 8, 13–14, 158
 in Bogota, 121–22
 cross-subsidization of affordable housing, 143n12
 Real Estate Investment Trust (REIT) funding, 75
 recommendations for, 19–20
 value capture. *See* value capture
"finger plan" development (Copenhagen), 4b, 53, 53f, 56f, 168
floating population, 145n25
floor area ratio (FAR). *See also* density
 in Ahmedabad, 10, 99, 103, 105–7, 154
 as barrier to transit-oriented development, 148
 in Bogota, 9, 10, 116, 118f, 123, 124–26, 154
 redevelopment limited by, 106
 value capture and, 192n14
freeway-to-greenway conversions, 66, 68–70

G

Gandhinagar, India, 108
gentrification, 165
German Agency for International Cooperation, 142n2
Germany
 land adjustment schemes in, 107
 transit ridership and economic productivity in, 52
greenbelt wedges, 53
Green Corridor project (Bogota), 128
greenfield development, 10, 100, 109, 125
greenhouse gas emissions
 automobile-dependent development and, 3, 32, 32f
 in Kuala Lumpur, 164–65
 in Seoul, 69
 in Stockholm, 57

greenways, 53, 58, 119, 131
Guangzhou, China, 129–38
    BRT in, 1, 129–33, 132–34*f*, 145*n*23, 179
    density regulations in, 156
    design issues in, 160
    public area improvements in, 134
    retrofitting problems in, 162
    transit corridor development in, 134–37, 134–35*f*, 137*f*
Guangzhou Municipal Engineering Design and Research Institute, 131
"guidance value"-based property taxes, 192*n*13
Gujarat Infrastructure Development Board, 99
Gujarat Urban Development Corporation, 99

H

Hammarby Sjöstad development, 57–60, 59*t*, 163
heat-island effects, 27, 35, 70
high occupancy vehicle (HOV) lanes, 116
highway construction
    automobile-dependent development and, 30, 33
    in Seoul, 65, 66*f*
Ho Chi Minh City, Vietnam
    design issues in, 160–62, 161*f*, 162
    transit corridor development in, 138–41, 139–42*f*
Hong Kong SAR, China
    as adaptive transit city, 7*f*, 49, 61–64, 63*f*
    demographics of, 50
    design issues in, 175
    environmental footprint of, 50
    FAR limitations in, 12, 156
    institutional framework in, 188–89
    private sector investments in, 23
    radial rail system in, 186
    transportation modes in, 90*t*
    value capture in, 3, 4, 183, 184–85
housing
    in Ahmedabad, 101–3
    in Bogota, 119–20, 121*f*, 126–27
    in Copenhagen, 55
    inclusive TOD and, 165, 182
    informal, 101–2, 165, 185
    regulatory framework and, 151
    in Seoul, 64, 69, 70*f*
    in Singapore, 72
    in Washington, DC metro area, 81
HOV (high occupancy vehicle) lanes, 116
Huangpu District (Guangzhou), 132
Human Transit (Walker), 171
Hyundai Group, 65

I

IBM study on commuter conditions, 30
IDU (Urban Development Institute, Bogota), 122, 149
incentive zoning, 79
inclusive transit-oriented development in Bogota, 126–27
    bus rapid transit and, 44
    challenges of, 165–67, 166*b*
    density and, 35
    recommendations for, 182
India. *See also* Ahmedabad, India
    greenhouse gas emissions in, 32, 32*f*
    institutional framework recommendations for, 150, 170, 170*b*
    Land Acquisition Act, 107
    motorization rates in, 30, 30*f*
    national development strategy in, 170, 170*b*
    National Urban Transport Policy, 97
    regulatory framework in, 12
    Rent Control Act, 107, 156
    traffic accidents in, 33
    Urban Land Ceiling Act, 12, 15, 100, 107, 143*n*8, 156, 176
induced traffic, 15
informal housing, 101–2, 165, 185
infrastructure
    in Copenhagen, 53, 54–55
    highway construction, 30, 33
    railways, 53, 55, 56, 74
    in Seoul, 65, 66*f*
    in Singapore, 72
    in Stockholm, 56
    in Tokyo, 74
    for water and waste management, 188
Institute for Research and Urban Planning (IPPUC), 82, 191*n*1
Institute for Transportation and Development Policy (ITDP), 130, 131, 134, 142*n*2, 160
institutional framework
    in Ahmedabad, 98, 103–4, 105*b*
    as barrier to integration of transit and urban development, 2, 39, 147–48, 149–51
    in Bogota, 116, 122–24, 123*f*, 124
    in Copenhagen, 189
    in Hong Kong SAR, China, 188–89

institutional framework *(continued)*
   in Ottawa, 85, 188
   recommendations for, 14–15, 167–73, 170*b*
   for redevelopment, 178
   in Singapore, 188–89
   urbanization and, 39
   value of, 188–89
interest groups, 163–65
intermodal transfer stations, 179
International Association of Public Transport (UITP), 50, 142*n*2
International Transport Forum, 142*n*2
IPPUC (Institute for Research and Urban Planning), 82, 191*n*1
"island valley" concept, 141, 141*f*
ITDP. *See* Institute for Transportation and Development Policy

J

Jakarta, Indonesia, urban growth in, 28*b*
Janmarg BRT (Ahmedabad), 96, 97–99, 98–99*f*, 110*b*, 148
Japan, land adjustment schemes in, 107, 178. *See also* Tokyo
Japanese National Railways, 78
Japan National Railway, 76
Jawaharlal Nehru Urban Renewal Mission (JnNURM), 97, 144*n*13, 170, 189
joint development. *See also* public-private partnerships (PPPs)
   in Hong Kong SAR, China, 62, 183
   in Tokyo, 77–78
   value capture and, 5–6
   in Washington, DC metro area, 81
JR Central (Central Japan Railway Company), 77, 78
JR East (Tokyo), 76
Junjing Gardens (Guangzhou), 137

K

Kalupur Narod corridor (Ahmedabad), 100
Kankaria Lake Park (Ahmedabad), 159
Kista Science City, Sweden, TOD renovations in, 61
Korea, Republic of. *See also* Seoul
   land adjustment schemes in, 178
   private automobile ownership in, 164
Kowloon-Canton Railway Corporation, 61
Kuala Lumpur, Malaysia, automobile-dependent development in, 164–65, 164*f*

L

Land Acquisition Act of 1984 (India), 107
land consolidation, 17, 74–75, 178
land prices. *See* property values
land regulations, 15, 36, 107
land speculation. *See* property values
laneway houses, 165, 166*b*
leap-frog development, 145*n*26, 163
Lee Kuan Yew World City Prize, 143*n*10
Letbanen (Copenhagen), 55
light rail
   Bogota's plans for, 128, 128*f*
   in Copenhagen, 55
   Ottawa's plans for, 89
   popularity of, 86
Liuyun Xiaoqu Community (Guangzhou), 137, 137*f*
Lizhiwan Canal (Guangzhou), 136
LOOT. *See* Territorial Ordinance Organic Law
Los Angeles, California
   density and traffic congestion in, 174–75
   transit investments in, 186
   value capture in, 184
low-income populations. *See also* inclusive transit-oriented development
   automobile-dependent development and, 32–33
   housing for, 119–20

M

Maritime Square (Hong Kong SAR, China), 62, 63*f*
Mass Transit Railway Corporation (MTRC, Hong Kong SAR, China), 5, 61, 62, 64, 183
Metrovivienda (Bogota), 109, 119–20, 121*f*, 166–67, 182
Mexico City, commuting times in, 33
mixed-use developments
   in Ahmedabad, 107
   density and, 175
   in Guangzhou, 136–37
   retrofitting problems and, 162
   transit-oriented development and, 36
   in Washington, DC metro area, 81
Mobility in Cities database (UITP), 50
Mobility Master Plan (Bogota), 127, 144*n*21
Moscow, Russia, commuting times in, 30–31
motorcycles, 29–30
motorization rates, 29–30, 30*f*
MTRC. *See* Mass Transit Railway Corporation
multisectoral planning, 169

Munich, Germany, transit ridership and economic productivity in, 52
municipal bonds, 103, 158

N

Nagoya Shinkansen station (Tokyo), 78
Nairobi, Kenya, commuting times in, 30–31
National Department of Statistics (DANE, Colombia), 119
National Urban Transport Policy (India), 97, 170, 170*b*
"necklace of pearls." *See* "string of pearls" development
network effects, 21, 188
new-town developments
    in Ahmedabad, 108
    in Copenhagen, 55
    in Seoul, 65
New Urbanism, 128, 145*n*22
New West (Ahmedabad), 108
nitrogen dioxide emissions, 69
not-in-my-backyard (NIMBY) resistance, 178, 188

O

OC Transpo (Ottawa), 87–88
"one-system approach," 38, 40*b*
open-system operations, 131, 179–80
Orestad, Denmark, rail infrastructure in, 55
Ottawa, Canada
    as adaptive transit city, 49, 84–89, 85*f*, 87–88*f*
    BRT in, 179–80
    demographics of, 50
    institutional framework in, 188
    regional planning and coordination in, 169
    strategic planning for, 168
    transportation modes in, 90*t*

P

PADDI (French planning organization), 140
park-and-ride facilities, 88
parking
    automobile-dependent development and, 33
    in Bogota, 116
    in Copenhagen, 55
    pricing of, 171
    private sector investments and, 43
    in Seoul, 68
    in Singapore, 72
    in Stockholm, 58
    TOD and, 37*b*
parks
    in Bogota, 117, 119
    in Copenhagen, 55
    financing of, 158
    in Stockholm, 58
pay-and-park systems, 107
pedestrian-oriented design
    in Ahmedabad, 107, 159–60, 179
    in Bogota, 116, 117, 118*f*, 126, 179
    in Copenhagen, 53, 179
    in Curitiba, 179
    density and, 175
    financing of, 158
    in Guangzhou, 134
    in Hong Kong SAR, China, 64, 179
    recommendations for, 16–17, 175
    in Stockholm, 58, 60–61
    TOD and, 37*b*
    transportation demand management and, 36
pilot testing of projects, 179
Pittsburgh, Pennsylvania, rail infrastructure in, 176
political commitment and continuity, 84, 170–71
pollution. *See* environmental conditions
polycentric growth pattern, 36
population density. *See* density
Por la Bogota que Queremos development plan, 111
POT. *See* Territorial Ordinance Plan
PPPs. *See* public-private partnerships
private automobile ownership
    in Bogota, 113
    in Copenhagen, 55
    economic development and, 29
    in Singapore, 72–73
    sprawl and, 25
    in Stockholm, 57, 60
    taxes and fees on, 55, 72, 171
    traffic accidents and, 31, 32
private sector investments. *See also* public-private partnerships (PPPs)
    in Ahmedabad, 100, 158
    in Bogota, 113, 119, 126, 158
    joint development and, 23
    redevelopment and, 187
    in Tokyo, 74, 75, 75*f*
    value capture and, 148, 184
    in Washington, DC metro area, 79
property development. *See also* redevelopment; transit corridor development
    brownfields, 17, 58, 100, 163
    "bull's eye" development, 79, 80*f*
    Constellation Plan development, 5*b*, 71, 71*f*, 168

property development *(continued)*
    "finger plan" development, 4b, 53, 53f, 56f, 168
    greenfields, 10, 100, 109, 125
    new-town developments, 55, 65, 108
    "string of pearls" development, 56, 79, 89
    in Tokyo, 74
    value capture and, 62
property taxes, 20, 103, 157, 184, 192n13
property values. *See also* value capture
    in Bogota, 113
    in Guangzhou, 136, 138
    in Hong Kong SAR, China, 62
    inclusive TOD and, 165
    regulatory framework and, 15, 151
    retrofitting problems and, 162
    in Seoul, 68–69, 70f
    sprawl and, 163b
    in Tokyo, 78, 78f
public housing in Ahmedabad, 101–3. *See also* inclusive transit-oriented development
public-private partnerships (PPPs). *See also* joint development
    in Ahmedabad, 99, 103, 158
    in Bogota, 120, 121, 158
    in Hong Kong SAR, China, 6, 183
    value capture and, 184
public spaces
    in Bogota, 117, 119
    in Copenhagen, 54
    financing of, 158
    in Guangzhou, China, 134
Public Transportation Integrated System (SITP, Bogota), 127
pulse-scheduling arrangements, 68
PZs (Zonal Plans, Bogota), 122

Q

quality-of-life index, 39

R

radial design, 21, 56, 71, 71f, 186
rail infrastructure
    in Copenhagen, 53, 55
    radial design, 21, 56, 71, 71f, 186
    in Stockholm, 56
    in Tokyo, 74
Rail+Property (R+P) programs
    in Ahmedabad, 109
    in Hong Kong SAR, China, 6, 61, 64, 183
Real Estate Investment Trust (REIT) funding, 75

recommendations, 167–89
    for Ahmedabad, 108–9
    for Bogota, 126–29, 128f
    for city-level planning, 173–80
    for institutional framework, 167–73, 170b
    for regulatory framework, 167–73
    for strategic planning, 168–69
    for value capture, 19–20, 182–85
redevelopment
    in Ahmedabad, 106–7
    in Bogota, 126
    brownfields, 17, 58, 100, 163
    density and, 13
    FAR limits and, 106
    greenfields, 10, 100, 109, 125
    institutional framework for, 178
    regulatory framework for, 12–13, 17
    transit investments and, 21, 187
regional coordination
    in Ahmedabad, 104–5
    as barrier to integration of transit and urban development, 8–9, 39, 148, 150
    in Bogota, 124, 125f
    recommendations for, 14, 169–71
Regional Council (Ottawa), 85–86
Regional Territorial Occupation Model (Colombia), 124, 125f
regulatory framework
    in Ahmedabad, 107
    as barrier to integration of transit and urban development, 2, 8, 12, 39, 148, 151–58
    in Bogota, 116–17, 124–26
    for density, 10–12
    for land and property development, 15, 36, 107
    recommendations for, 14–15, 167–73, 188–89
    for redevelopment, 12–13
    urbanization and, 29, 39
    value capture and, 185
REIT (Real Estate Investment Trust) funding, 75
Rent Control Act of 1949 (India), 107, 156
Republic of Korea. *See* Korea, Republic of
retrofitting issues, 13, 162–63
Rio+20 Conference (2012), 25

S

Sabarmati Riverfront Development Project (Ahmedabad), 100, 101b, 104, 108, 163

San Francisco, California
    land-use shifts in, 176
    radial rail system in, 186
    redevelopment in, 187
São Paulo, Brazil
    transit ridership per capita in, 83
    unplanned densities in, 41, 42f
secondary suites, 165, 166b
sectoral master plans (Bogota), 122
sector silo behavior, 8, 9, 150, 151
Seoul, Republic of Korea
    as adaptive transit city, 49, 64–70, 66–67f, 69t, 70f
    BRT in, 67–68, 67f
    demographics of, 50
    density in, 10, 152
    FAR limitations in, 12, 156
    market adaptation in, 6, 183
    transportation modes in, 90t
Shanghai, China, FAR limitations in, 154
shared vehicle fleets, 37b, 58, 72
Shinagawa Shinkansen station (Tokyo), 77
short-term demands vs. long-term vision, 15, 148–49
Siemens AG/McKinsey study on Stockholm's carbon dioxide emissions, 57
Singapore
    as adaptive transit city, 3, 4–5b, 49, 70–73, 71f
    Constellation Plan development in, 5b, 71, 71f, 168
    demographics of, 50
    density in, 10, 152
    FAR limitations in, 12, 156
    institutional framework in, 188–89
    strategic planning for, 168
    transportation modes in, 90t
SITP (Public Transportation Integrated System, Bogota), 127
Skarholmen, Sweden, TOD renovations in, 61
SkyTrain (Vancouver), 86
smart fare cards, 68
social inequity, 25, 32–33. See also inclusive transit-oriented development
Sodra Lanken tunnel project (Stockholm), 61
South City tunnel project (Stockholm), 61
South Korea. See Korea, Republic of
Spanga, Sweden, TOD renovations in, 61
sprawl
    automobile-dependent development and, 3, 35
    in Bogota, 111

    land speculation contributing to, 163b
    private automobile ownership and, 25
    urbanization and, 27
Stockholm, Sweden
    as adaptive transit city, 49, 56–61, 59–60t
    brownfield development in, 163
    environmental footprint of, 50
    Hammarby Sjöstad development in, 57–60, 59t
    market adaptation in, 6, 183
    mixed-use development in, 175
    transportation modes in, 90t
    transport demand management in, 60–61
strategic planning
    in Bogota, 122–24
    recommendations for, 14, 168–69
"string of pearls" development, 56, 79, 89
subsidies, 13, 171, 191n4

T

Tama Den-en Toshi (Tama Garden City, Tokyo), 74
tax abatements, 176
tax increment financing (TIF), 17, 192n11
tax policy
    betterment taxes, 20
    on private automobile ownership, 55, 72, 171
    property taxes, 20, 103, 157, 184, 192n13
    recommendations for, 176
TDM. See transportation demand management
Tehran, Iran, urban growth in, 27b
temporary migrants, 145n25
Territorial Ordinance Organic Law (LOOT, Colombia), 9, 124, 144n20, 150
Territorial Ordinance Plan (POT, Colombia), 12, 122, 144n19, 149
Texas Transportation Institute, 174
Tianhe District (Guangzhou), 131
Tianjin, China, FAR limitations in, 154
TIF (tax increment financing), 17, 192n11
timed-transfer arrangements, 68
time pollution, 33
TOD. See transit-oriented development
Tokaido Shinkansen line (Tokyo), 77
Tokyo, Japan
    as adaptive transit city, 49, 74–78, 75–78f

Tokyo, Japan *(continued)*
  demographics of, 50, 75
  FAR limitations in, 12, 156
  market adaptation in, 6, 183
  private sector investments in, 23
  radial rail system in, 186
  redevelopment in, 187
  transportation modes in, 90*t*
  value capture in, 3, 4, 6, 183, 185
Tokyo Metro, 76
Tokyo Station City, 76, 77*f*
Tokyu Corporation, 74, 75
toll revenues, 60–61, 171. *See also* congestion pricing
Toronto, Canada
  land-use shifts in, 176
  radial rail system in, 186
  transit investments in, 186
Town Planning Scheme (Ahmedabad), 103–4, 105*b*, 109, 158, 165
traffic accidents, 31, 32
traffic calming, 36
traffic congestion
  automobile-dependent development and, 25, 30, 33
  in Bogota, 111, 113
  bus rapid transit and, 89
  density and, 154
  in Guangzhou, 129
  in Ho Chi Minh City, 138
  in Seoul, 65
  in Singapore, 73
  in Tokyo, 75
transit corridor development
  in Ahmedabad, 100–101, 101*b*, 102*f*
  in Bogota, 113–16, 114*b*, 115*f*, 117–18*f*
  in Guangzhou, China, 134–37, 134–35*f*, 137*f*
  in Ho Chi Minh City, Vietnam, 138–41, 139–42*f*
"transit first" policy, 82, 86
The Transit Metropolis: A Global Inquiry, 49
transit-oriented development (TOD)
  in adaptive transit cities, 49–94. *See also* adaptive transit cities
  in Ahmedabad, 109
  constraints on, 39–41, 41*t*, 147–65, 153*f*, 155*b*, 157*f*, 160–61*f*, 163*b*, 164*f*
  defined, 37–38*b*
  in developing countries, 95–146. *See also* developing world
  integration of transit and urban development
  inclusive. *See* inclusive transit-oriented development
  in India, 170, 170*b*
  land use and, 3–7, 33–41, 34*b*, 35*f*, 37–38*b*, 40*b*, 41*t*, 42*f*
  preconditions for, 17, 18*f*, 176, 177*f*
  promotion and implementation of, 19, 180–82
  prototypes for, 19, 181
  recommendations for, 19, 175–80, 177*f*
  sustainable development and, 33–41, 34*b*, 35*f*, 37–38*b*, 40*b*, 41*t*, 42*f*
  transportation demand management and, 19, 36, 181
  typologies, 19, 180–81
transit ridership
  in adaptive transit cities, 50, 51*f*, 52*t*, 90*t*
  in Ahmedabad, 98
  in Bogota, 110, 144*n*17
  density associated with, 50, 51*f*
  in Ottawa, 87
  in Washington, DC metro area, 80
TransMilenio BRT (Bogota), 9, 109, 111–13, 112*f*, 114*b*, 130*b*, 148
transportation demand management (TDM), 3
  in Ahmedabad, 109
  in Bogota, 116–19, 118–19*f*
  in developing countries, 96
  in Singapore, 72–73
  in Stockholm, 60–61
  transit-oriented development and, 19, 36, 180, 181
Transportation Research Board Committee on Developing Countries, 142*n*2
trinary road system design, 82–83, 83*f*
trunk-line services, 36, 111
Tvärbanan (Stockholm), 58

U

UITP (International Association of Public Transport), 50, 142*n*2
ULCA. *See* Urban Land Ceiling Act of 1976 (India)
Unified Traffic and Transportation (Planning & Engineering) Centre (UTTIPEC), 159
United Nations Centre for Regional Development (UNCRD), 142*n*2
United Nations Development Programme (UNDP), 165
unregistered migrants, 145*n*25

UPZs (Zonal Planning Units, Bogota), 122, 123
Urban Development Institute (IDU, Bogota), 122, 149
urbanization, 26–29, 27–28b
Urban Land Ceiling Act of 1976 (ULCA, India), 12, 15, 100, 107, 143n8, 156, 176
Urbanplanen (Copenhagen), 55
Urban Renovation Company, 122
urban villages, 145n25
UTTIPEC (Unified Traffic and Transportation (Planning & Engineering) Centre), 159

V

Vällingby, Sweden
    suburban renewal projects in, 61
    TOD in, 57, 58
value capture
    in Ahmedabad, 109, 158
    in Bogota, 158
    FARs and, 192n14
    in Hong Kong SAR, China, 62, 183
    joint development and, 5–6
    long-term TOD goals and, 148
    recommendations for, 19–20, 182–85
    in Tokyo, 6
Vancouver, Canada
    inclusive development in, 165, 166b
    light rail system in, 86
vehicle kilometers traveled (VKT) per capita, 50, 51f, 57, 71. *See also* transit ridership

W

Washington, DC metro area
    as adaptive transit city, 49
    private sector investments in, 23
    redevelopment in, 187
    transportation modes in, 90t
    value capture in, 6–7, 184, 185
Washington Metropolitan Area Transit Authority (WMATA), 7, 81
waste management, 59, 188
water supply, 27, 58–59, 188
"whole journey" approach, 159
World Bank
    on barriers to integrating transit and urban development, 39
    Eco^2 Cities initiative, 25, 38–39, 40b
    Ho Chi Minh City BRT system development by, 138–39, 139f
    on TransMilenio's impact, 114b
    transport-oriented development and, 25

Z

Zengzhou, China, FAR limitations in, 154
Zhongshan Avenue (Guangzhou), 129, 131, 132
Zonal Planning Units (UPZs, Bogota), 122, 123
Zonal Plans (PZs, Bogota), 122
zoning regulations, 43, 79, 178, 192n7. *See also* regulatory framework
Zurich, Switzerland, transit ridership and economic productivity in, 52

ECO-AUDIT
Environmental Benefits Statement

The World Bank is committed to preserving endangered forests and natural resources. The Office of the Publisher has chosen to print **Transforming Cities with Transit** on recycled paper with 30 percent postconsumer fiber in accordance with the recommended standards for paper usage set by the Green Press Initiative, a nonprofit program supporting publishers in using fiber that is not sourced from endangered forests. For more information, visit www.greenpressinitiative.org.

Saved:
- 10 trees
- 4.5 million BTU of total energy
- 1,256 pounds of CO_2 equivalent of greenhouse gases
- 6,879 gallons of wastewater
- 401 pounds of solid waste

green press
INITIATIVE